THINKING SPACE

Tavistock Clinic Series

Margot Waddell (Series Editor)

Recent titles in the Tavistock Clinic Series
(for a full listing, please visit www.karnacbooks.com)

Acquainted with the Night: Psychoanalysis and the Poetic Imagination, edited by Hamish Canham & Carole Satyamurti

Addictive States of Mind, edited by Marion Bower, Rob Hale, & Heather Wood

Borderline Welfare: Feeling and Fear of Feeling in Modern Welfare, by Andrew Cooper & Julian Lousada

Childhood Depression: A Place for Psychotherapy, edited by Judith Trowell, with Gillian Miles

Contemporary Developments in Adult and Young Adult Therapy. The Work of the Tavistock and Portman Clinics, Vol. 1, edited by Alessandra Lemma

Consultations in Psychoanalytic Psychotherapy, edited by R. Peter Hobson

Creating New Families: Therapeutic Approaches to Fostering, Adoption, and Kinship Care, edited by Jenny Kenrick, Caroline Lindsey, & Lorraine Tollemache

Engaging with Complexity: Child & Adolescent Mental Health and Education, edited by Rita Harris, Sue Rendall, & Sadegh Nashat

Inside Lives: Psychoanalysis and the Growth of the Personality, by Margot Waddell

Living on the Border: Psychotic Processes in the Individual, the Couple, and the Group, edited by David Bell & Aleksandra Novakovic

Looking into Later Life: A Psychoanalytic Approach to Depression and Dementia in Old Age, edited by Rachael Davenhill

Managing Vulnerability: The Underlying Dynamics of Systems of Care, by Tim Dartington

Oedipus and the Couple, edited by Francis Grier

Organization in the Mind: Psychoanalysis, Group Relations, and Organizational Consultancy, by David Armstrong, edited by Robert French

Reflecting on Reality: Psychotherapists at Work in Primary Care, edited by John Launer, Sue Blake, & Dilys Daws

Sent Before My Time: A Child Psychotherapist's View of Life on a Neonatal Intensive Care Unit, by Margaret Cohen

The Anorexic Mind, by Marilyn Lawrence

The Groups Book. Psychoanalytic Group Therapy: Principles and Practice, edited by Caroline Garland

The Learning Relationship: Psychoanalytic Thinking in Education, edited by Biddy Youell

The Many Faces of Asperger's Syndrome, edited by Maria Rhode & Trudy Klauber

Understanding Trauma: A Psychoanalytic Approach, edited by Caroline Garland

Unexpected Gains: Psychotherapy with People with Learning Disabilities, edited by David Simpson & Lynda Miller

Waiting to Be Found: Papers on Children in Care, edited by Andrew Briggs

"What Can the Matter Be?": Therapeutic Interventions with Parents, Infants, and Young Children, edited by Louise Emanuel & Elizabeth Bradley

Working Below the Surface: The Emotional Life of Contemporary Organizations, edited by Clare Huffington, David Armstrong, William Halton, Linda Hoyle, & Jane Pooley

Work Discussion: Learning from Reflective Practice in Work with Children and Families, edited by Margaret Rustin & Jonathan Bradley

Young Child Observation: A Development in the Theory and Method of Infant Observation, edited by Simonetta M. G. Adamo & Margaret Rustin

THINKING SPACE

Promoting Thinking about Race, Culture, and Diversity in Psychotherapy and Beyond

Edited by

Frank Lowe

Foreword by

M. Fakhry Davids

KARNAC

First published in 2014 by
Karnac Books
118 Finchley Road
London NW3 5HT

British Library Cataloguing in Publication Data

A C.I.P. for this book is available from the British Library

ISBN: 978–1–78220–059–8

Edited, designed, and produced by Communication Crafts

Printed in Great Britain

www.karnacbooks.com

To my children:
Kwame, Yohannes, and Moyenda

CONTENTS

SERIES EDITOR'S PREFACE   ix

ACKNOWLEDGEMENTS   xi

ABOUT THE EDITOR AND CONTRIBUTORS   xiii

FOREWORD   xvii

Introduction
    Frank Lowe   1

1   Thinking space: the model
    Frank Lowe   11

2   Race and our evasions of invitations to think:
   how identifications and idealizations may prevent
   us from thinking
    Onel Brooks   35

3   Between fear and blindness:
   the white therapist and the black patient
    Helen Morgan   56

4   Is it coz I'm white?
       David Morgan   75

5   Being "black" in the transference:
       working under the spectre of racism
       Jonathan Bradley   85

6   The complexity of cultural competence
       Inga-Britt Krause   109

7   "Class is in you": an exploration of some
       social class issues in psychotherapeutic work
       Joanna Ryan   127

8   Psychoanalysis and homosexuality:
       keeping the discussion moving
       Juliet Newbigin   147

9   Paradoxes and blind spots:
       an exploration of Irish identity
       in British organizations and society
       Aideen Lucey   166

10   Dehumanization, guilt, and large-group
       dynamics with reference to the West, Israel,
       and the Palestinians
       Martin Kemp   184

11   The August 2011 Riots—them and us
       Frank Lowe   211

APPENDIX: THINKING SPACE EVENTS   229

REFERENCES   235

INDEX   255

SERIES EDITOR'S PREFACE

Margot Waddell

Since it was founded in 1920, the Tavistock Clinic has developed a wide range of developmental approaches to mental health which have been strongly influenced by the ideas of psychoanalysis. It has also adopted systemic family therapy as a theoretical model and a clinical approach to family problems. The Clinic is now the largest training institution in Britain for mental health, providing postgraduate and qualifying courses in social work, psychology, psychiatry, and child, adolescent, and adult psychotherapy, as well as in nursing and primary care. It trains about 1,700 students each year in over 60 courses.

The Clinic's philosophy aims at promoting therapeutic methods in mental health. Its work is based on the clinical expertise that is also the basis of its consultancy and research activities. The aim of this Series is to make available to the reading public the clinical, theoretical, and research work that is most influential at the Tavistock Clinic. The Series sets out new approaches in the understanding and treatment of psychological disturbance in children, adolescents, and adults, both as individuals and in families.

Thinking Space springs from the collaborative work of the "Thinking Space" discussion forum, initiated by the volume's editor, Frank Lowe, twelve years ago and run by him ever since. As the book makes clear, this is a very distinctive forum, bringing together, as it does, a broad spectrum of thinkers and writers from a wide variety of disciplines. The hallmarks are honesty, courage, loyalty, and a shared commitment to facing the uncomfortable truths that are expressed in the areas examined. These areas are those of diversity, race, and culture, and the truths are about hard-to-acknowledge and not always conscious attitudes and beliefs of one's own, but also those of others—hence the subtle interlacing of internal worlds and external realities.

These choppy waters have been beautifully and consistently navigated over the years, as is attested in the pages that follow. The forum does, indeed, as the editor states, constitute a "container for thought"—a "mental space" (Young, 1994a) in which the participants can learn and develop, in a wide variety of settings. In the current world climate, the scope of the book feels acutely topical, as a wide range of experiences and contexts are examined and reflected upon. As befits public sector work, several chapters concentrate on racial differences between clinician and patient. But the net is cast far wider than such contexts, complex though they may be. Other chapters explore, with sensitivity and learning, issues of class in psychotherapeutic work; of homosexuality and psychoanalysis; of Irish identity in British organizations and society; of group dynamics in relation, for example, to Israel, Palestine, and the West; of the recent riots in Tottenham and elsewhere. When these huge issues are swirling around, it can be difficult to think straight—or indeed to think at all—in the consulting room. These pages address such areas too, with a depth, honesty, and quality rarely seen, nor available to read about, in clinical, by contrast with academic, settings. These are topics that are more easily evaded than engaged with. But in *Thinking Space* the engagement *is* undertaken. The fruits of years of serious discussion, driven by the absolute necessity to understand the world more deeply and more thoroughly, are laid out in the chapters of this book. How important it is to have such a publication in the Tavistock Clinic Series, a book that proudly gives voice to so much that underpins the Clinic's work and identity and hopefully will do so more extensively in the future.

ACKNOWLEDGEMENTS

This book is the product of people who have supported Thinking Space out of recognition that certain disadvantaged groups or their experiences have been excluded or marginalized in psychotherapy as in wider society. They are too numerous to mention by name, but they include those who have contributed chapters to this book, as well as those who have spoken at, chaired, and attended Thinking Space meetings during the past eleven years. There are, however, some individuals who have been critical in helping to create and run Thinking Space whose contribution must be acknowledged. They are Onel Brooks for his solid support and comradeship; Beverly-Foster Davis and Vicky Howells for their excellent administrative support; Agnes Bryan and Maxine Dennis for their helpful critical perspectives; Lois Thomas for helping to organize and develop Thinking Space over the past two years; and Deirdre Moylan, Louise Lyon, Jeannie Milligan, Robin Anderson, and Matthew Patrick for their vital professional and managerial support.

In putting together this book, I have been privileged to have had the editorial support of Margot Waddell, whose wisdom and attention to detail helped to make my task easier. I would like to thank Aideen Lucy and particularly Martin Kemp for their helpful comments on chapter drafts and for their support in bringing the book to completion. Finally, I would like to express my gratitude to my sister, Doris, and brothers, Godwin and Carlisle, for their unwavering support and to my wife, Gloria, for her patience, assistance, and belief in the project at every stage.

ABOUT THE EDITOR AND CONTRIBUTORS

Jonathan Bradley is a consultant child and adolescent psycho-therapist working with adolescents and young adults at the Tavistock and Portman NHS Foundation Trust. His clinical work has been carried out in both clinic and school settings, among ethnically diverse populations. He has played a major role in trainings linked to child psychotherapy, including the lead role in a 2- to 3-year MA in Psychoanalytic Observational Studies. He is joint editor with Margaret Rustin of *Work Discussion: Learning from Reflective Practice on Work with Children and Families* (2008), a book that is linked to an element in the Observation Course. He has held a number of roles within the Tavistock: he was Chair of the Race and Equality Committee, with the task of formulating and developing the Trust's response to Race Relations legislation, and has played a prominent role in the running of Group Relations Events (Leicester model), which offer the possibility of experiential learning in areas such as equality and ethnicity.

Onel Brooks completed a doctorate in philosophy before working in the field of psychotherapy, then training as a psychoanalytic social worker and as a psychoanalytic psychotherapist. He is a UKP-registered psychoanalytic psychotherapist in independent practice and a senior lecturer in Psychotherapy, Counselling and

Counselling Psychology at Roehampton University, where he contributes to the Research Centre for Therapeutic Education, which is in the Psychology Department. He is a member of the Philadelphia Association and contributes to the training there.

Martin Kemp is a psychoanalyst and psychoanalytic psychotherapist (BCP, BPF, BPA). He worked in Africa as a teacher and as a support to technical aid projects before spending ten years as Director of The Lorrimore, a voluntary organization based in the London Borough of Southwark providing social support to people with long-term mental health difficulties. He has worked at Open Door, the adolescent therapy service, and as a staff consultant to several residential facilities for young people. He is currently in private practice in South London.

Inga-Britt Krause is a social and medical anthropologist and a Consultant Systemic Psychotherapist. She has carried out ethnographic work with high-caste Hindus in Nepal and with British Sikhs. As a systemic psychotherapist she has worked for over twenty years in the NHS and has helped set up Specialist Services for Asian Communities in London. Her publications include *Therapy Across Culture* (1998), *Culture and System in Family Therapy* (2002), and *Culture and Reflexivity in Systemic Psychotherapy: Mutual Perspectives* (2013, editor), as well as many papers on medical anthropology and cross-cultural psychotherapy. She is currently a Training and Development Consultant in the Tavistock and Portman NHS Foundation Trust.

Frank Lowe is a psychoanalytic psychotherapist and Head of Social Work in the Adolescent and Adult Directorate at the Tavistock Clinic. Before joining the Tavistock in 2001, he was a Social Services Inspector with the Department of Health and had been a manager for over twelve years of local authority mental health and children services. He has developed services at the Tavistock to help improve access to psychotherapy for black and minority ethnic young people, teaches on several Tavistock courses, and is the Course Organizer of Understanding the Emotional Needs of Care Leavers. He has written several papers on working with adolescence, race, and psychotherapy and has a long-standing interest in making psychotherapy more accessible to poor and marginalized communities.

Aideen Lucey is an independent organizational consultant and executive coach. She is an associate at Tavistock Consulting, where she was previously a principal consultant. She is a visiting consultant at IMD and Insead European business schools. She provides consultancy to a diverse group of clients, from practitioners and managers in the mental health field to executives in large international organizations. Her primary area of interest relates to how people make (or fail to make) meaning at work, and she is currently pursuing a professional doctorate on this topic. Her practice is underpinned by a first-class degree in social science and a Master's degree in psychodynamic approaches to consultancy. She co-edited (with Laurence Gould and Lionel Stapley) *The Reflective Citizen: Organizational and Social Dynamics* (2011).

David Morgan is a Fellow of the British Psychoanalytical Society and a training analyst with the BPA and the IPA. He was formerly a Consultant Psychotherapist at the Portman Clinic for over twenty years and is now a Consultant Psychotherapist for WBUK, a support organization for Whistleblowers. He is Joint Editor (with Stan Ruszczynsky) of *Violence, Perversion and Delinquency* (2007). He is in private practice.

Helen Morgan is a Fellow of the British Psychotherapy Foundation and is a training analyst and supervisor for the Jungian Analytic Association within the BPF. She works mainly in private practice as an analyst and also supervises in both the individual and the group setting. Her background is in therapeutic communities with adolescents and in adult mental health. She was chair of the British Association of Psychotherapists for four years until February 2008, during which time she was involved in setting up an ongoing project to explore issues of race and ethnicity in the organization. She has written on issues of racism within the supervisory relationship and in psychoanalytic psychotherapy organizations as well as in the clinical setting.

Juliet Newbigin is a senior Psychoanalytic Psychotherapy member of the British Psychotherapy Foundation and a member of the Foundation for Psychotherapy and Counselling. She works in private practice. She has taught seminars for a number of years at WPF Counselling and Therapy on the impact of significant differences—those of gender, sexual orientation, and ethnicity, for example—on the clinical relationship.

Joanna Ryan is a psychoanalytic psychotherapist, supervisor, and researcher. She is a member of the Site for Contemporary Psychoanalysis and trained at the Philadelphia Association, London. She was Visiting Fellow at Goldsmith's College, University of London, from 2004 to 2008, while conducting a research project on social class and psychoanalysis. She is co-author (with N. O'Connor) of *Wild Desires and Mistaken Identities: Lesbianism and Psychoanalysis* (reprinted 2003), and author of *The Politics of Mental Handicap* (1987), as well as many other publications. Her recent publications include "Elision and Disavowal: The Extrusion of Class from Psychoanalytic Discourse and Practice" (*Sitegeist*, 2009).

FOREWORD

M. Fakhry Davids

To those of us troubled by the collective silence in our discipline on matters of race and diversity, it is a special pleasure to welcome this timely and thoughtful book. It is not only the fact that its editor, Frank Lowe, has brought together a number of excellent professionals who raise their voices, mostly in a highly personal way, in this neglected area that is so impressive. Significant as it is, this contribution from Lowe is surpassed by an even greater one: namely, his initiative in setting up the Thinking Space project—described fully in his introductory chapter—at the Tavistock Clinic, which is the premier psychotherapy training institution in the NHS. Most of the contributions in this volume originated in the Thinking Space forum. The significance of this achievement can be appreciated by reminding ourselves of the context in which it occurred.

In 1983, recognizing how poorly the needs of minority patients were being served within mainstream psychotherapy services in the capital, Jafar Kareem established the Nafsiyat Intercultural Therapy Centre here in London. A sense of being marginalized,

---

M. Fakhry Davids, a psychoanalyst, is the author of *Internal Racism: A Psychoanalytic Approach to Race and Difference*, published in 2011.

misunderstood, and treated in a racist way ran as a common thread through these patients' experience of seeking help, which exacerbated their psychological difficulties. There was therefore an urgent need to provide for them—hence the need for Nafsiyat—but as the experience of these patients became known, it also underlined the failure of mainstream services to adapt to the changing demographic of the capital. There was some considerable anxiety that a service catering specifically for minority patients might in itself contribute to the marginalization of their needs and undermine their legitimate demand—as citizens—to be accommodated within the mainstream.

In the intervening thirty years, the face of London has changed even further into what is now a truly multiracial and multicultural metropolis. Its inclusive ambience, which is even more remarkable for acknowledging difference and containing points of tension that inevitably arise, was even lauded as an asset in the capital's successful bid for the 2012 Olympic Games. Many of the contributors to this volume remind us, however, that within our predominantly white profession issues of race and diversity remain largely invisible. Yesteryear's struggle to address our minority group patients is mirrored by today's struggle to attract minority group professionals to our ranks, with the perspective they might bring currently beyond reach. Yet we seem oblivious to this as a difficulty, as if we were colour blind, and pay a heavy price for it. When it comes to considering and debating matters across the boundaries of race, class, and culture—not academically, but in the more personal way that our profession demands—we freeze up and become defensive. It may seem obvious, but it is worth stating that we then enter a vicious circle: the more these issues remain invisible, the less familiarity we have with them; the less our familiarity, the less our ability to bring them into a proper psychoanalytic conversation. This shortcoming, in turn, is easily covered over by conceptualizations of racial difference that make them secondary to supposed psychological essences. As a profession interested in depth psychology, our non-engagement with these issues is thus justified on the grounds that they are "more superficial"; this in turn limits our opportunities for engaging fully and properly with them. Compare this with how we are able to engage with issues of gender and generation difference that arise in the consulting room and beyond, where we are able to free associate and to think creatively and at depth. This capacity flows directly from the fact that in consulting rooms up and down the land, oedipal dynamics, when they arise, are assiduously pursued and worked with. The same cannot be said of our attitude to racial difference.

The problem about racial difference is indeed complex, difficult to address, and resistant to change. As if to remind me of this, as I write fresh revelations are surfacing that, despite all the time and money that has already been invested in trying to uncover what went wrong in the police handling of the racist murder of Stephen Lawrence, there has been yet a further cover-up, this time of police attempts to smear the Lawrence family when resources should have gone into apprehending his killers. Again, there are to be two inquiries . . .

Trying to bring these issues into the open is, therefore, a daunting task. When it is a black person who undertakes it, a further layer of complexity is added in the form of an assumption—mostly unspoken—that he has a personal issue about his race, a chip on his shoulder. And so there is a further danger that his attempt to bring things into the open may itself become marginalized.

Seen in this context, we can appreciate the magnitude of the achievement that Frank Lowe's development of his Thinking Space initiative represents. What I find so impressive is that though one could make a political case that this development is essential both for our profession and in a *national* health service required to serve all without prejudice, this is not the path he chooses. Instead, he makes a clear and measured psychoanalytic case for a Thinking Space dedicated to issues of working with racial and cultural difference. I find his argument both coherent and compelling, and it is easy to see how this clarity of purpose succeeded in creating an atmosphere experienced by presenters—myself included—as clearly tolerant, respectful, and facilitating. It is also marked by intense curiosity and interest in the subject that leads to lively debate and engagement. Creating and sustaining such an atmosphere speaks to Lowe's deep inner strength and quiet determination to pursue a difficult, not to say daunting, task whose rightness he never doubts. His admirably steady hand is revealed in some of the vignettes he discusses.

Lowe's achievement in creating a Thinking Space thus speaks for itself. That he has been able to do so within the mainstream represents very significant progress in the attempt to get race and difference taken seriously. Publishing some of the work that arose from that initiative takes things a step further: it allows the conversation to extend beyond the events themselves. The result is this book, *Thinking Space*, with rich, varied, and thought-provoking chapters that make a real contribution to bringing this subject out of the shadows. It deserves to be widely read by newcomers and experienced practitioners alike—in our profession and beyond—and I hope that they might be stimulated to join in.

THINKING SPACE

In human affairs, however, thinking is but a snare and a delusion unless the unconscious is taken into account. I refer to both meanings of the word, 'unconscious' meaning deep and not readily available because of the pain that belongs to its acceptance as part of the self.

D. W. Winnicott,
"Thinking and the Unconscious" (1945, p. 169)

Introduction

Frank Lowe

> "Socrates . . . introduced the idea that individuals could not
> be intelligent on their own, that they needed someone else to
> stimulate them. . . . His brilliant idea was that if two unsure
> individuals were put together, they could achieve what
> they could not do separately: the truth, their own truth for
> themselves. By questioning each other, dividing each of these
> into parts, finding the flaws, never attacking or insulting, but
> always seeking what they could agree between them. . . ."
>
> Theodore Zeldin (1995, pp. 33–34)

Anti-discriminatory practice was an important part of my training as a social worker in the 1980s. Racism, sexism, ageism, and other forms of discrimination were accepted as external and internal realities that had a negative impact on the health and social well-being of individuals, families, and communities. However imperfect this aspect of the training might have been, race equality and anti-discriminatory practice were and still remain at the core of social work values. In contrast, my training as a psychoanalytic psychotherapist during the 1990s treated the issues of cultural diversity, racism, and other forms of discrimination as of little importance or not meriting serious thought and attention in the training of psychotherapists.

During four years of psychoanalytic theory and practice seminars, my year group had one seminar on intercultural therapy, facilitated by Jafar Kareem, a pioneer of intercultural therapy in the UK. Jafar was angry about there being only one seminar on the subject and communicated to us his ambivalence about accepting the invitation to teach. On the one hand, he saw agreeing to teach this single seminar as colluding with tokenism; on the other, he felt that on balance he should use the opportunity to impress on trainees—the future leaders of the profession—the importance of thinking about how psychotherapy should become more accessible and helpful in its practice to more disadvantaged groups in society. While there has been some improvement, it would not be an exaggeration to say that thinking about racism and other forms of discrimination towards "the other" continues to be a marginal issue in psychotherapy.

In April 2002, I started a monthly learning forum called "Thinking Space" at the Tavistock Clinic, in order to promote thinking about race, culture, and diversity in psychotherapy. There was growing recognition that there was little or no real exploration of these subjects at the Tavistock Clinic or in many psychotherapy, health, and social care organizations in the UK (Audit Commission, 2004b; Gordon, 1993a, 2004; SCIE, 2006). Race, culture, and diversity are complex, emotionally charged, and anxiety-provoking subjects, and thinking about racism and other forms of hatred of difference is beset by difficulties inside and outside the individual. Internally, we all carry blind spots, including blind spots about our destructiveness—in particular, a propensity to project on to others characteristics that we cannot bear in ourselves. Externally, it is difficult to find a space where one could really talk and think with others about diversity[1] in a way that is emotionally truthful and that helps one to learn and develop.

I had learnt from previous experiences, both as a participant and as a facilitator of diversity learning events, that facilitating discussion, thinking, and learning about these subjects was extremely challenging and required an ability to work with immense complexity, including unbearable feelings or states of mind. Perhaps in an attempt to avoid the discomfort of this complexity, there exists in many organizations an essentially superficial approach to matters of race, culture, and diversity. First, staff learning and development needs in these areas tend to be addressed in a tokenistic way at brief or "one-off" learning events, often held in order for the organization to be seen to comply with diversity legislation or in response to a complaint or crisis around diversity. Second, good-quality diversity training is rare. Professionals regularly report feeling that the complexities and challenges they face in working with diversity are either poorly addressed or not addressed at all. Instead, they often feel "preached at" or report that courses simply provide basic information about dos and don'ts regarding diversity legislation or, even worse, attempt to teach about "other cultures" in ways that seem close to promoting cultural stereotypes.

Furthermore, at such learning events, there is often a stressful atmosphere, which paralyses thinking and learning. In such spaces, it can feel as if one's survival is at stake, and a fright, fight, or flight response tends to predominate. At one extreme, participants can be frightened of speaking their minds out of anxiety that it will cause offence and lead to catastrophe. At another extreme, there can often be immense hurt and anger when participants speak openly; discussion and thinking may then quickly deteriorate into a war-like atmosphere of attack and counter-attack around a perception that a participant had, for example, expressed a racist view. This unpleasant experience can reinforce the view that it is unsafe and unwise to share one's thoughts and engage in meaningful discussion about diversity issues.

Another difficulty with the subject of diversity is that it is frequently plagued by "black-and-white" or "them-and-us" thinking. For example, it is common to split people into those who are anti-racist or racist, feminist or sexist, in support of homosexuality or homophobic. These divisions encourage stereotyping and mutual projections between individuals on both sides of the divide, and this is another barrier to thinking and learning. It is as if we cannot be good and bad, loving and hateful, anti-racist and racist, rather than either/or. This habit of splitting people into "goodies" and "baddies" is a childish type of thinking, which is a form of lying or of not facing the truth about ourselves and others.

Having said that, it is, of course, important to distinguish between what people think and what they actually do. For example, a person who consistently supports anti-racist initiatives is arguably more helpful than someone who opposes all anti-racist initiatives on the basis that they are unnecessary. The danger is for this anti-racist person or others to assume that because someone is an anti-racist activist, she or he can never be racist.

It seems that underlying the numerous difficulties that beset thinking about diversity is our ability unconsciously to tell lies—not least to ourselves—which is a fundamental human problem regarding our capacity to look at and think about the whole self honestly, including our hateful and destructive aspects. It is therefore ironic, distressing, but in some ways also chastening that a profession that possesses expertise helping people to think about, understand, and find better ways of dealing with their problems should be so uninterested in thinking about racism and other forms of hatred and their psychological impact. There was and still is a need for more "mental space" (Young, 1994a),[2] individually and socially, to develop thinking about diversity. Despite some increase in thinking about diversity within the psychotherapy profession in recent years, there continues to be a severe lack of mental space, especially *regular space*, to discuss and think about the challenges of diversity. This is, to me, a major barrier to learning and one that reinforces the culture of superficial engagement with these issues.

Given the many obstacles to thinking about diversity, it was clear that if the Thinking Space forum was to succeed in achieving its core objective of promoting thinking and learning in this area, it was imperative that its organizers created and maintained a safe and emotionally containing environment—or, in the words of Young (1994a), a place that was "a container for thought". The atmosphere and boundaries that promote engagement, discussion, thinking, and learning would need to be consistently held, if participants were to feel able to speak openly and to learn, without fear that they would be attacked for doing so.

This book is a celebration of eleven years of Thinking Space at the Tavistock Clinic[3] and a way of sharing some of the thinking, experience, and learning gained over these years. Thinking Space functions, among other things, as a test-bed for ideas, and many of the chapters began as presentations or discussions at Thinking Space (the exceptions being chapters 3, 7, and 8) and were encouraged and developed by the experience. Chapter 11, in fact, was born out of two Thinking Space discussions about the August 2011 Riots. These chapters do not seek to provide a coherent theory or set of views. On the contrary, they are very diverse—and decidedly so, as finding, expressing, and developing one's own personal idiom

(Bollas, 1992) involves emotional truthfulness and is an important part of getting to know oneself, both of which are important prerequisites to getting to know the other.

In chapter 1, I describe Thinking Space: its aims, theoretical underpinning, practice methods, and values. Drawing largely on psychoanalysis—in particular, the ideas of Melanie Klein and Wilfred Bion—I describe how we sought to develop thinking, not as an abstract activity, but as a means of better getting to know the self and the different other. This involves meeting with others to reflect on and reconsider our relations with ourselves and diversity in a facilitative environment. I emphasize that knowledge of ourselves—particularly our capacity to use others for our benefit, be it to cope with primitive anxieties or for power, money, or glory—is critical to an understanding of racism and other forms of hatred towards people categorized as being different.

In chapter 2, Onel Brooks cautions us to take seriously our capacity for self-illusion and to not believe that we—especially psychotherapists—are necessarily thinking when we say we are thinking. He argues that being psychoanalytically sophisticated or trained does not enable someone to think better about race or other forms of hatred. Onel shows that this is because our identifications and idealizations of theories and models can become a way of evading thoughtful engagement with many things, including racism or diversity. Drawing on Wittgenstein, he questions whether we can really think if we do not want to hurt ourselves.

Chapters 3, 4 and 5 are explorations by white therapists of their responses to race and cultural differences in the consulting room. Helen Morgan (chapter 3) was one of the first white British therapists to explore how a white therapist thinks about and works with racism in her clinical work. In this updated version of her paper first published in 1998, Helen identifies difficulties that include how feelings of shame and guilt can prevent the white therapist acknowledging racism and exploring issues concerning difference that arise from the transference. David Morgan (chapter 4) provides a candid personal reflection on how unprepared he was to work with patients from different cultural and racial backgrounds. He identifies how his work with such patients was threatened at times by his cultural bias and prejudices. David does not attempt to airbrush his difficulties in working with difference; while his frankness at times may make uncomfortable reading, it has an authenticity that is rare and necessary if we are to make progress.

Jonathan Bradley (chapter 5) describes how his understanding and technique as a white psychotherapist was challenged in his work with two patients (one black, one white)—in particular, by images from dreams that came up in the process of their therapy. In one case, he was treated as if he were a black nanny in the transference, and he had to think what this meant, how to respond, and whether he would be colluding with racism. Jonathan demonstrates well the complexity of this terrain, which can feel like a mental minefield and requires great patience, care, and thought with the patient to carefully gather, one step at a time, aspects of truth as a means towards finding a way through. He demonstrates the clinical value of the concepts of projection and projective identification to understand the unconscious getting rid of unwanted and unbearable feelings. But Jonathan is also aware that these concepts can be used defensively by psychotherapists as a way of not looking at or of defending against their own evacuations of unwanted and unbearable feelings on to the patient. This chapter convincingly shows that these pitfalls can be avoided if therapists continually find the space to review their practice (probably especially with patients from different racial and cultural backgrounds to themselves, given the history of silence, avoidance, guilt, and shame in this area) and explore the meaning of their reactions and responses to their patients.

Chapter 6 focuses on culture in ways that highlight the complexity of the concept, as a process that is both unconscious and conscious, has internal and external meanings, and is dynamic and contextual. Inga-Britt Krause helpfully sketches this out and argues against a superficial, tick-box approach to cultural competence. She shows, however, that tick-box approaches have a powerful appeal because they absolve individuals both from developing an understanding of diversity as well as from self-reflection.

Chapter 7 is a rare paper on social class in psychotherapy, which has been updated by the author. Drawing on a research study, Joanna Ryan reports that although there is much knowledge and experience of social class in psychotherapy, it is seldom formally discussed or written about in the profession. She argues that class has a far-reaching psychological impact, but there seems to be a class-blind ideology within psychotherapy that obscures or denies the psychic pain of class inequality. Joanna believes that class is a hidden subject in psychotherapy because feelings about inequality often cannot be faced openly and worked with therapeutically and that there are as yet no frameworks for discussing social class issues in psychotherapy.

Chapter 8 is an important chapter on homosexuality. Juliet Newbigin shows how psychoanalysis arrived at a more fixed view of heterosexuality as normal and homosexuality as pathological. How and why did psychoanalysis as a reflective and thoughtful profession allow itself to reach such a prejudicial and uncritical position—and, more pertinently, did so without critical reflection, open discussion, and review? Was this a consequence of psychoanalysis firmly becoming part of the status quo—reflecting and reinforcing the dominant values of the culture in which it has gained acceptance and achieved status? Whatever the reason or reasons, this chapter provides a salutary lesson for the profession and at least requires all of us to think seriously about whether we are as reflective, neutral, and unaffected by the prejudices of our culture as we like to think we are. Juliet applauds the 2012 position statement by the British Psychoanalytic Council that a homosexual orientation is not evidence of pathology, but she contends that discussion and thinking about homosexuality should continue within the profession and on our training courses. This is needed, she argues, because being open-minded, curious, and self-questioning are vital to being consistently analytic.

The last three chapters explore the unconscious role and function of certain groups in society and how near impossible it is to talk and think about them. Aideen Lucey (chapter 9) explores how Irish identity is used unconsciously in British organizations and society. She identifies a number of paradoxes, including how the Irish in Britain are treated as both the same as but different from the British and how they can also seem to be both proud and ashamed of their Irish identity. She uses these paradoxes to show how a blind eye is being turned on issues to do with Irish identity in Britain among both the Irish and the British. Aideen argues that the Irish are a part-object to the British and continue to be recipients of specific projections that are a legacy of British colonialism. However, Irish identification with some of these projections makes it difficult for them to speak out about their experience, and there is a psychological investment for others in keeping it that way.

Martin Kemp (chapter 10) responds to the proposition that within Britain there is a divide between private and public discourse about the Israel–Palestine situation. As addressing the issue gives rise to immense anxiety, Martin believes that this suggests the presence of disturbing unconscious factors that need to be explored. He argues that a complex relationship between European and Israeli guilt has locked Britain and the West into a position where the price of atoning for Western anti-Semitism in the past is our participation in the dehumanization of the Palestinians in the present. He challenges the widespread belief that the stance of psychotherapy as a profession in this and other situations should be characterized by neutrality, and he suggest instead that the true ethics of the profession should have at its heart a commitment to universalism and human rights.

In chapter 11, I look at the response to the August 2011 Riots and in particular David Cameron's view that the riots were caused by "pockets of our society that are not only broken, but frankly sick". I argue that to understand the riots requires as much of an examination of those who did not riot (us) as those who did (them). I also put forward the idea that the riots were both a manifestation of a deep malaise and an unconscious request for this to be recognized, understood, and thoughtfully contained.

Despite differences, there are some common themes that run through these chapters. They include the view that we all internalize to varying degrees the racist, sexist, and other forms of hatreds of difference within our culture. Also, that we all use others, through splitting and projection, to feel better about ourselves and that differences such as race, culture, and class are used as a means of dehumanization and domination by those more powerful. The black, the Jew, the woman, the gay, the working-class person, the Palestinian is not a whole person but a stereotype, a part-object, and is in effect dehumanized. All the chapters argue that what is hated in the different other is what is feared in the self and that to avoid repeating the violence of earlier generations, we must remember our own traumatic experiences and how we have been damaged by them. However, saying this serves to remind me of the need to acknowledge the severe limitations of this book.

Thinking Space does not seek to provide an explanation or theory of racism and other hatreds of difference. I do not think a psychological theory or a single discipline can provide such a theory, because racism and others forms of oppression are determined by a number of factors, not least economic and political ones. Finally, while I agree with Aristotle's view that thinking is the most powerful and divine of human abilities and that we "must, so far as we can, make ourselves immortal, and strain every nerve to live in accordance with the best thing in us; for even if it be small in bulk, much more does it in power and worth surpass everything" (in Ross, 2005, Book X, p. 8), I also believe that the power of thinking on human behaviour should not be overestimated, because it is often thwarted by our primitive anxieties, self-interest, and desires for power, success, and wealth. Nonetheless, Aristotle is fundamentally correct, for, as the thinking species, our capacity to think using our hearts and our minds is the best thing we have, and we should do all we can to make use of this facility for the benefit of all.

Notes

1. Diversity is used here to refer to groups who experience prejudice, discrimination, and disadvantage on the basis of socially significant differences such as class, gender, race, culture, sexuality, faith, age, or disability. The term is used as a short-hand for inequalities between groups in society in terms of access to services, employment, and life chances and how this reflects and contributes to differences in wealth, power, and status between groups in society (see Audit Commission, 2004b).

2. Young (1994a), in the Preface to his book *Mental Space*, describes mental space as "a congenial place for thinking, for reflecting, for rumination, for nourishment. It connects readily to comforting boundaries—containment, being held in mind. It also connotes capaciousness, relative freedom from being crowded, from mental claustrophobia." Thinking Space sought to be a mental space of this kind.

3. The Appendix contains a list of all the presentations at Thinking Space since 2002.

CHAPTER ONE

Thinking space: the model

Frank Lowe

"The disturbance of the impulse of curiosity on which all learning depends, and the denial of the mechanism by which it seeks expression, makes normal development impossible."

W. R. Bion (1959, p. 108)

Thinking Space was set up to develop the capacity of staff and trainees at the Tavistock Clinic to think about racism and other forms of hatred towards difference in ourselves and others. Drawing on Bion's (1962) distinction between "knowing" and "knowing about", the latter of which can be a defence against knowing a subject in a deeper and emotionally real way, Thinking Space sought to promote curiosity, exploration, and learning about difference, by paying as much attention to how we learn (process) as to what we learn (content). The establishment and design of the forum was determined not so much by theoretical considerations, but by my many years of experience as a participant in and facilitator of "diversity" learning events. This has taught me that the subjects of race and racism tend to arouse strong feelings such as anxiety, guilt, shame, and anger. This emotional maelstrom often created numerous barriers to thinking and learning at such events. These included:

» fear of saying what one thinks because one might be severely criticized or labelled as racist

» saying what is politically correct to gain approval or acceptance

» being silent because of anxiety about getting it wrong and offending someone

» witnessing or becoming part of extremely angry exchanges between participants regarding who is right or who is wrong, or who is racist or anti-racist

» feeling upset, guilty, and ashamed about the unedifying behaviour of oneself and or others and deciding to give such events a wide berth in future.

These experiences were a particular spur to the idea of creating the Thinking Space forum, as a space that could enable participants to engage constructively with the feelings and dynamics that tended to emerge around the subject of race and culture in a way that did not derail or stop thinking and learning. However, there were a number of other factors that led to this initiative, which I would like to mention before outlining the model of practice developed and its theoretical underpinnings.

The lack of thinking about race, culture, and diversity in psychotherapy

There is growing evidence that social and economic inequality in British society is increasing and that prejudice and discrimination against people on the basis of their race, culture, class, gender, sexuality, religion, and age is still widespread. Psychoanalytic practitioners have, however, been largely silent about these hatreds, and a largely colour-, culture-, and class-blind approach continues to pervade the psychotherapy profession (Bhugra & Bhui, 1998; Gordon, 1993a, 2004; Kareem & Littlewood, 2000; Lowe, 2006b; Morgan, 1998; Thomas, 1992; Young, 1994a). Furthermore, despite increasing racial and cultural diversity in Britain, psychotherapy—particularly psychoanalytic psychotherapy—continues to be a largely white middle-class profession. This reinforces the perception, still common today, that psychotherapy, especially psychoanalytic psychotherapy, is a white middle-class "privileged" activity. There have, of course, been initiatives taken by a number of pioneering individuals and organizations—such as Sue Holland (1992), who worked with depressed women on the White City Estate; Jafaar Kareem (1992), who created Nafsiyat to provide intercultural therapy; and Luise Eichenbaum and Susie Orbach (1987) and the Women's Therapy Centre—which counter this perception. These individuals and organizations sought to make psychotherapy more accessible and responsive to the needs of the working class, ethnic minorities, and others in disadvantaged or oppressive circumstances. But while there is much to celebrate from these efforts, psychotherapy, in the main, continues to be largely the preserve of the better-off. There are many barriers, other than finance, to accessing psychotherapy by disadvantaged communities. These include prejudicial assumptions and attitudes towards them by psychotherapists and a lack of interest in developing psychotherapy services that are more accessible and responsive to people from adverse social and cultural circumstances (see Altman, 2010; Bhugra & Bhui, 1998).

There is also little or no attention paid in the selection and training of psychotherapists to issues of prejudice and discrimination on the basis of race, culture, religion, class, or sexuality. There is a widespread assumption that these are political issues and, as such, ones that are not within the purview of the psychoanalytic practitioner because psychoanalysis is concerned primarily with the internal world. This perspective assumes, erroneously, that there is no relationship between the external world and the internal world of the individual and that issues of race, culture, class, or sexuality are not vibrant aspects of the internal world that affect our feelings, fantasies, perceptions, identities, and relationships. This institutional attitude is, among other things, a defence against facing the reality of class and race in the profession and its implications. The unwillingness to think about the white middle-class nature of psychotherapy in terms of its membership, values, and clientele, on either an individual or an organizational basis, is a defence against guilt about an investment, probably unconsciously, in maintaining the status quo. There are a number of defences that are commonly used to prevent engagement with racism and other forms of exclusion—in particular, avoidance, denial, and turning a blind eye. Steiner (1985) helpfully says about "turning a blind eye" that "we seem to have access to reality but choose to ignore it because it proves convenient to do so. I refer to this mechanism as turning a blind eye because I think this conveys the right degree of ambiguity as to how conscious or unconscious the knowledge is" (p. 161).

Thinking Space was set up because the psychotherapy profession turns a blind eye to its whiteness and its lack of diversity, and, when it does not, too often its approach is tokenistic. Most courses have one or two seminars on race or culture as an add-on, not as a thought-through and integral part of the training. While tokenism, or turning a blind eye, may provide some short-term relief, I believe it undermines self-confidence and competence within the profession as regards working with diversity and strengthens common underlying fears that these issues are too overwhelming to deal with. This is tremendously sad because psychoanalysis has the tools, both theoretically and clinically, to make a vital contribution to understanding and addressing these problems and their vicissitudes. Peter Fonagy wrote in his introduction to a book on taboos in psychotherapy that "Our clinical experience and our training have taught us that change requires taking the human mind places where it least wishes to be. Taking the analyst's mind to these domains is in the best interest of unencumbered work, which is obviously in the best interests of our patients" (Fonagy, 2009, p. xvi). Promoting thinking about racism and other forms of exclusion within psychotherapy is, I believe, also in the interests of good analytic work and in the best interests of patients.

The poor reputation of race equality training

Recognition of the problem of racism and other forms of discrimination in British society led to the development of anti-discrimination legislation and equal opportunity policies to ensure fair access to jobs and services. These required organizations, particularly in the public sector, to develop Race Equality Plans, as well as Inclusion Strategies supported by training programmes to enable staff to achieve better representation of excluded groups among staff and users of their services. These equal-opportunity and valuing-diversity initiatives, while well intentioned, spawned a culture of "political correctness". There was an official mantra of commitment to equalities by most organizations, but in actuality this was poorly implemented in practice and had little impact on outcomes (see Audit Commission, 2004a; Lowe, 2006a). Race equality training was often regarded as a critical component to developing anti-discriminatory practice and achieving better race equality outcomes but was generally found unhelpful or disappointing (see Bhavnani, 2001). The Stephen Lawrence Inquiry (Macpherson Report, 1999), for example, was critical of "race awareness" and "cultural diversity" trainings' failure to tackle colour blindness, ignorance, and the denial of racism in the police force. The generally poor reputation of race equality training is due to a number of factors. These include:

1. The unrealistic expectation that such training courses will eliminate or significantly reduce racism in individuals or organizations.

2. A tokenistic, or "tick-box", approach by organizations and their staff to such programmes, driven by the need to be seen to comply with legislation and policy. This approach has led to an increasing reduction in the length of such trainings across a number of organizations, and many are now as brief as an hour or two per year as part of a mandatory training programme for all staff.

3. Resistance to engage with such trainings because of vested interests, conflicts, and anxieties, which are sometimes unconscious, within individuals, teams, and organizations.

4. A collusion between commissioners and providers of such training to knowingly settle for a superficial training intervention into the highly complex and multifaceted problem of racism, which is highly resistant to change not only in individuals and organizations, but in society as whole.

In short, equality legislation and policy, while seemingly tackling exclusion, may have created an environment where prejudice and discrimination have become more hidden or covert and in many ways been driven even further underground. Race equality training is too often limited and superficial and, paradoxically, has unwittingly become part of a culture that resists tackling racism, while stating the opposite. A more genuine engagement with the reality of race and racism is needed, one that goes beyond the superficial surface of clarifying current legislation and policy and seeks, instead, to unpack the multiplicity of factors that are involved in racism, such as financial gain, greed, and self-interest, including its internal-world dimension.

On not wanting to think about racism in the self: resistance, self-illusion, and the need for critical reflection

No person is fully aware of every aspect of him/herself. (This is because part of our mind is unconscious, and as a result we are not aware at times, or sometimes ever, of some of our impulses, phantasies, thoughts, and behaviours.) Freud found that there was a resistance to becoming conscious of our unconscious. Resistance or "not wanting to know" is a defence to protect the ego from anxiety, pain, and threats to its survival. People use a number of defences—most commonly, splitting, denial, and projection—as a way of not knowing about themselves, attributing to others feelings and characteristics that they find impossible to bear in themselves. It is worth pointing out that some of these views of the human mind, developed by Freud and his followers, in fact predated psychoanalysis. A number of writers, including Feuerbach (1841) and Marx (1844), have argued that human beings have an immense capacity for self-illusion and are prone unconsciously to project on to God, for example, attributes that, in actuality, belong to them.

I have learnt from experience through working with professionals in the helping professions that many do not want to think about whether they may be racist. When asked to do so, even in the gentlest way possible, most get anxious, and a few would get angry in response to what they perceive as "being terrorized". One participant on a psychotherapy course responded to this request by saying that he was fed up with thinking about racism and that there are other issues such as class to think about. This is not an uncommon response to the invitation to think about racism. What does it mean? It can mean a number of things. Possibilities include that the individual who spoke:

» was simply angry about the continual prioritization, in his experience, of race over other issues such as class
» had transferred his feelings of anger from previous settings to a new setting—a seminar on race and psychotherapy—as a result of being asked to think about racism in himself
» was expressing feelings of anger about the task, not just for himself, but unconsciously on behalf of the group or at least for some others in the group

»   was expressing his and the group's resistance to doing the task in order to avoid painful feelings such as anxiety, guilt, and shame about their racism.

It seems easier to acknowledge the existence of racism, and other forms of hatred in the abstract, in "fascist groups" or in those individuals whose words or behaviour are clearly and obviously racist than it is in oneself. It is much more difficult, it seems, to explore and think about racism when it is covert, subtle, or nuanced. Such an endeavour seems to arouse strong resistance, and a wide range of defences are usually mobilized to undermine, paralyse, or destroy such initiatives. A number of theorists (e.g., Altman, 2010; Kovel, 1988) argue that racism is a ubiquitous part of Western culture and that no individual is unaffected by it. Davids (2011) goes further and argues that internal racism is a normal part of the mind but is extremely defended against by a defensive organization in the mind. A defensive organization, he explains, protects against anxiety more effectively than do individual defences, but it exerts a stranglehold on development, in particular limiting the individual's capacity to relate, especially to the racial other (Davids, 2011, p. 40). As a result, it is quite common that there are many who deny and project their racism and are resistant to change. However, it is also possible to get to know one's own racism.

In general, people who have suffered exclusion, such as Jews and black people, seem willing to talk about racism and being discriminated against (Wilson & Francis, 1997), but those who do not suffer such experiences are generally much less willing to do so. It should, however, not be assumed that Jews or black people are exempt from resistance to thinking about racism in themselves or that they do not also experience feelings of anxiety, guilt, and shame when they attempt to undertake this task. The works of Fanon (1967), Lipsky (1987), and Alleyne (2005) highlight that black and minority ethnic people can and do internalize racist values, which can result in feelings of self-hate and rage towards themselves and other black people. If Davids (2011) is correct—and I think he is—the operation of an unconscious defensive organization undermines the black or minority ethnic person's ability to free him/herself from racism in his or her mind. As Jung (1990, p. 49) argues, it is the fear of the unconscious which impedes self-knowledge and is also the gravest obstacle to developing a wider understanding of others.

Marx's (1973) early work on freeing humans from alienation from themselves is considered by many as the birth of critical theory. Critical theory, according to Habermas (1972), does not regard the individual as always aware of the meaning of his or her actions, nor does it consider reality, as it appears to be, the truth. It espouses that what is presented as facts must be examined critically as there are usually hidden factors operating that should be uncovered and brought to awareness. Critical theory believes that the aim of any theory should be human emancipation. Psychoanalysis is regarded by Habermas (1972) as a model example of critical theory because its practice involves methodical and critical self-reflection. According to Habermas, the experience of reflection is the act that frees the individual most to become a subject. Freud puts this more specifically: he wrote that psychoanalysis aims "to strengthen the ego, to make it more independent of the super-ego, to widen its field of perception and enlarge its organization, so that it can appropriate fresh portions of the id. Where id was, there ego shall be" (1933a, p. 80). Psychoanalysis can and does help people to achieve greater self-knowledge, particularly of their previously denied and split-off aspects. As I will show later, its methods play an important role in Thinking Space to facilitate thinking about racism in the self and in others.

Lack of curiosity or interest

In my experience, there are always some people who, for various reasons, do not want to take part in any learning event that aims at thinking about racism in themselves or in others. Their reasons tend to range from not regarding such learning as personally necessary, fearing being attacked because of their experience of previous trainings, and thinking that these events are always neither helpful nor worthwhile. Underneath this attitude is a belief that race equality or diversity events are by their nature unsophisticated and aggressive and, in phantasy, are facilitated by unsophisticated others who lack understanding and are preoccupied with dirt. These people simply do not trust "the people who are involved in such events". With this experience in mind, it seemed to me that managing low expectations and hostile projections was probably the most significant consideration in the way in which Thinking Space was to be organized, publicized, and chaired.

The aim of Thinking Space

The aim of Thinking Space is to promote thinking and learning about issues of diversity in psychotherapy—in particular, race and culture but also class, homosexuality, gender, faith, and disability. I believed that, by creating a space to think about issues that have historically been excluded or marginalized in psychotherapy training, such a space would contribute to their exploration becoming more acceptable, manageable, and normative in the profession.

In its aim to promote thinking rather than to provide the answer, Thinking Space draws on the tradition of the Work Discussion Group at the Tavistock Clinic (Rustin & Bradley, 2008). According to Rustin (2008), "The theory of work discussion as pedagogy is that the seminar leader's task is the creation and sustaining of an atmosphere of enquiry in the group characterized by curiosity, scepticism, fellow-feeling, debate, differences, so that the unknown can become less unwelcome and new thoughts, questions, and perceptions find fertile ground" (p. 12). To achieve this it was vital to be able to contain the anxiety that these subjects arouse in order to share knowledge and experiences in an open and non-defensive way (Lowe, 2006a).

However, given that difference (gender, race, culture, religion, sexuality, etc.) has frequently been a vehicle for human destructiveness, then the risk of repetition of destructiveness is real, even in settings that aim to do the opposite. Layton (2006b) has pointed out that living within a culture of hierarchies of class, race, gender, and so forth is wounding for all, but particularly for those at the bottom of these hierarchies, however much this may be repressed or disguised. We know that, in general, there is a tendency for those less powerful to identify with those with power and to internalize the negative attributions about them (see Dalal, 2002; Moss, 2003), although not always without conflict (Layton, 2004a). The risk of re-enactment of the destructive dynamics of racism and other forms of exclusion is perpetually present, and one that has to be contained, thought about, and used to enable participants to learn from experience rather than to repeat it.

The risk of re-enactment

A few years ago, I went with a colleague to listen to Joy DeGruy Leary, an American psychologist, speak about "Post Traumatic Slave Syndrome" at a Black History Month event. Her thesis was that African slaves experienced many traumas during slavery which led them to adopt strategies to survive, many of which have had a dysfunctional impact on their psyches and behaviours. These adaptations to trauma continue to operate today, she argued, as they have been transmitted from one generation to the next, largely unconsciously. One example of this is the distrust that was encouraged between slaves by slave owners. Higher status jobs and privileges were used as rewards for loyalty, which would be withdrawn or denied to any who showed any hint of disobedience or threat. As a result, a high-status, or "house", slave was often treated with suspicion, contempt, and even hatred because he or she was regarded as being in bed with the "oppressor".

DeGruy Leary concluded her inspiring speech by saying to the audience that there was work that black people still needed to do in order to heal the injuries of their history. It was therefore amazing that, not long after a warm and rousing ovation, an energetic and hopeful atmosphere was suddenly brought to an end by a ferocious attack on a senior black health professional on the Discussion Panel for being a "traitor to his people". The speaker argued that the panel member had failed to protect and support a black mental health patient in the psychiatric system and therefore should not be on this panel. He was supported by a small group around him, who heckled and shouted at the panel member. It took some time for the chairperson and others to restore order, and at one point the conference seemed to be at risk of imploding.

The speaker was clearly in the grip of an overwhelming anger that he felt he needed to express towards a black professional whom he had expected to protect and support black people in the psychiatric system. He used the conference to say what a bad black man this panel member was, and he seemed to have either assumed that his view would simply be agreed with by all at the conference or that the conference would replace its original task and become a court that heard the case for and against the panel member whom he had alleged to be a traitor to his people.

This illustrates that the aim to learn and progress can be thwarted by forces—often unconscious—that seek expression that

seem impossible to stop. In this case, the speaker and his supporters had consciously decided to attack the panel member, as they
thought this was the appropriate thing to do. They clearly did not
consider what impact their behaviour would have on the event,
which they seemed to support. When asked by the chairperson to
consider this, they were unable to do so for some time, possibly
because they were so consumed by their rage towards this panel
member.

I think this speaker and his supporters' behaviour was a repetition of the very past that we had gathered to remember and learn
from. However, the way in which the issue of betrayal by the
"house slave" was brought up seemed more like a repetition of
the trauma of slavery than a way of transcending it. My colleague
and I left the conference angry and despairing and wondered about
the black community's capacity to heal the injuries of its history.
Freud (1914g) has argued that we are prone to repeat what we do
not remember and that we must find the courage to not simply
see the illness within a contemptible enemy but also in ourselves.
He argued that to heal, we must keep in mind our impulses rather
than act them out, and to dispose of them through the work of
remembering, thinking, and working through instead of action.

What is thinking?

Thinking is a broad term, referring to a mental operation, non-
directed or directed, conscious or unconscious, that is involved in
learning, considering, or making sense of an experience or subject.
There are many types of thinking and thinking styles. Thinking
Space is less concerned with abstract thinking and more with getting to know and understand oneself and one's relationship with
the "different" other. Psychoanalysis—in particular, the work of
Klein (1946), Bion (1962), and Bollas (1992)—seemed highly relevant to Thinking Space because the theories it provides about both
thinking and its development most informed the approach we took
to creating the Thinking Space environment.

Klein (1935, 1946) thought there were fundamentally two modes
of thinking: the paranoid–schizoid position, which is the most
primitive type of thinking and predominates in early infancy,
and the depressive position, which is the more mature mode of

thinking. In the paranoid-schizoid position, the individual defends him/herself from pain by splitting feelings into good and bad and then projecting into others those feelings that she or he cannot bear. By contrast, depressive-position thinking occurs when the individual is able to integrate feelings and is thus able to see himself and the other as a whole person with good and bad aspects. This ability is described as the depressive position, because of the painful recognition by the individual that she or he has hateful and loving feelings towards the same person. Klein described these two modes of thinking as positions, not stages, because the individual, she argued, will oscillate between being depressive and paranoid-schizoid throughout life, but is more likely to be paranoid-schizoid when under stress.

Racism is a classic example of paranoid-schizoid thinking, in which the processes of splitting and projection dominate. Notions about black and white people are a product of paranoid-schizoid thinking, which we have inherited from history. In our culture, a white person, for example, might think that black people are primitive and white people are civilized, therefore believing that such people do belong to opposite categories: black = primitive (inferior) and white = civilized (superior). This person can be described as operating in the paranoid-schizoid mode, because of the clear strength of splitting and projective processes in his or her thinking. The division of people into opposites can be interpreted as a reflection of repressed feelings of inferiority which this individual cannot bear, ones that are projected on to black people, who are then looked down upon. The process of splitting and projection of unwanted parts of the self on to others is common because it gives relief from anxieties that arise from difficulties in containing our conflicting needs and feelings. Projection creates external figures that are disliked and feared, and it is hard to take back our projections because this makes us anxious and deflates our idealized image of ourselves. Additionally, it may also be difficult to differentiate between our projections and the reality about a person or group that we hate. As there is, however, a tendency among professionals, particularly helping professionals, to deny feelings of racial prejudice, these feelings are more likely to be split-off and projected on to others. This enables racist feelings to be located outside the self and for a self-image of fair-mindedness to be maintained.

In the depressive position, individuals are able to give up self-idealization and face the complex reality of their feelings about both themselves and black people, which is likely to produce feelings of anxiety, guilt, and concern. In this position, there is a real desire to make reparation for one's less-than-ideal character to work for a better understanding of oneself and one's relationship to others. Working in the depressive position also enriches the ego's belief in its good capacities and helps the individual to become more confident in the ability to contain his or her destructive aspects and to grow.

Drawing on Melanie Klein's work, the psychoanalyst Wilfred Bion (1962) was particularly interested in the process of getting from the paranoid-schizoid position, the primitive form of thinking, to the depressive position, the more complex form of thinking. According to Bion, the acquisition of the capacity to think as an emotional experience of getting to know oneself or another, which he called K (Know), develops as a result of a relationship between the mother and the baby, in which the mother is able to contain the baby's projections. Bion argued that if the mother is able to contain the baby's projections, and help it to tolerate frustration and to make sense of its incomprehensible feelings, the baby will, over time, introject this capacity to think, to make sense of experiences, and to get to know itself and others. He also regarded as "minus K" the avoidance of knowing and truth. There are others who support the view that the development of thinking is dependent on the relationship with primary others. For example, the work of Fonagy and Target (1966, 1997) also argues that the reflective, or mentalizing, self develops from the exchanges with another mind in a safe, sensitive, and thoughtful relationship. In short, there is growing research evidence to show that a secure attachment facilitates the acquisition of the reflective function (Fonagy, Steele, Steele, Moran, & Higgitt, 1991).

The importance of containment and reverie

If Thinking Space were to achieve its aim, it was vital that the anxieties and passions aroused by the subjects of race, culture, and so forth were contained and could be thought about and worked with. Containment occurs by making sense of the individual's feelings and making these feelings understandable and tolerable. To be able to do this, the person attempting to contain—that is, the container—must be receptive to the individual's feelings and have the capacity for what Bion calls "reverie"—to empathize and think about the other's feelings and state of mind, as well as to bear the pain that that individual cannot tolerate. The willingness to receive, empathize, and think about the person's communication not only helps the container to understand the person's communication but also enables the individual who is communicating to better tolerate his or her unbearable feelings. Bion argued that if a person repeatedly has the experience of being thought about (kept in mind) and understood, he will acquire through introjection and identification the capacity to think and to know psychic qualities in himself and others.

It is well known that an individual's capacity to think is very likely to diminish when he or she is highly anxious, or under great stress, or is in the grip of powerful feelings. Therefore, providing a containing environment is clearly vital if we are to help anxious or stressed participants to bear their difficult feelings in order to maintain or regain their capacity to think. I also believed that repeated experiences of containment around diversity issues at the Thinking Space forum would lead to an internalization of a thoughtful "object"[1] or an internal mental space in participants that would increase their capacity to tolerate, understand, and better deal with anxiety and pain about diversity issues, both in themselves and in others. Bion (1959) argued that thinking does not produce thoughts but that thought is born out of relationships with other minds and is intricately linked with the processing of emotional experience. Thinking Space, therefore, aimed to provide an opportunity for those who were curious enough to engage with other minds in order to contain and process difficult and unbearable experiences in relation to diversity. This process, I believed, was more likely to produce real emotionally integrated knowledge about oneself and difference that would lead to a more grounded understanding about race, culture, and diversity.

In brief, through ongoing participation in Thinking Space, we sought to develop participants' capacity to reflect on their own selves and on other selves through safe, meaningful exchanges from the heart and mind.

Developing thinking

Bion (1962) reasoned that the task of getting to know oneself and others was challenging because it requires an active relationship between the person seeking to know (x) and the person who is getting to be known (y); as result there are four key factors that affect the task of getting to know (thinking) which should be borne in mind:

1. the need to know oneself in order to differentiate oneself from the other;
2. the nature of the relationship between person x and person y;
3. that getting to know someone is often painful;
4. the commitment of x and y to truth and their capacity to maintain contact with and affirm reality.

This process can result in K (trying to know): the individual can be seen or experienced as trying to know. Alternatively, if too anxious or unable to tolerate frustration, pain, and envy, the process will result in the avoidance of K and truth, which Bion called minus K (–K). These ideas about thinking, the conditions that promote it, and the hazards that can lead to –K are all extremely useful to both the conceptualizing and the running of Thinking Space.

In psychoanalysis, patients are encouraged to say "whatever comes to mind", without any censoring, even if the emerging thoughts and feelings are believed to be unacceptable. At Thinking Space events, we encourage free association because we want to engage with the entire person, not just the conscious self, in order to facilitate unconscious thinking, because we believe that it is perfection—not imperfection—that is a block to getting to know oneself and others. But more importantly, free association is a gateway to the unconscious and opens up the possibility of greater engagement of the whole personality and of deeper psychic work.

Christopher Bollas is a psychoanalyst who is particularly interested in the unconscious as a source of individual truth, self-knowledge, and creative thinking. Drawing on the work of Wilfred Bion and Donald Winnicott, Bollas (1992) argues that unconscious thinking initially requires the facilitating presence of others, and this leads to the formation of what he calls genera which results in the development of new perspectives on self and other. He regards the dialectic between conscious and unconscious thinking as like the relationship between waking and dreaming. Unconscious thinking, he believes, is like dreaming, an oscillation between condensation and dissemination of thoughts and experiences. It is not a complex self reflecting on its experience; it is a more like being lost in thought (Beck, 2002).

Bollas use the term "object" broadly to mean anything that affects the psyche, and this includes a parent, a person, a group of people, a place, works of art, and so forth. An object, argues Bollas, can be experienced as a structure, as memorable, as related to certain concepts, and as a transient container for projection. It can also evoke or be used in different ways—such as sensationally, structurally, mnemonically, conceptually, and symbolically—to stimulate unconscious thought. He distinguishes between traumatic and generative objects: the latter facilitates genera leading to individual truth and self-knowledge.

According to Beck (2002), there are six characteristics of conscious thinking that are relevant to Bollas's ideas about the dialectic between conscious and unconscious thinking:

1. It begins with stopping, or withdrawal from, practical involvement with the world and becoming in touch with ourselves.
2. It involves a turning-away from reality, as directly perceived, and a turning-towards the mind, which includes memories, opinions, hypotheses, concepts, etc.
3. It is like a conversation between different parts of the mind.
4. It can take a number of forms, including logical, objective, or subjective thinking.
5. It is always in relation to the thoughts of others—for example, parents, friends, teachers, society. Most thinking is passive thinking—that is, thinking the thoughts of others. But some thinking is active thinking—that is, when we think for ourselves, which is more likely to lead to insight.
6. It is always connected to the concept of truth, but just as there are different types of thinking, so there are different kinds of truth.

Thinking Space sought to create an environment that promoted these characteristics of thinking—getting in touch with ourselves, turning towards the mind, conversation and dialogue, promoting active thinking, and identifying truth. Therefore, we particularly sought to create an environment that promoted thinking by being containing and facilitative, one that was felt safe and emotionally holding and gave permission for presenters and participants to test out their thoughts and ideas with each other in order to develop insights and understanding. Thinking Space can be thought of as functioning as an evocative object, engaging the psyche intensely and stimulating unconscious thinking, which leads to psychic change and the development of new perspectives on self and other.

Bollas's (1992) idea of genera as a form of internal work that results in an important new way of seeing the world seems to describe the process that we seek to facilitate in Thinking Space. He describes genera as a process of psychic incubation of experiences of facilitative parents or others who contribute to the evolution and successful elaboration of the individual's personal idiom. This process involves emotional experiences, ideas, feelings, words, all unconsciously constellating to become the nuclei of genera, which in time will return to consciousness as acts of self-enrichment. Bollas argues that this process happens in therapy, where the psychotherapist and patient collaborate to construct psychic structures that can change the patient's view of him/herself and the world. However, he points out that the incubation of genera can be, and usually is, the work of great personal struggle and conflict, and, as with any change of one's status quo, it involves tolerating uncertainty and emotional turbulence (Bollas, 1992, p. 70).

The model:
key values and methods to promote thinking

Thinking Space sought to find ways to stimulate curiosity about race, culture, and diversity in psychotherapy by establishing an ongoing learning forum about these subjects and inviting emotionally truthful and thoughtful speakers who would model trying to know as well as stimulate feeling and thinking. The values and methods listed below were regarded as critical to achieving our aims.

Values

» Thinking Space events should be as safe as possible, which means that all participants should be treated respectfully, and that the ordinary rules that operate at learning events should be adhered to.

» To not promote a particular view at Thinking Space but to foster openness to different perspectives and encourage discussion and debate.

» To not assume that there is one correct answer or "the truth" but to consider that there may be many truths.

» That it is ok to explore and to make mistakes as part of the learning process.

Methods

To:

» create a relaxed and informal atmosphere

» encourage participants to free-associate—say anything that comes to mind in response to the presentation and in discussions

» encourage participants to cooperate with and challenge each other in order to learn and develop

» encourage and support the group and the individual to expand capacity to accept, tolerate, and work with anxiety, conflict, and ambivalence

» allow and support participants to take responsibility to work things out for themselves

» regard the pain, frustration, difficulties, and imperfections of trying to know as a critical, valuable, and normal part of the process of getting to know and learning

» encourage participants to have a receptive mind and consider new ways of looking at things

» tolerate strong feelings or "emotional storms" for long enough so that they can be thought about and given meaning

» attend to thoughts and feelings at the margins

» face the truth of one's experience and share one's genuine reflections

» try to achieve and retain a "balanced outlook".

The role of the chairperson

The chairperson ensures that each Thinking Space event keeps to its task by adhering to the above values and encourages the use of the above methods—in particular, fostering a friendly and tolerant but challenging atmosphere and ensuring that individuals and the group adhere to the boundaries that support dialogue and reflection. Following a presentation, the chairperson encourages participants to free-associate and to speak as freely as possible to the large group about their responses to the material, which can include addressing questions to the speaker or sharing feelings, thoughts, personal experiences, opinions, information, and so forth. The speaker may or may not respond to these responses at this stage. But the chairperson would always provide an opportunity for participants to discuss their response to the presentation, in pairs or small groups. She or he would also think about the group's response to the presentation as a way of understanding the subject at hand, how it can impact on those involved, and what might be helpful in addressing the situation. The chairperson would pay attention to the atmosphere in the room, non-verbal communication, the handling of the speaker's material, and significant incidents.

In many ways, the chairperson functions as a nurturing but firm parent, encouraging and enabling participants to remain in touch with their own thoughts and feelings as well as to communicate these in safety. Simultaneously, the chairperson needs to model the capacity to tolerate conflict and difference and, at the same time, to appropriately name avoidant, defensive, and other behaviours that stop/hinder the group in carrying out its task. For, as Bion (1961) has pointed out, groups can resort to basic-assumption functioning as a way of not getting on with the task—for example, taking flight from the subject at hand or getting into a fight with the organizers of the event by blaming them for the painful and upsetting feelings aroused by the material. These dynamics often create a good–bad split, with the bad often located outside the self or the group, because it is too unbearable to consider that the threat may be within the self or the group. The chairperson may offer an interpretation to help the group think about the possibility that the bad object may be a projection of something within that, it is feared, cannot be contained and thought about.

An example to illustrate

Aideen Lucey's presentation at Thinking Space in 2009, "Paradoxes and Blind Spots: Reflections on Being an Irish Woman Working in Mental Health and Organizational Consultancy in Britain", well illustrates the atmosphere and experiences in Thinking Space, as well as some of the issues that tend to emerge and how they are addressed in the group. The following is not a comprehensive or objective record of the event but a summary of what most struck me about it. I do not aim to provide details about Aideen's thoughts on the subject, as they are reproduced in the chapter that she has contributed to this book (chapter 9). My focus is on the emotional experiences that her talk aroused and some of the insights and learning that participants seemed to glean from the reflections and discussion that ensued.

Anxiety has been a constant theme in Thinking Space, for both presenters and participants. The vast majority of speakers have been extremely anxious about presenting to the forum, even those with extensive, even international, experience of lecturing and public speaking. Aideen therefore was not unusual. She was worried that she might inappropriately expose things about herself in a way that would diminish her in the eyes of colleagues. But worse than the fear of shame was guilt about possibly betraying the Irish community by talking about things ("washing dirty laundry in public" or "exposing family secrets") that should be kept private or discussed only within the Irish community. She was also anxious that, by speaking honestly about her experiences of stereotyping and discrimination in Britain, she was in some way being ungrateful to or betraying her English colleagues and the England that had, in many ways, been good to her.

After her presentation of approximately thirty minutes, there occurred a series of powerful cathartic outpourings from a number of participants. Initially this felt like an Irish "coming-out". A few people, including some whom I and others had not ever thought of as Irish, spoke about their "unspoken experiences"—experiences they had never spoken about in public or in therapy. These included being sent as a child to elocution lessons, in order, ostensibly, to get rid of any trace of Irishness. Several spoke of often being seen as a terrorist during the IRA's campaign on the British mainland in the 1980s. One person talked about not being assumed to be Irish either in Ireland or in England because he was black. A few said that being frequently confronted by the common stereotype of the Irish in Britain had, at times, left them feeling ashamed of being Irish.

Aideen's feelings prior to her presentation of fearing inadequacy, shame, and guilt began to look less personal and could be thought of as an unconscious identification with projections received by the Irish in England. A woman born in England, whose grandparents from Poland settled in the UK during World War II, talked about her painful childhood experiences as a result of her Polish roots. She confessed that because she was born in England, she has hidden her Polish heritage for some time, but much more today than in childhood. This is due to the common stereotypes of Poles as part of an invading mass of East European migrants abusing Britain's too generous welfare state and reducing wages or taking jobs from British people as au-pairs, cleaners, and craftsmen of all descriptions.

Reclaiming split-off parts of the self

What is remarkable about these reflections is not so much the pain they describe but the fact that they have been unspoken. It seems that people of Irish descent within the psychotherapeutic, analytic, and mental health community have been fearful or ashamed of speaking about experiences in their organization, and sometimes in therapy, out of fear that it would not be handled well, that it might be experienced as an attack, or as an act of trouble-making, or as a lack of gratitude. But the discussion was not just a release of painful emotions, it was also a reclaiming of part of the self—one's cultural heritage that had become split-off and kept at the periphery.

Aideen's presentation had given permission for the "inappropriate or unacceptable" experiences to be voiced, and, in so doing, emotional conflicts—some unconscious—could be brought out into the open for thought and exploration. As Aideen pointed out, the issue of her being Irish was paradoxically both known and invisible simultaneously. However, the acknowledging of cultural heritage, denied or otherwise, was not the end. Rather, it was a beginning of further reflections about the reasons why people migrate to Britain from Ireland. It was thought that this was not simply about jobs and opportunities but included escaping something oppressive.

This led to a discussion about the domination of Ireland by the British, and then by the Catholic Church, and how both forms of colonization have had both a negative and positive impact on the Irish people, on their culture and identity.

The chairperson of this particular Thinking Space had, as is often the case, little more to do than to be a non-intrusive but facilitating presence. Prior to the event, as chairperson I supported Aideen with her anxieties about presenting by listening to her and asking her to articulate what her worst fantasies were about the approaching event. I informed her that most previous speakers had been anxious, and I suggested that it might be worth thinking about her anxieties as not just personal but that they may be part of the material that she wants to present to the group. At one point during the event, I had to point out to the group of about twenty-five participants that there seemed to be an assumption that only people of Irish descent could talk, and, if this was the case, was there a fear that talking between the English and the Irish participants might lead to a fight? This comment highlighted to the group a relative silence from the non-Irish members, but this was not taken up, and the discussion was brought to an end soon after, because of time. It was clear that we had touched upon a range of significant issues that would have benefited from much more thinking and dialogue in general, but also among Irish people living in Britain, as well as between the Irish and English.

Discussion

Thinking Space is usually an emotionally moving and thought-provoking event, and Aideen's presentation at the forum illustrates that well. The primary purpose of bringing people together is to talk and to think about difference. In this example, the fright, flight, and fight response was contained, and a silence about being Irish in Britain was broken. However, the relative silence of non-Irish participants may have reflected guilt and/or anxiety about speaking, out of fear that it might result in a fight, or even murder.

Nonetheless, the participants in this Thinking Space, especially those who were Irish, learnt about the "unspoken experiences" not only of the Irish but of other minorities who are recipients of projections, stereotyping, and discrimination and of some of the negative effects that this can have on their feelings about themselves and their heritage. They also developed a better understanding that there are painful racial dynamics that occur below the surface, intrapsychically, interpersonally, and within mental health organizations, which are rarely brought out into the open for thought and discussion. This state of affairs invariably disadvantages minorities, as their painful experiences are not recognized and there is no space to talk about this. In other words, there is immense resistance, consciously and unconsciously, to exploring these issues as it is felt to be a threat to the status quo—the dominant power relations that exist.

Psychotherapy—in particular, the psychoanalytic tradition, especially in Britain—has always had a preponderance of practitioners from abroad, some from minority ethnic backgrounds. These include Sigmund Freud, Anna Freud, and Melanie Klein, who were Austrian Jews; Hanna Segal was from Poland; Masud Khan was from Pakistan; and Wilfred Bion, an Anglo-Indian, was born in India. Despite this, hardly anything has been written about the experience of race or ethnicity within their work, or of living in the UK. This silence dates back, I believe, to Freud himself. I think that Freud's desire for his ideas to be accepted as universal by the Christian establishment in nineteenth-century Austria, and not be dismissed as nothing more than a "Jewish science", has contributed to this paradoxical culture of silence within psychoanalysis about ethnicity, culture, and racism. However, psychoanalysis itself teaches us that we must court the unfamiliar, be curious about what is absent, and pay particular attention to what is on the margin of awareness, as these are likely to lead to the parts of the individual's internal world that are most unbearable and have become split-off and separated from the conscious self.

Conclusion

Thinking Space is an event, influenced by critical theory and psychoanalysis, that seeks to promote thinking about diversity. This is achieved by creating an environment where people can meet to listen, talk, and reflect on the thoughts and feelings aroused in them by what they have experienced and to try to interpret, make sense of, and understand what has been communicated. Communications can, of course, occur on conscious, preconscious, and unconscious levels, often simultaneously, and participants are encouraged to pay attention to all thoughts and feelings, even the most marginal. The chairperson's task is to create and maintain a non-judgemental atmosphere that can keep the group to its task: that of being curious and receptive to different ideas; of holding seriously thoughts and feelings at the margins of awareness; and of containing difficult emotions and allowing each other to listen, talk, and think without violence or coercion.

This is not to say that Thinking Space is a paradise, that participants do not experience difficult feelings, such as frustration, anger, shame, fear, or disappointment. However, it is the ability to endure these experiences of relative disintegration that can lead to psychic change—to what Bion refers to as the PS–D (paranoid-schizoid–depressive) balance. It is the experience of feeling fear and worrying about being exposed, attacked, even annihilated by others, and then discovering, in interaction, that these fears can be contained, that you can participate and survive, that leads to discovering new knowledge and growth and, with it, the creation of new ideas and meaning. Of course, as in the example above, not every question is answered, and some things are clearly not known. But to acknowledge that one doesn't know is an important type of knowing, and to bear not knowing and be committed to getting to know is an invaluably rich capacity.

Thinking Space is not a neutral or value-free space. It is committed to understanding and learning about racism and other forms of human oppression based on difference, not in the abstract but in ourselves and others. It seeks to do this because with greater knowledge of self and others, we—not just psychotherapists and mental health professionals—are more likely to be aware of our capacity for destructiveness and, in so being, are better equipped to prevent unnecessary harm and suffering for the benefit of all, not just the immediate victims of such hatreds.

Note

1. Bollas (1992) uses the term "object" broadly to include a structure, a place, a group of people, and so forth. I believe that Thinking Space can be internalized as an object that can evoke containment and stimulate unconscious thought. More is said about Bollas's ideas later in this chapter.

CHAPTER TWO

Race and our evasions of invitations to think: how identifications and idealizations may prevent us from thinking

Onel Brooks

This chapter argues that our identifications and idealizations often make it very difficult for us to think about most matters, including race. So when we think that we are thinking about race and culture, we may not be; we may be better described as engaged in protecting ourselves, our theories, and our subgroup. Psychotherapy can offer us an easy path to thinking that we are thinking when we are not. To the extent that psychoanalysts and other psychotherapists are busy acting out their own tendencies to idealize, identify, and denigrate—their own tribalism, their own implicit or explicit claim to be better than other psychotherapists— they do not give us reasons to be confident in their ability to think about issues to do with race, for they show that they are caught up in the very issues that they need to be thoughtful about.

This chapter is not part of an attempt to construct a theory or model or some set of generalizations about race, racism, and psychotherapy. Indeed, it indicates the author's misgivings about any such enterprise. For even if some interesting and useful psychotherapeutic theory of race and racism could be constructed, the argument of this chapter would still apply to it, in that this theory or model could easily become a way of evading thoughtful engagement with notions of race, ethnicity, and culture and the part such notions play in what we say, do, and believe.

This chapter claims that there are many ways to decline an invitation to think about race, and that one way of doing this is to talk about race by falling back on our favoured way of talking about it, as we reassure ourselves that we are being thoughtful, when we may not be doing much more than reassuring ourselves and imposing a system of belief or a model on the space where thinking might take place.

If this chapter appears to fail to provide convincing definitions of the terms it uses, and to discuss directly and compellingly notions such as "racism", "the racist", "racist states of mind", "the internal racist", "institutional racism", and so on, it does this partly out of an anxiety that sometimes in being preoccupied with catching the whale, we may trample on and be unable to see the particular flora and fauna, the humble plankton and little fishes that provide the whale with its habitat and renders it mighty. In other words, if this chapter "fails" to discuss such terms, "fails" to try hard to pin them down and make it clear what they really mean, it does so partly out of a fear that in trying to write about how we fail to think, it may, through being focused on such terms, fall foul of what it sets out to identify and consider—namely, our failures to think about difficult matters, and, in particular, matters to do with race, and our tendency to confuse thinking about a matter with repeating what others tend to say about it. This chapter is part of an attempt to value small nets, attentiveness, and patience and to be wary of smothering our thinking in theoretical constructs. However, it may be possible that the reader is misled by talk of "small nets, attentiveness, and patience"; she or her may think that the author is claiming that the only response in situations where race, culture, or any other difference that often evokes discomfort, pain, and indignation is involved is quietism—meek and passive contemplation. This chapter is neither meek nor passive in what it argues. A work that is concerned with our difficulties in thinking is not necessarily a work that claims that there is never a time for action, especially if what, how, and when is carefully thought through. And we must not assume or try to present the issues so that thinking is presented as if it is not a kind of action that is of immense importance in our lives, including in psychotherapy. This chapter is a doing, it is a sustained critique of some tendencies in psychoanalysis that get in the way of our being able to think. It tries to show or illustrate how our evading or declining our opportunities to think can be violent or can contribute to violence towards others. It should be clear, too, that although this chapter is primarily concerned with notions of race, ethnicity, and culture, what it has to say goes beyond these matters

Wittgenstein's question and invitation

It is 1939 and the most important philosopher of the twentieth century, Ludwig Wittgenstein, is walking by the river in Cambridge with his student and friend, Norman Malcolm, when they see a newsvendor's sign announcing that the German government has accused the British government of being the instigators of the recent attempt to assassinate Hitler with a bomb. Wittgenstein remarks, "It would not surprise me at all if it were true." Malcolm writes:

> I retorted that I could not believe that the top people in the British government would do such a thing. I mean that the British were too civilized and decent to attempt anything so underhand; and I added that such an act was incompatible with the British "national character". My remarks made Wittgenstein extremely angry. He considered it to be a great stupidity and also an indication that I was not learning anything from the philosophical training that he was trying to give me. He said these things very vehemently, and when I refused to admit that my remark was stupid he would not talk to me anymore, and we soon after parted. [Malcolm, 1980, p. 32]

Wittgenstein may not have been the easiest man to get on with, but it is difficult to accuse him of being the sort of man who does not think, and who cares more about keeping his friends happy and maintaining a good opinion of them or himself, rather than about thinking carefully and honestly. Here he does seem to have a point. What was Malcolm thinking? What is "national character" anyway? Do philosophers (or psychotherapists) have the right to throw such terms around, or is philosophy (and psychotherapy) something more like a practice of being scrupulously concerned about what we might mean, imagine, assume, or be trying to do when we reach for such terms? Was the Empire acquired and retained by "civilized" and "decent" means exclusively? Was he thinking or displaying a reflex, asserting something consistent with his prejudices and idealizations, caught up in what we might want to regard as an imaginary or at least partial picture of what it means to be British? Did Malcolm see *himself* as "civilized" and "decent" and so identified with the essence of being British? (Who was he leaving out of this category? What gets you into this club?) Was it too much of a challenge to his own sense of himself and what he held dear to even consider the accusation for a moment? A space for thinking and talking was not opened up here.

Although this incident did not end their friendship, it ended their practice of going walking together, and it remained an issue between them. Five years later, in 1944, Wittgenstein wrote to Malcolm about this incident and how shocked he was by the "primitiveness" of Malcolm's comments about "national character". (Of course, "primitive" is an interesting term, and hardly unrelated to our discussion.) Wittgenstein wrote to Malcolm:

> I then thought: what is the use of studying philosophy if all that it does for you is to enable you to talk with some plausibility about some abstruse questions of logic, etc., & if it does not improve your thinking about the important questions of everyday life, if it does not make you more conscientious than any . . . journalist in the use of the dangerous phrases such people use for their own ends. You see, I know that it's difficult to think well about "certainty", "probability", "perception", etc. But it is if possible, still more difficult to think, or to try to think, really honestly about your own life & and other peoples' lives. And the trouble is that thinking about these things is not thrilling, but often downright nasty. And when it's nasty then it's most important. . . . You can't think decently if you don't want to hurt yourself. . . . [Malcolm, 1980, pp. 39–40]

Wittgenstein and Nietzsche are very much concerned with how we are easily misled, confused, and seduced by language, ideas, pictures, or images of who we are and what we are doing. They are concerned with how our words, terms, and conceptions muddle and flatter us and often obscure from us what we are doing. Both are ferocious critics of the lazy, the complacent, the fearful, and the formulaic and insist on the importance of thinking honestly, courageously, and creatively about oneself and others, even if it hurt, even if it means that you find yourself isolated or cast out of the group (Nietzsche, 1887, Sections 2, 319, and 335, for example). For them, thinking is not and cannot be cleverness or fidelity to a set of convictions or a system; thinking involves intellectual integrity, conscience, and moral courage, and it often leads to difficult and uncomfortable places.

Wittgenstein's question addressed to psychoanalytic practitioners might read: what is the point of being able to speak with some plausibility about "the Oedipus complex", "the unconscious", "attacks", "projective identification", "transference", "counter-transference", and the like if we do not try to think really honestly about our own lives, the lives of other people, and our relationships with them.

It is not being disputed that some psychoanalysts do try to think honestly about these matters. What is being claimed is that what passes for thinking in psychoanalysis, including thinking about race, often has little to do with intellectual integrity, courage, and being prepared to inhabit uncomfortable places, that what passes for thinking is usually a matter of saying what those in one's group tend to say. What is being claimed here is that where there is a system of thought or beliefs, there is also the danger that it restricts as well as facilitates thought. Where there is a group that may see itself as being in the right (and few groups do not), maintaining their own sense of themselves as the group that is in the right is likely to get in the way of its members being able to think about themselves, others, and the very thing that they claim to be in the right about. Psychoanalysis does not seem to be an exception to this argument. What is being disputed in this chapter is the idea that being psychoanalytically sophisticated or trained enables us to think better about race in particular. Psychoanalytic concepts can help us to think or be used to foreclose thinking.

To take such claims as yet another example of Freud-bashing, as anti-psychoanalysis, is perhaps to demonstrate one of the contentions of this chapter: that it is easy to react in the way that Malcolm reacted in the story above, as if an illegitimate and unwarranted attack is being made on what we hold dear and that, therefore, it must be dismissed rather than thought about.

Self-love or narcissism as an obstacle to thinking

It is 2006 and an important child and adolescent psychotherapist, Anne Horne, is writing about the state of psychoanalysis in Britain. Commenting on "those who would cling to narrower identifications and supposed orthodoxies", Horne tells us that "such 'orthodoxy' brings its own dilemmas". She continues:

> The greatest issue facing psychoanalysis in Britain today, paradoxically, is not the assumed threats from other psychological approaches or even the slowness in establishing an evidence-base. It lies for many of us in the incapacity of the profession to analyse its own tendency to idealization. [Horne, 2006, p. 19]

Horne has interesting and useful things to say about this "pathological idealization", how this is "institutionalized", and how psychoanalytic practitioners can come to depend upon "ideal internal objects". "Such a process", she writes,

> often brings an accompanying reluctance to question the ideas and tenets of one's theoretical forebears and carries with it an assumption that what one is taught are "set" and "right" techniques and principles. [p. 20]

Whether this is the greatest issue facing psychoanalysis today or not, the incapacity of those professionals who regard themselves as psychoanalytic or psychodynamic practitioners to think about their own tendency to idealize and identify with psychoanalysis is certainly an issue, and an issue that can be related to the notion of self-love or narcissism.

Laplanche and Pontalis (1973) state that identification is a "Psychological process whereby the subject assimilates an aspect, property or attribute of the other and is transformed, wholly or partially, after the model the other provides" (p. 205). Rycroft (1988) tells us that identification is "The process by which a person either (a) extends his identity into someone else, (b) borrows his identity from someone else, or (c) fuses or confuses his identity with someone else" (Rycroft, p. 67). The idea seems to be that the person feels himself to be extended into the other, to borrow from or be enhanced by or confused with this other person or thing. There is a sense of expanding our sense of who and what we are, of the binding-up of our sense of who and what we are with the acquired qualities of the other person, object, idea, or body of doctrine.

Idealization is a "Mental process by means of which the object's qualities and value are elevated to the point of perfection" (Laplanche & Pontalis, 1973, p. 202); the object is "aggrandised and exalted in the subject's mind" (p. 203). The idealized person or thing needs to be perceived as perfect, and anything that does not fit in with the illusion of perfection must be ignored or denied (Rycroft, 1988, p. 67).

For Klein (1946), the tendency to idealize the good breast is a "characteristic feature of the earliest relation to the good object" (p. 9). Frustration and anxiety, she argues, impels the infant to seek comfort and protection from the good object when anxiety of a persecutory nature is great; but when persecutory anxiety is great, "the flight to the idealized object becomes excessive, and this severely hampers ego-development and disturbs object-relations" (p. 9).

Klein seems to be telling us what the idealized object is needed for, what we seek to bring about by believing in and creating it: she seems to be telling us that we need the ideal object to help us to feel protected from a sense of being persecuted, or, rather, from the fear that we may be attacked, got at, damaged, or destroyed. It beats whistling, or it is a form of whistling when we are afraid of the dark and lurking bogeys. It is a comforting illusion; however, by writing that it "severely hampers ego-development and disturbs object-relations", Klein might be read as telling us that idealization provides us with some comfort but it helps to prevent us from growing up and relating to others. Helping others to grow up and relate to other people might be one way of talking about what we might hope for from psychoanalysis. We might be concerned that it seems that psychoanalysts, too, are sometimes caught up in their own comforting illusions and may have trouble growing up and relating to others.

Narcissism, Laplanche and Pontalis helpfully tell us, is "love directed towards the image of oneself" (Laplanche & Pontalis, 1973, p. 255), and referring to Lacan, they describe narcissism as "the amorous captivation of the subject by [his own] image" (p. 256). It refers to self-love and a love of oneself in which what is loved is not what one is, but very much caught up in how we would like to see ourselves, in our defence against our sense of loss and other pains, including our defence against our potential for coming to know how we are not as perfect and as loveable as we might like to see ourselves.

Freud (1930a) allows us to hear a narcissistic voice when in his discussion of the injunction "Thou shalt love thy neighbour as thyself", he remarks, "He deserves it if he is so like me in important ways that I can love myself in him; and he deserves it if he is so much more prefect than myself that I can love my ideal of my own self in him" (p. 109). Here Freud seems to be telling us that the supposed love of the other can be but a path to self-love. A little later in this work, he observes that "It is always possible to bind together a considerable number of people in love, so long as there are other people left over to receive the manifestation of their aggressiveness". This is said in the context of his discussing "the narcissism of minor differences", where he seems to be saying something about how it is people who are physically close to each other and similar to each other who are locked in rivalry with each other, and apparently wanting to see themselves as different to and better than the other group (Freud, 1930a, p. 114).

In speaking of narcissism or self-love, we are speaking about our identifications and idealizations, our comforting illusions, and our refusal to be more aware of what might puncture or deflate our imaginary picture of ourselves. In idealizing psychoanalysis and holding on to the fantasy that we are identified with it, and therefore share in its perfection, we do not put ourselves in the position to think about psychoanalysis, race, or anything else.

Trans-ideological acknowledgement and beyond

From Horne's comments—and not only from them—we might get the impression that the "narcissism of small differences" is still a feature of the psychoanalytic world. She quotes Gregorio Kohon as reminding us that in the world of British psychoanalysis, "analysts would never be found quoting from colleagues of any of the rival groups". This might be regarded as remarkable, if it means, as it seems to, that Kleinians would not be found quoting contemporary Freudians or ego psychologists or that Freudians find it too difficult to acknowledge that a follower of Klein or someone who thinks of herself as Winnicottian, and therefore an Independent, has something interesting to say. Horne also quotes Eric Rayner as acknowledging that between psychoanalysts "there is frequent acrimony about group-ideological matters". Horne seems to be making a plea for "trans-ideological acknowledgement of sources" (Horne, 2006, p. 21). She seems to mean that psychoanalytically trained practitioners should be generous enough to acknowledge when they have read something interesting or useful but written by a psychoanalytically trained practitioner who is not actually a part of their own school of psychoanalysis, their own subgroup. As well as joining Horne in this hope for some generosity between the subgroups or schools of psychoanalysis, we might want to go further and urge what may be referred to as extra-ideological acknowledgements of sources and influences, the perhaps audacious idea that we might be able to acknowledge that psychotherapists who do not belong to the same subgroup as us through training— including psychotherapists who do not consider themselves to be "psychoanalytic" and writers who do not identify themselves as psychotherapists—often have interesting and useful things to say.

The voices from outside psychoanalysis are interesting and useful to the practice of psychotherapy. A diet of what is said and written in our own subgroup tends to lead to our saying what those around us tend to say, but to pride ourselves on our thoughtfulness. We cannot take it that a person who has a narcissistic attachment to psychoanalysis or one of its subgroups, who identifies with its teachings, dogmas, and celebrities, a person who idealizes psychoanalysis, is a useful person to turn to when we are concerned with how the notion of race can frequently contribute to restrictions to our regard for others, apply the brakes on our capacity for reverie—our being able to allow thoughts to come to us—and dull our appreciation of our relatedness to others, for such a person is caught up in what we need to think about. By being caught up in denigrating "them" and idealizing "us", we do not offer grounds for confidence in our ability to think about race or any other difference between people. Whatever else may be said to be involved in racism, it seems plausible to state that thinking in terms of them and us tends to be part of it.

Some of us practitioners of psychotherapy seem to find comfort in feeling ourselves to belong to a small group or sect, practitioners who are faithful to the right ideas, who hold our convictions, who are sufficiently like them. Wittgenstein and Nietzsche might argue that this safety in sameness, this longing to belong to the people who are right, cannot be taken as an indication that we have much in the way of intellectual integrity, moral courage, and the ability to inhabit unpleasant, uncomfortable, and lonely places. We might wonder whether there is any indication that we are able to think about anything and be concerned that there is something partial, a bias about belonging to a group of people in this way, a way of binding oneself to others, as long as there are others to hate, denigrate, and feel superior to others who are regarded as "different".

Where Horne writes about "The Independents", that group of psychoanalysts who see themselves as somewhere between Freud and Klein, she speaks of their adopting "a very British position" by compromising in the face of disputes; "we", she writes, "do not seem to be creatures of extremes" (Horne, 2006, p. 18). Here again, we might argue, are issues to do with identification, idealization, and narcissism, the very issues Horne is discussing. A picture or image is held of what it means to be British, and it might be very gratifying for us to think of ourselves as belonging to this group when it is seen in this way. This might remind us of Wittgenstein and Malcolm in 1939. Perhaps a less idealized and narcissistic picture of what it means to be British—one that is from what we might refer to as a more "depressive position"—might dare to include some acknowledgement that along with a talent for compromise in some situations, there have also been "extremes", including domination and intransigence. For this is also a country that beheaded a king, played a major part in the slave trade, created and maintained an empire (and not solely, presumably, due to its ability to compromise), excelled at gunboat diplomacy, and sometimes attacked other countries for gain. Britannia did not rule the waves simply through her talent for compromise. We might find ourselves, with an eye on Wittgenstein's question above, asking what is the point of studying psychotherapy and being able to think well about notions such as defence, projection, projective identification, narcissism, displacement, transference, and so on if, when it comes down to it, we are at least as likely to project, displace, omit what is inconvenient to remember or acknowledge, discriminate against others, and be narcissistically involved with the ideas rather than think about them? What is the use, Wittgenstein might prompt us to ask, of so much analysis, supervision, and study of psychoanalytic concepts if we are still so clearly caught up within an imaginary view of what we are, what we belong to, and how other people are deficient? Wittgenstein and Nietzsche might say that there is little here that resembles thinking; little that indicates conscientiousness, a willingness to go where it is "downright nasty" to be; and much that indicates that safety, security, and comfort inside the party is what is being sought.

Anyway, who might we be talking about when we claim to be able to compromise? Who do we want to say is incapable of being reasonable? All of us who have been trained as psychoanalytic practitioners ought to be familiar with the idea that we can ascribe to the external world "things that clearly originate in his own ego and ought to be acknowledged by it" (Freud, 1930a, p. 56). When we think we are talking about others, we may be talking about ourselves. This might prompt us to watch our tendency to imply that other people are extremists, dogmatic, and unable to be rational and ourselves be more concerned about whether we are the other people of whom we speak.

It is not clear why we might think that race is something that will yield up its secrets only to our subgroup, tribe, or preferred colleagues. Nor is it clear why a group of people who are narcissistically attached to their own groups and theories will be able to see and love anything other than themselves and the theories they are so identified with that these theories serve as extensions and paths back to themselves. Why might we not suspect that often when we claim to be talking about race, we may be seen as talking about and talking to ourselves, using our favoured terms and ideas?

Evading and accepting the invitation to think about race in practice in institutions

This chapter is not concerned with advancing or refuting theories, but with the argument that our attachment to our theories, our group, and our image of ourselves as thoughtful practitioners may make it difficult for us to be able to think about any issue, including race. The second part of this chapter focuses on illustrations of how, in practice, opportunities to think about race are evaded, declined, or accepted.

I am the only black man working in a therapeutic community for "emotionally disturbed adolescents". Early one morning we learn that a group of boys have just absconded, so I, along with two of my male colleagues, whom I like very much and get on well with, go with two boys to look for the missing residents. We spot them in a field, climb over the fence, and give chase. It is apparently quite good-natured. All the boys are caught, and we walk back to the fence to climb over. I have a good relationship with the boy I have caught, in so far as this boy has good relationships with anyone. He is laughing and joking, and we are the last to climb over the fence to return to the community. Suddenly this boy begins to scream abuse and threats at one of my colleagues and reaches with his right hand into the breast pocket of his jacket. Instantly convinced that he is reaching for a knife, I find that I have clamped my right hand on his right hand, thereby preventing him from producing the knife. He is struggling, swearing at me now, and trying to hit me, but I have him firmly and won't let go. I think that any minute now my colleagues will jump over the fence and help me hold on to him to make the situation safe. This does not happen. We slip, fall, and roll around in the mud: I end up on the bottom but I still have my right hand clamped on his so that he cannot use the knife. I am thinking, "In a minute now . . . In a minute now . . . Any minute now". In fact, neither colleague climbs over. Two of the other boys come to help us, and together we take the knife from the boy who is threatening to use it. I am left feeling suspicious, betrayed, and confused. Where were my colleagues? Why had they not helped me? I am unable to speak to them about this, and they seem unable to say anything to me about it. It is as if I am unable to think about it clearly, as if something shameful has happened, or might happen if I managed to think more clearly about it.

Around that time I begin to notice that the large axe, with the long handle, which is usually kept under lock and key in the shed, tends to be in the sleeping-in room when it is my turn to sleep in. I make enquires about why it is there and who is leaving it there, but I am unable to clear up this mystery: no one owns up, and no one knows anything. I ask some of my colleagues whether the axe has been left in the room when it is their time to sleep in; they tell me that this has not happened. Sometimes, if things are hectic, I just hide it under the bed rather than take it back to the shed in the night, and I return it in the morning. However, the next time I arrive to do a sleep-in, it is there again.

This is a period in which there are many violent incidents, especially at night. One night one of the larger boys threatens to beat up one of the smaller boys. I put myself between the two boys, and looking up at the aggressor—because he is taller than me!—tell him that he was not going to hit anyone. He insists that I cannot stop him. No one can. And he threatens to flatten me too. Another boy is egging him on. The senior member of staff sends me to the sleeping-in room. I do as I am told, although I think it is a mistake and that if adolescent boys such as the boy making the threats are not firmly met by the adults, they often get drunk on their feeling of omnipotence, as well as frightened, and this is sometimes disastrous for them and those around them. This thought came from an understanding of Winnicott's work and a number of incidents where adolescent omnipotence led to difficult and unpleasant incidents. I also dislike bullying and being bullied.

As I walk into the sleeping-in room, there is the axe looking at me. The noise level and the atmosphere in the house speak of an orgy of violence to come. In my impotence to do anything to prevent this, I have an image of my standing there in front of the two boys, axe in hand, frightening them into behaving. I smile to myself, think that this is crazy and that I have to take this image to supervision. I hide the axe under the bed, sit down, and try to think about what is going on. The sounds of things being smashed, people screaming and running makes me decide that my being sent to my room, as if I am the aggressor, no longer stands, so I follow the noise. Outside, the boy who was being threatened has clearly been hit, the senior member of staff is trying to restrain and calm the boy who was threatening to do the hitting, and the boy who had been doing the egging-on has a huge gatepost in his hand and is just going from window to window smashing every pane of glass with it. I approach him, call him by his name, and say that's enough! Stop! He suddenly turns to me and lifts the gatepost, as if to cave my skull in with it. I react by grabbing him, putting him on the floor, and taking the post from him, so that he cannot use it to damage me or anyone or anything else. I hold up the weapon, as one might hold up a book or pen or some other object that one is talking about, call him by his name, and say, feeling disbelief, "I can't believe that you would have hit me with *this*!" I have a good relationship with this boy and know that he will punch and kick me in anger, but I feel very shocked and upset that he would do something that might kill me. The boy looks frightened and says that he was not going to hit me with it, he was just trying to scare me.

I learn the next day that the senior member of staff had said to the other senior staff that the most frightening time for her was to see a member of staff who is usually so calm, dependable, and laid back standing over one of the boys with a huge post in his hand, about to do him some serious damage with it. Fortunately, she continued, he managed to restrain himself. I am dumbstruck. I am again the threat rather than the one threatened. Again I feel betrayed and as if my actions and my sense of who I am are sucked into and swept along in a scenario I did not write or authorize and from which there is no escape.

In our staff group, the colleague who was the target of the threats and abuse at the fence, when I was rolling around in the mud on my own with the boy who was reaching for his knife, says that he is tempted to say that he did not climb over, as he could have done in seconds and usually would do, because if the boy wanted to attack him, it would be better if he did not try to hold on to the boy. He adds, however, that he can be more honest than this. The boy had been giving him hell for weeks, and he had had enough. He confessed to having the urge to do violence to this boy and to having the thought that if I am left alone with an angry boy who is waving a knife around, I might have to hit or beat him up, in order to protect myself. He said he was hoping that being left in this dangerous situation would lead to my doing for him what he was just about preventing himself from doing. This helped me to make sense of my suspicions as well as my confusion and sense of betrayal. Race was not mentioned. My suspicions involved thoughts and feelings about race, but I thought it wise not to raise it yet.

I mentioned in that group that this axe kept on appearing in the sleeping-in room when it was my turn to sleep in, but apparently not when others are sleeping in, and that the axe had been there again on the night when the house was smashed up and a number of people were hit. The facilitator was visibly alarmed. She told me that a number of my colleagues had been to see her privately, claiming that they were at the end of what they could take and sharing their fantasies about seriously injuring one of the young people. She told me never to sleep with the axe under my bed and claimed that she thought that I was being set up to act out something for the staff group: the one who injures one of the young people. She added that she did not think that it was coincidental that I was the only black man on the staff group, and that my being offered and egged on into this position may have much to do with some unconscious things about race.

I felt relief that she had spoken openly about race and that it was less easy to dismiss me as being a bit mad or having "a chip on my shoulder" if I then spoke about race.

A number of points can be made about these experiences. First, I am not accusing my former colleagues of being racist, insensitive, or therapeutically unsophisticated—I am claiming that they were quite the opposite. Yet the incidents I have related happened, and I found it extremely difficult to talk about race and was, for a time, left feeling set up and vulnerable.

Second— and this is a crucial point—if colleagues who are psychotherapeutically sophisticated and prepared in many ways to be honest, who like me as I am fond of them, can manoeuvre me into situations where they hope I will do their violence for them, and if this has something to do with my colour, then how often does this happen in institutions, sophisticated psychotherapeutically or not, in businesses, in schools, with people who are less able or less prepared to be so honest?

Third, it is crucial to emphasize that the organization *did* address race through the consultant it employed. It would be unrealistically stringent to claim that a good organization is one in which issues to do with race, or any other difficult issue, for that matter, never arise; the question is whether these issues can be spoken about and responded to thoughtfully, rather than the organization or its individual members reacting with indignation and denial whenever there is any suggestion that race may be an issue. It is crucial for an organization to have spaces for thinking together that are spaces for thinking together, rather than spaces for persuading itself that all is well, others are deluded, and it is always someone else who is at fault.

Fourth, some years later, I tried to speak to my analyst about the knife and the axe and other issues that seem to be related. She was quick to make a case for it having little or nothing to do with race, but a lot to do with my being a fit and strong young man at the time. Yes—but I was certainly not the only man there who was fit and strong. What concerned me about my analyst's response was both its speed and its dismissal of race, together with an apparent conviction that I was really talking about my Oedipus complex and my concerns about *her* racism. Her apparent confidence that she knew that what I was saying about race was a code for oedipal matters and the transference made me feel as if she was not able to listen and think with me about this matter but had to dismiss it for supposedly "deeper" issues that she, in many ways, felt more comfortable with.

It is important to say that her taking my reflections on these incidents as a code about the transference led to my no longer talking about these incidents but about my relationship with her and the thought that I was covertly accusing her of being racist. We might say that I had the impression that she did not want to talk about my memories of a time in my life when I was doing something very difficult alongside colleagues whom I am still fond of; she wanted me to talk about the transference.

Finally, it could be said that her remarks were blunt instruments when something more delicate was needed. Why would she take up my telling her about these experience as my concerns about her racism rather than as possibly about her being someone who might not help me when I needed help (when I am struggling with a boy who has a knife), or as someone who might treat me as if I am the aggressor when I am being threatened (as I felt at the time that the senior member of staff did)? Why, indeed, might she not have made a comment about my wondering whether she would be like the group facilitator, who was clear and direct about what she thought was going on, and whom I experienced as helpful and caring? Her belief in her own model, her apparent conviction that she knew what I was talking about and why, long before I had any thoughts about what and why, meant that she was not able to think with me nor allow me to think.

It has nothing to do with race

I am one of two black men in an organization in which psychoanalysis is the dominant model. Two black women join the organization in junior positions; I supervise one of them. The other black man is my manager. After a number of months without anything out of the ordinary being apparent to me, my supervisee suddenly declares that she and the other black woman are taking out a "sexual harassment" grievance against the other black man; however, as they are afraid of him, she wants me to ask him to meet with them now and to be there when they tell him this. I am stunned and feel myself to be in a difficult position. I feel even more so when I learn that both of these black women have been supported in their decision to take this step by a white woman in the organization, who has a history with this black manager. I am concerned that through their discussions with her, the language is now "sexual harassment" and "grievance procedure"; it is not that there is something about what he has done or the way he is that they need to talk to him about. I protest about not being included at all in any of the discussions and suddenly being put in this position. My supervisee reminds me that I am a man (not something I had forgotten) and am perceived as friends with this man. I inform her that we are not unfriendly to each other, but we are hardly "friends". Where does the idea come from that we are friends? It seemed to have a lot to do with our being the only two black men in the organization. Well, it could have been worse: they might have decided that we were related!

I do what I can to help these two women to air their grievances to the man they are accusing, hoping, stupidly maybe, that we might think together about the situation. No argument is being made here that there is never a time or a situation in which grievance procedures need to be resorted to. But Wittgenstein's question haunts. For what is the use of studying psychoanalysis, having psychoanalytic supervision, and being in psychoanalytic therapy, as I and some of my colleagues were and had been for some time, if we do not try to talk to the people around us about our feelings, our thoughts, and our relationships with them? If we skip talking to each other and just take out grievance procedures? However, as I go to get him, my being given no time to think about it, and my inviting him to a meeting so that he can be accused publicly, make me feel as if I have been set up to do the dirty work and am caught up in a well-spun web.

Although he comes to the meeting, looking puzzled and asking what it is about, the women are unable to tell him what they experienced him as doing, and they flee from the meeting. Things escalate very quickly. I find myself in the director's office.

The director, a psychoanalytic psychotherapist, claims that as the two women accusing the black man of sexual harassment are black, race cannot be a factor. Politely, I ask her if this follows, and after a while and a little thought, she acknowledges that it does not.

I wonder what she is thinking or if she is thinking: surely many things go on between black people that are about race and racism! Any thought of mentioning that there is a white woman involved, who for years has been making comments about this manager's incompetence and her ability to do a better job than he does, leaves me when I begin to realize that I am being cross-examined and accused.

Why and how did you manage to turn a blind eye to this for so long? Did you not want to see it? I explained that my supervisee had not mentioned it until the day she asked me to invite him to meet with us; I had certainly experienced them as being quite flirtatious together, with quite a bit of sexual banter, but I saw no indication that she was upset by it and had no reason to raise it with her. "Well, were you part of it?" No! "Why not?" (Strange question: now I feel as if I have to produce a justification of why I have not harassed my supervisee or behaved in such a way that she might feel harassed by me.) It was, I said, because I generally don't get into that sort of banter at work, and it seemed to be clearly inappropriate with a young woman I am supervising. She then tells me that I had wanted to do it too but felt unable to because of my position. She even speculates that I had projected my desire to abuse my position with this young woman into my manager, who had acted this out for me. Puzzled, confused, and aware that I might be said to be in no position to speak for my unconscious, aware that disagreement can easily be termed "denial", and not at all convinced about her right to use interpretations in this way in this situation, I find myself simply stating that this is not so and pointing out that the young woman would not have come to me for help if she had felt that I was part of it.

I was unhappy with my responses and the way I had handled the whole matter. Part of my unhappiness lies in the thought that my own self-love, my vanity, was very much involved in how things turned out. Perhaps it was omnipotent of me to react to being told about a group of women taking out a grievance procedure against a black male colleague by thinking that I could and should do something to get the people involved to talk to each other about how they relate to each other. Perhaps my image of myself as someone who sorts things out and gets to the bottom of things was in that situation problematic, for I did not give enough thought to the possibility that I was being invited into something from which there was no escape and that, because I am a black man, I would be likely to be seen as being in league with the other black man.

My self-interest, too, could be said to have asserted itself when on realizing that I was being accused, I abandoned all thought of being part of trying to clear the matter up and found that I was trying to save my own skin, rather than trying to help us to appreciate the significance that seemed to be attributed to possessing such skin.

It also dawned on me slowly after the event that had I refused to help these women to arrange a meeting with the accused man, had I simply told my manager what my supervisee had told me but refused to be a part of the meeting, this might have been taken as an indication by the director and the rest of the organization that I was in league with him. It does not seem to have been a situation that I could emerge from unscathed.

It could be said that psychoanalytic concepts were used in a way that was abusive to both of the black men, and perhaps all the people concerned, because they prevented thinking and enabled speculation driven more by concepts and ideas and the organization's desire not to think about race and the complex situation between individuals.

It can also be said that what happened misused psychoanalysis. No argument is being made here that race was the only factor, but although I attempted to stop the director quickly dismissing race as a factor in the accusation, it was dismissed, and yet it seemed to persist in the notion that the two black men in the organization were probably in it together. The speed at which race was dismissed, and the use of a theoretical model to implicate and accuse me and to frame this whole experience, meant, I contend, that this whole incident could not really be thought about. The institution had no space or will to think about race and found a way to dismiss it as an important factor, while it appeared to be doing a lot of work.

Nearly twenty years later I ran into the director at an event where there were mainly psychotherapists. Perhaps I do not need to say that there are usually very few black people at these events. I went over to say "Hello". Her response was something like, "Oh I thought it was you, but I wasn't sure. All black people look the same to me. I know that it is not politically correct to say this, but I am going to say it anyway."

It is possible to utter such a sentence while believing that we are substantiating the claim that we are able to think for ourselves, in spite of "political correctness" and other fetters to our freedom of thought. This is to identify with those people who have swum against the current bravely, the group of people who have put their own integrity and need to speak the truth above what is prudent and common in their time. However, this seems as if it is an indication of someone who is amorously captivated by her own image of herself: when we express ourselves in clichés, we might be suspicious about whether we are thinking and brave and are in the same company as Nietzsche, Wittgenstein, Freud, or Ferenczi. Furthermore, it is easy to understand how an English person who has just arrived in China, and has hardly ever seen Chinese people, might have difficulties distinguishing between the people she sees, but not so easy to understand how a person who has lived and worked with black people in London as colleagues and clients for over thirty years might say this. It took me some time before it occurred to me that this was part of the problem then and still is her and our problem now: black people are seen as part of a mass term, not individual people, and they are, therefore interchangeable.

What, we might ask, is the use of studying and practising psychoanalysis in London for many years, and being able to talk about the unconscious, denial, hostility, and attacks, if, far from being interested in, embarrassed, or appalled by your inability to recognize other people, you actually turn this into a source of pride, an apparent refusal to be cowed by something called "political correctness"? It is difficult to see how an opportunity to think about race might be accepted for someone who seems to be so proud of her difficulties with it.

Conclusion

The author of this chapter cannot claim that he is outside of self-love and its seductions, or that he does not belong to any groups, has no colleagues or friends, and does not admire any thinker or other therapist. The examples above indicate that he is caught up in the difficulties of thinking about race and that there are many groups that he may see himself as being involved with. The argument of this chapter is not that we can escape from self-love into some objective selfless perspective on ourselves and others, or that we must not in any way be involved with, admire, or be identified with others. This chapter argues that the issue is whether we are able to begin to think about our self-love and narcissistic attachments, to take a more thoughtful and sceptical position to claims about right and wrong ways of seeing things and, in particular, the claim that our particular group must be in the right. The issue is whether we can worry more about the possibility that, when we think that we are thinking about race, or anything else for that matter, we may not be thinking.

There are at least two possible criticisms of this chapter. The first is that the illustrations used are too revealing. A wiser or more prudent man would have disguised the material and written about his "supervisee" or "client". This would have worked: the material could have been used in this way. Having presented the material in the way I have presented it exposes me. Others can now analyse the material and pronounce on my pathology or feel that they are in a position to tell me how I should have handled these situations differently (and their knowledge of who is "ill" and how they are ill, and how matters should be handled, often has much to do with what those in their sub-group tend to say and write). Furthermore, and this is the second criticism, the reader might not believe that what I have reported happened. I have no interest in preventing people from expressing their opinions and reactions, but it does need to be pointed out that to write a paper that comments on the lack of intellectual honesty, courage, and willingness to occupy uncomfortable positions in some psychoanalysis, and yet to pretend that my experiences belong to a "client", "supervisee", or "friend", is obviously problematic. If this practice is widespread in psychoanalysis, and it has been since Freud, this seems to support the argument of this chapter. Finally, as for that reader not believing what he has read, what needs to be said here is that this reader might consider whether this might be his way of evading or declining the invitation to think that this chapter constitutes.

CHAPTER THREE

Between fear and blindness: the white therapist and the black patient

Helen Morgan

T his chapter is an attempt by a white psychotherapist to consider issues of racism and how they might impact on the work in the consulting room. There are two main features of this first statement that I want to emphasize by way of introduction. The first is that I intend to explore questions of difference in colour, and not issues of culture. This is not because I believe that matters of cultural differences in the consulting room are not interesting, or that culture and race are not often conflated, but, rather, that there is something so visible, so apparent, and yet so empty about colour that to include a discussion of culture can muddle the debate and take us away from facing some difficult and painful issues. A black patient may come from a culture more similar to my own than a white patient, yet it is the fact of our colours that can provoke primitive internal responses that are hard to acknowledge and face.

Clearly there are many differences such as culture, class, gender, sexuality, and so forth that form divides within the wider society and where the power balance is asymmetrical. But those are the subjects of other papers elsewhere. It is my experience that when the subject of race and psychotherapy arises among white therapists, we often quickly widen the question out to include other issues. It is as if we are trying to swallow up this difficult subject and lose it in a generality of difference. I am always struck by how very hard it is to think about racism, for it is essentially such an irrational phenomenon and yet one that is so insidious and pervasive. Colour blindness, ignoring difference of this nature, is more comfortable, but I believe it to be a denial and a defence against a complex array of emotions that includes anxiety, fear, guilt, shame, and envy. No wonder we do our best to avoid the subject.

The other point I wish to make is that this chapter is written from the perspective of the white therapist. It is the only position I might have any authority from which to speak. There are worryingly few black people entering this profession, but it seems that those who have are impelled by their experience in the consulting room with both black and white patients to consider matters of racism. Some have written of their subsequent thinking. On the other hand, there is a notable paucity of writing from white therapists on this subject. Paul Gordon conducted a survey of psychoanalytic psychotherapy trainings and equal opportunity policies in 1993 and concluded:

> . . . not only that few organisations had actually done anything meaningful in this respect, but that many simply did not regard it as a problem and some completely misunderstood the issues. [Gordon, 1996, p. 196]

Because this is an essentially white profession within a society where white holds power, the white therapist can go through life avoiding this matter altogether, assuming it to be a problem only for black colleagues. Pressures to think about it may be dismissed as mere fashion and political correctness. I will suggest that we as individuals, our work, and the profession in general are the poorer for such avoidance.

A paper by Bob Young on how little the issue of racism is addressed within training organizations is entitled "Psychoanalysis and Racism: A Loud Silence" (1994b). There is a silence generally within our profession concerning racism, but I believe also that a silence can too easily develop in the consulting room. It is a dangerous silence for the therapy because it contains too much background noise for it not to infect all the other work we try to do. A frequent response by the black patient is to stop and leave therapy, often silently. Another response is not to enter in the first place—which is the loudest silence of all.

Psychotherapy—"What's race got to do with it . . . ?"

In its essence, psychotherapy is a process of an individual therapist working with an individual patient. In that work, a relationship develops that is specific to those two individuals. The focus is on the vicissitudes of the internal world of the patient and how it emerges transferentially within that relationship. The terms "black" and "white" are definitions of collective categories of so-called race. Racism involves such collective definitions which carry a process of de-personalization, seeing only the characteristics ascribed to that category and not the individual. What, therefore, has such a topic to do with the business of psychotherapy?

Assuming racism to be a non-issue for psychotherapy is tempting. However, I believe that racism forms a backdrop that exists for any therapeutic encounter. It is a form of pathology and, therefore, should be open to the exploration of therapy. It is so for our white patients and needs, therefore, to be available to analysis where it appears. When a black patient enters therapy, because of the effects racism will have had on him or her, these experiences will be present in the room. Power differences, both real and perceived, between a white therapist and a black patient will exist, and we need a way of exploring them, especially when they occur as transference resistances.

Racism

In "The Good Society and the Inner World", Michael Rustin describes the concept of "race" as "an empty category":

> . . . differences of biological race are largely lacking in substance. Racial differences go no further, in their essence, than superficial variations in bodily appearance and shape—modal tallness of different groups, colour of skin, facial shape, hair, etc. Given the variations that occur within these so-called groups, and give rise to no general categorisations or clusterings . . ., it is hard to find any significance in these differences except those that are arbitrarily assigned to them (. . . even physical visibility has been lacking in important cases of racism as a ground of distinction—the Nazis compelled Jews to wear the Star of David because they were not readily identifiable as Jews . . .). Racial differences depend on the definition given to them by the other

. . . and the most powerful definitions of these kinds are those which are negative—definitions that we can call racist. [Rustin, 1991, p. 58]

The emptiness of this category "race" emphasizes the irrational foundation of racism. Any analysis of these foundations has to include a political and economic perspective. Colonization and the riches of power and wealth that were exploited by white Europeans in the past, and the continuation of such exploitation in the process of globalization, require moral and psychological constructs as a justification for the exploiters. Exploration of the psychology behind and within the process can be helpful if it goes alongside other approaches. In his paper "Souls in Armour", Gordon argues that:

Psychoanalysis cannot provide a theory of racism, although it can—and should—be part of one. Racism is in the material world as well as the psyche and our attempt to understand it—like our attempts to understand all other phenomena—must be in two places at once. [Gordon, 1993b, p. 73]

Those who have considered the subject of racism from a psychoanalytic perspective focus on different possible aspects. Rustin sees racism as akin to a psychotic state of mind. The mechanism includes a paranoid splitting of objects into the loved and the hated, and the racial other becomes the container for the split-off, hated aspect, which is then feared and attacked. Rustin argues that it is the very meaninglessness of the racial distinction in real terms that makes it such an ideal container, for no other complications of reality can intrude. Splitting mechanisms include idealization as well as denigration. The latter is mobilized and expressed in political speeches that refer to excrement and the terror of floods of immigrants taking over the country. The former is evident in the idealization of African Caribbean youth culture and the attribution of abilities in sport, music, and dance. This process of idealization carries with it the dynamics of envy.

Frank Lowe suggests that it is useful to consider white racism as a borderline phenomenon, as it

helps us better understand the white's inability to make contact with the black other because it arouses immense anxiety and there is a fear of loss, of fragmentation or dissolution of self and identity. [Lowe, 2006b, p. 59]

Davids (2011) argues that it is because the racist thought is unconscious, universal, and operates at a pre-verbal level that it leads to such a sense of rupture and immobilization of thought. In his model he posits three steps: The first is the perception of a difference between ourselves and the "racial other". The second is where the designation of this "racial other" provides a container for unwanted aspects of the psyche which are split off and projected. The split is a mechanism for protecting the subject from unbearable anxiety, which is rooted in the experience of infantile helplessness and dependency. It is his introduction of the third step which takes us beyond the usual understanding and offers a more complex way of thinking about the internal processes. Here, Davids argues that an "organizing internal template" is established to "govern the relationship between subject, now free of his unwanted aspects, and object, now containing them" (p. 30). The purpose of the template is to cover up the racist nature of the first two steps, which otherwise would provoke unbearable shame and guilt, and to provide a construct whereby subject and object are given strictly defined, unchallengeable roles and relationships. As long as these roles are complied with and the subject stays loyal to the organization, safety and freedom from the original anxiety is assured. Although allied to the concept of the pathological organization posited by Steiner (1987), Davids argues that this template of inner racism is rooted in the ordinary infantile experience of helplessness and so is a feature of the "ordinary" mind and is not, in itself, pathological.

Farhad Dalal (2002) draws on the works of the group analyst S. H. Foulkes and the sociologist Norbert Elias to present a post-structuralist understanding of how social groups, as well as the subsequent power relations between them, are established. He argues that racist labelling is constructed in order to maintain a hierarchical ordering forming what he terms the social unconscious. This ordering means that such differentiations as white positivity and black negativity are, in fact, constructs deeply imbedded in society, language, and the psyche, but which come to be accepted as natural. Dalal uses the ideas of the Chilean psychoanalyst Ignacio Matte-Blanco with those of Elias to show how differences are created and then maintained so the more powerful become idealized and the less powerful marginalized and stigmatized. The implications of his argument are that differences such as skin colour cannot be overcome with well-intentioned wilful efforts on the part of either individuals or governments through legislation and that we must accept that we are born into a racist society and operate with racist psyches.

Stephen Frosh (1989) argues that racism is a response to modernity and the fragmentation that is experienced. The move to a more pluralistic society together with the dismantling of much of the external forms of superego control carried by the established institutions, such as church and state, may mean greater freedom, it but places a considerable strain on the individual ego to manage that freedom and hold the depressive position. The fragile ego, fearful of fragmentation, must find ways of defending itself. The need is to establish a boundary between self and other and to then define the other as inferior and thus the self as superior. Hated feelings can be projected into the other and feared, envied, and attacked. Frosh predicts that the retreat to fundamentalism and the growth of racism will be the key problem for modern society.

From a Jungian perspective, James Hillman in his paper "Notes on White Supremacy" explores the meaning of the colours white and black:

> Our culture, by which I mean the imagination, beliefs, enactments and values collectively and unconsciously shared by Northern Europeans and Americans, is white supremacist. Inescapably white supremacist, in that superiority of whiteness is affirmed by our major texts and is fundamental to our linguistic roots, and thus our perceptual structures. We tend to see white as first, as best, as most embracing, and define it in superior terms. [Hillman, 1986, p. 29]

In his paper "The Soul of Underdevelopment", presented to the International Congress for Analytical Psychology in Zurich in 1995, Roberto Gambini quotes a statement of the Pope at the time of the conquest of South America: "There is no sin below the Equator." Gambini notes that:

> In sixteenth Century catholic Europe, the shadow was kept under relative control by ethical institutions and civil law. . . . The shadow stayed in the corner, pressed for a way out to be lived and projected. Thus, when a vast geographical area was opened under the rubric, "Here it is allowed," the shadow disembarks on the shore and runs free, proclaiming gladly: "I made it! This is home!" [Gambini, 1997, p. 142]

Hillman talks of the projection of the shadow onto the black population. The very nature of white and its equation with light, bright, and innocent means it cannot include the dark within it. He suggests that "whiteness does not admit shadow, that its supremacy rejects distinctions and perceives any tincture as dullness, stain, dirt or obscurity" (Hillman, 1986, p. 40). White, therefore, casts its own white shadow and casts it into the black.

The concept of projection of the shadow into the other who is then feared, hated, envied, and so forth allows a generality that leaves open the question of what that shadow aspect might consist of. Different so-called racial groups—the Jew, the African, the African Caribbean, the Asian, the Middle Eastern, and others—all carry separate collective projections and evoke various primitive responses. The threat each category is perceived to contain, from a white racist perspective, is seen to be different in each case, as is what is perceived to be enviable. Each is seen to be available to carry an aspect of the white shadow. The effect of the process in each case is one of depersonalization and dehumanization.

Furthermore, I am not saying that the process of shadow projection is the prerogative of white people only. To do so would be to engage in a reverse form of splitting, assuming pathology to belong to white people and health to black people. This would be to deny the facts and to idealize the other. However, I do want to keep focused on white racism, for two reasons. One is that the power balance between white and black in this society is not symmetrical and needs to be owned as a reality. The second is that my concern in this chapter is the white therapist and the implications of white racism for him or her.

The white liberal

The racist self is an ugly creature and one to which we wish to give no house room. This ugliness has expression in such groups as the British National Party (BNP), the Ku Klux Klan, apartheid, and so forth. It does untold harm to the black "Other" who is the recipient of the evacuation of the hated parts of the racist self and who then is hated and attacked. Their existence is also a problem for the white liberal in that, in themselves, they provide a container into which we can project the racist self.

When we consider racism as a splitting or projective mechanism, it is easiest to focus on the extreme forms of overt racist attack,
genocide, slavery, and exploitation. Of course, this is important,
but the danger can be that those of us who do not engage in such
acts of hatred and who abhor such groups can retreat to a fairly
comfortable position of disassociating ourselves from the whole
process. Racism is a pervasive business, and it gets into everything
and everyone. I doubt whether there is any black person living in
this country who hasn't been subject to it in some form or another
in their life. But nor am I, as a white person, free of it. Like everyone else, I grew up in a racist society, and it would be a supreme
statement of omnipotence to say that it has not got into me too.
When we attempt to disassociate ourselves from the phenomena,
I believe that this is denial and another sort of defence, a defence
against something ugly we fear in ourselves.

Julian Lousada describes two traumatic aspects of racism in his
paper "The Hidden History of an Idea: The Difficulties of Adopting
Anti-Racism":

> There are, it seems to me, two primary traumas associated with
> racism. The first is the appalling inhumanity that is perpetrated
> in its name. The second is the recognition of the failure of the
> "natural" caring/humanitarian instincts and of thinking to be
> victorious over this evil. We should not underestimate the anxi-
> ety that attends the recognition of these traumas. In its extreme
> form this anxiety can produce an obsequious guilt which under-
> takes reparation (towards the oppressed object) regardless of
> the price. What this recognition of a profoundly negative force
> fundamentally challenges is the comfort of optimism, the back
> to basics idea that we are all inherently decent and that evil
> and hatred belong to others. Being able to tolerate the renuncia-
> tion of this idea, and the capacity to live in the presence of our
> own positive and destructive thoughts and instincts is the only
> basis on which the commitment to change can survive without
> recourse to fundamentalism. [Lousada, 1997, p. 41]

This trauma of racism, therefore, is not, in Lousada's view, just the
horror of the racist act, but the problem for us all that it exists. The
problem for the white liberal is not only the negative racist feelings
we may have towards the black "other", but our need for denial of
them out of guilt and shame.

On being white

When I first began to think about these issues, largely via my contact with black friends, colleagues, and clients, I found that the previous basic assumptions about my own identity were challenged. Growing up as a white person in a white society, I had no cause to question either my culture or my colour. If asked to describe who I was, I would not have even considered defining myself as white.

Doubtless such primary assumptions exist for all human beings. However, I cannot imagine a black child growing up in this country who does not have to face, fairly early on, that he or she is black. The luxury of it never crossing my mind that I was white is not allowed the black person. I call it a "luxury" because of the sense of ease that being permitted to take an aspect of my identity for granted brings. But I wonder. Taking something for granted is a near relative of it being unconscious.

In his book *Partisans in an Uncertain World*, Paul Hoggett says:

> . . . uncritical thought will not simply be passive but will actively cling to a belief in the appearance of certain things. It actively refuses, rejects as perverse or crazy, any view that may contradict it. To think critically one must therefore be able to use aggression to break through the limitations of one's own assumptions or to challenge the "squatting rights" of the colonizer within one's own internal world. [Hoggett, 1992a, p. 29]

He goes on to suggest that if the movement of thought is to be sustained, the act of aggression must be followed up by the act of play. He quotes Winnicott:

> The creativity that we are studying belongs to the approach of the individual to external reality. . . . Contrasted with this is a relationship to external reality which is one of compliance, the world and its details being recognised but only as something to be fitted in with or demanding adaptation. [Winnicott, 1971, pp. 68, 65]

Given the fact of global colonization by white Western Christian culture, those us who are defined as belonging to such a culture can, if we choose, avoid external pressure to make that act of aggression that challenges the "squatting rights" of the internal colonizer. But not noticing this figure who inhabits at least a corner of our minds demanding compliance does not mean that it does not exist. I suggest that we are the poorer if we do not attempt the act of aggression to break through our assumptions, for they then remain an area of internal life that is unexamined. The tenacity of the uncritical thought that actively clings to a belief in the appearance of certain things in Hoggett's quote may give us a clue to the tenacity of the fact of racism despite legislation and attempts at training. For me to think differently about my place in the world and the privileges it has brought me requires an undoing of a well-laid system of assumptions about myself. The fact that those assumptions existed and continue to exist does not make me an inherently bad person, but to break through their limitations is hard work. For Hoggett to then suggest that I am required to take it further into the area of play is asking a lot. This is not an easy subject to "play" with. It raises feelings of guilt, shame, envy, denial, and defiance, all of which are hard enough to face in the privacy of one's own life. To explore it publicly can bring up in me a fear of getting it wrong, of saying the unforgivable and of exposing a badness in me.

I wish now to consider work with two patients, one white and one black, to illustrate the issues as I perceive them in therapeutic work.

A white therapist and a white patient

J was a white woman in her late forties who at the time of the incident described below had been in therapy with me for several years. She arrived at one session disturbed and shocked. J was a social worker in an inner-city area. She had been working with a client for some time and had become emotionally close to this young woman of 18, whom she saw as vulnerable and abused. That day the client had told J that she had started going out with a black man she had met in Brixton. J's immediate reaction to this news had been one of fear and loathing; this was followed by real distress at her own "unthinking" reaction. J considered herself to be a rational liberal person who was used to having black colleagues and friends and thought she had "worked through" issues of racism.

J reported the news and her reaction at the start of the session but hastened to assure me that she had had a chance to think it through and things were OK now. She realized her reaction had been from a stereotype of a black man and she was ashamed of her initial response, which she considered primitive and racist. Soon she was on to another subject and apparently the matter was over and done with. I was struggling to work out what might be going on here. The telling me of this event had the feel of the confessional, where J was telling her secret "sin" to me. It seemed that the telling of the secret was enough and, with a sigh of relief, we could both move on.

In this she seemed to be appealing to my "understanding" as another white woman on two levels. One was a recognition of the stereotypes conjured up by the words "black man" and "Brixton". The other was a liberalism that had no truck with such silly notions. Both expectations were accurate. The questions in my mind, then, were: What was her immediate response about in terms of her internal world? What was she defending against in the shame and the wish to move on? What was being re-enacted in the transference?

Despite an uncomfortable feeling in the room, I returned to the subject of the client's boyfriend and tried to explore her associations more explicitly. Brixton, it emerged, was like London's "Heart of Darkness". It was for J a vibrant, but fearful, place, which both repelled and fascinated her. Locating this black man in Brixton imbued him with both excitement and fear. J imagined this man to be sexually active and attractive, and she feared what he might do to her client. She was able to acknowledge both her fear of him as threat, and her envy of the client having this exciting sexual object. She feared he might have AIDS, and had already imagined the man making the young woman pregnant then abandoning her. The fear of the aggressive, contaminating, and feckless man was evident.

Clearly there are some complex processes occurring here that were specific to the internal world of my patient. For the purpose of this chapter I want to emphasize a few main themes. Put simplistically, one theme was how she had projected a primitive animal male sexuality onto the man, and an innocent pure femininity onto the client who had to be protected. But there was also the issue of her sense of "badness" and shame at having these feelings. After all the work she had done on herself in developing her awareness of her racism, she still was capable of such "bad" thoughts. These thoughts had intruded into her mind like an aggressive attack. In themselves they were shadow aspects which penetrated, left her with a shitty baby and then abandoned her. The client, perceived as the victim of the black man, was also "innocent" and "pure" of such nasty thoughts.

In seeing the black man through her initial lens which she defined as "racist", she employed a mechanism of projecting the aggressive, physical and sexual masculinity onto him and the innocent feminine victim onto the white female client. As such it was a projective defence. However, the more difficult issue to explore was how her denial of her racist feelings was also a defence against her own aggressive and penetrating thoughts. By telling me of the initial reaction and the subsequent process back to a more comfortable position she was inviting me to collude both with her initial disgust and with her subsequent shame. We were to be "in this together". Her "confession" followed by the response "it's all right now" seemed to be an appeal for me to ally myself with the aggressive intruding thought, with the innocent female victim and the rescuer who protected my patient from this attack by denial.

What I want to emphasize for the purposes of this chapter is the following:

1. "Bad" intolerable aspects of aggression and sexuality were projected onto the black man and onto Brixton. As with all projections, their acknowledgement allows the possibility of their withdrawal and these "bad" aspects integrated into the self.

2. The projection itself was experienced as a thought that was invasive and intolerable as it evoked shame, guilt, and anxiety.

3. The patient tried to resolve a dilemma by "confessing" the initial reaction to me and then making a speedy retreat from the subject. Shame and anxiety led her to avoid exploring the projective processes and their potential access into internal structures.

4. Because both the racist "bad" thought and the shame this produced echoed in me, the patient's invitation to collude with her avoidance was tempting. I was required to face and accept my own responses in order that there was permission for the patient to explore some important material. While these responses may

have been used unconsciously by my patient to support her avoidance, they were not of themselves countertransference responses. They were more general processes familiar to me as a white individual, living in a white racist society.

A white therapist and a black patient

D is a woman of African descent who was brought up abroad. In her mid-fifties when she first came to see me, she was the eldest of four having come from a religious family where a strict, sometimes harsh discipline was imposed on all the children. This discipline was often experienced as arbitrary, and D responded by retreating into a fantasy world inside herself. It was only in her late teens that she discovered that she had been adopted when she was 6 months old and that her "mother" was, in fact, her aunt who had just married at the time of D's birth. They had then had three children of their own. The birth mother left the area, and all contact with her was lost after the adoption. The identity of the father was not known by the adoptive parents.

At our initial interview, I raised the fact of the black/white differences between us. She assured me that this was not an issue, that she was used to living in a predominantly white culture and knew that she was unlikely to find a black therapist anyway. It made no difference to her. In my experience this is a common response. I know there is an argument that the therapist should wait for things to come up in the material and not refer to these matters unless the patient does. On the issue of difference in colour, I disagree. I believe that, given power issues and possible anxiety the patient may be feeling about my response as a white person, it is a lot to expect that a black patient will risk raising the issue him/herself. Stating that the difference is noticed and acknowledged by the therapist and that it can be talked about gives permission for the matter to emerge at a later date.

D was very polite and well-behaved in her sessions for some time, and, while the work went on, there was a sense of a lack of engagement. It was only after the first long break came that any negativity surfaced, when she began to miss occasional sessions. We both understood this to be an expression of anger and a re-enactment of her "disappearance" from the family as a child, but it remained a theoretical understanding and was not felt in the room by either of us. Gradually I became aware of a feeling in me in her sessions of wanting her to leave. I would look at her on the couch, and the phrase that came into my mind was "cuckoo in the nest". More to the point, she was a "cuckoo in my nest" and I did not want her there.

Usually, of course, when I have negative thoughts about patients I am reasonably able to accept them, welcome them even, as a countertransference feeling and therefore of an indication of what is going on. This time I was also aware of an urge to push this feeling away. I felt I "should not" feel this way towards her, and an effort was required to stay with the thought. Eventually I said something about the wish for us not to be together. She seemed relieved and said she had been feeling she did not belong, that being in therapy was a betrayal of herself and maybe not right for her. There followed a period where she verbally attacked therapy in a contemptuous way, describing it as tyrannical and against people thinking. Implicit in her attacks was her superiority to me. I had been taken in by this tyranny, while she remained free. At one point she was saying how she feared that I would—and she meant to say "brainwash" her, but what she actually said was that I would "whitewash" her.

She was initially shocked by the idea that she was relating to me as a colonial, imperial power that could take her over with my mind. She was well read and understood theoretical constructs regarding transference, and she began to "wonder" whether her fear of brainwashing was about her fear of the therapist/mother. Her invitation to me was to interpret in terms of her internal world only. There were, indeed, thoughts about an engulfing adoptive mother who disciplined harshly, of her struggle to fit in with what is around her and only able to assert herself by leaving. I felt, however, that we needed to take care. All that was in the "brainwashing" scenario. Something more complex was expressed in that of the "whitewash", something we both might be finding difficult to face.

Staying with the subject of colour and the difference between us, she began to express a disparagement of blackness. She said she had been relieved that I was white when she first met me, because of a sense that a black therapist would be second rate and she wanted the best. She was deeply ashamed of these feelings as a woman who was politically aware and dismissive of the mimicry she saw in some black people. The self-denigration in this was evident and illustrated how the black individual on the receiving end of white shadow projections can internalize this hostility and turn it into an attack on the self.

However, my job was to explore with her which aspects had been introjected by her and how this related to her internal world. From infancy, D retained a sense of abandonment. She was the odd one out, without understanding why. She had to be good to hold onto her mother's love, but she still kept getting beaten for crimes she did not always understand. Her general feeling throughout was of not being good enough, and her sense of belonging was extremely tenuous. Her rage at this had had no expression as a child, except in fantasies of suicide. She could only cope with the situation by imagining there was something fundamentally wrong with her.

The fact of being black in a white society fitted this sense of not belonging. Her experiences of racism had provided an unconscious confirmation that she was "bad" and deserving punishment. Despite political alignment with the black movement, her internal sense remained that of being an outsider, of being wrong and somehow dirty. White meant belonging and white meant what she was not: good, successful, and of value. My whiteness meant she could get close to the source of what was good, but she had to be careful that she did not antagonize me through any exposure of her "bad" rage.

As we explored the self-loathing inherent in her "secret" disparagement of "black", her comments switched from a denigration of the blackness of herself to a denigration of my whiteness. This was done largely through her accounts of the racism she had experienced. She seemed to be challenging me to take up a position. Was I allied with these white others, or would I join with her in her attack and become black like her? What was not to be allowed, it seemed, was our difference. I was to be for her or against her.

Whichever category was to be deemed superior to the other, the insistence that one had to be superior served to perpetuate the perception of me as "Other". "Other" with a capital "O" as, this way, I was being safely removed behind a shield of categorization.

Thus D could defend herself against the anxiety of her longing to become one with me and the terror of expulsion. If I rejected her, it could be because she was black and bad, or because I was white and bad. The pain and frustration of me being different and separate from her could be avoided.

In his paper "Racism and Psychotherapy: Working with Racism in the Consulting Room", Lennox Thomas describes a similar experience of a white therapist working with a black patient who was in supervision with him. Thomas says: "it is difficult for the therapist to recognise that the unconscious does not distinguish between colour as far as the perpetrators of pain are concerned" (Thomas, 1992, p. 138).

In the same paper, Thomas cites the concept, put forward by Andrew Curry, distinguishing between the pre-transference and the personal transference. This, to my mind, is a useful distinction. The pre-transference is described as

> the ideas, fantasies and values ascribed to the black psychotherapist and his race which are held by the white patient long before the two meet for the first time in the consulting room. Brought up in the society which holds negative views about black people, the white patient will have to work through this before engaging properly in the transference. The white psychotherapist too will need to deal with this when working with black patients. . . . This pre-transference is constituted of material from the past: fairy tales, images, myths and jokes. Current material, in the form of media images, may serve to top up this unconscious store of negative attributes. [Curry, 1964, quoted in Thomas, 1992, p. 137]

Dorothy Evans Holmes in her paper "Race and Transference in Psychoanalysis and Psychotherapy" (1992) considers the way that references to race can give access to transference reactions in the therapeutic situation. In the following extract she quotes from an earlier paper of hers:

> . . . often it is said that patients' racist remarks in therapy constitute a defensive shift away from more important underlying conflict. . . . While it is the therapist's ultimate aim to help the patient understand the protective uses of defences, this aim can best be achieved *only after* the defences are elaborated. [Holmes, 1992, p. 3]

For my patient D, the early loss of the mother, and the later felt tenuousness of the bond with the adoptive mother, constituted the pain that lay at the centre of her self. It was this pain and her consequent rage that had to enter the therapy and be survived before transformation could occur. White and black as placed in opposition to each other served as a vehicle to keep us apart and away from an engagement with each other.

This opposition formed a dividing line, provided by the wider society, and we were perceived to be on opposite sides. The line both exists in reality and is an internal, defensive construct. We both needed, I believe, to acknowledge its external reality and its consequences for each of us. As the white therapist, I was required to explore my pre-transference and where this colluded with the racist line. My shame and guilt had also to be owned internally. D needed to know I knew about the line and accepted its reality for her. A too-hasty interpretation of her response, as only a recapitulation of the original pain and the original defence, would have been a defensive denial on my part of a real divide.

However, the analytic stance required an understanding that the divide was also being used as a defence and that this had to be elaborated to give access to transference reactions. The generalities of race had to be interpreted and understood in terms of the specifics of her internal world and the transference. To do so, we had to withstand an engagement that held the possibility of aggression and hate.

The wish to make everything all right and deny anger and hatred in the relationship was rooted in D in her original childhood scene where her anger was not allowable. She was, in many senses, the cuckoo in the nest, not a real part of the family and not conscious of why. She had had to defend against her angry, destructive thoughts because she could be rejected altogether. Such a sense of not belonging was re-enforced by her move to another country, but also by her experience of being a black woman in a white world. In the transference, she had to take great care that she did not upset me, for her aggressive impulses could be so destructive she could do me damage.

On my side, I did not actually fear her anger or aggression. More problematic was the possibility of shame at having any racist thought about her. It was the fear of shame that was potentially more debilitating and paralysing. It seems to me that, in order that we could work together, D and I had to hold two positions simultaneously, of "remembering" that she was black and I was white, and of "forgetting" it.

Conclusion

There are, it seems to me, a variety of routes a white therapist can take in our attitude to work with a black patient.

The first is to ignore the issue. This is a form of colour blindness and, in my view, a denial—a denial of difference and a denial of uncomfortable feelings this difference may invoke in both and in the relationship. It has the appearance of good therapeutic practice for it seems to be seeing the individual and not the category. A consequence of this is that, should the patient bring material of racist experiences, the therapist will interpret it only in terms of the patient's internal world. A reality is not acknowledged and an abusive situation reinforced by the denial of the reality of the abuse.

The second is to acknowledge that there is an issue, but it is one that exists for the black patient alone. It recognizes that the patient is likely to have experienced overt racism in his or her life, and that needs to be acknowledged and understood. This, I believe, still removes the problem to outside the consulting room and can be a defence on the part of the white therapist against his or her own racist responses and therefore against shame and guilt. The responsibility for the pre-transference is left on the shoulders of the black patient.

The third is to recognize that if I acknowledge a racist backdrop to our society, then as a white person I too cannot be free of the phenomenon. I also have inherited a prejudicial veil that forms before my eyes when I see the blackness of the individual. Such a veil is likely to include an embroidery of guilt, shame, and envy given that the relationship for the white liberal as opposed to the extreme racist is complicated by the hatred of the internal racist. Such shame is likely to prevent us from working through the reality of the external situation to an interpretation of the meaning of the situation for the individual.

Following on from this is a fourth position, which also recognizes that racism will affect the relationship between us and that there is a power differential inherent in that relationship over and above the power relationship that both exists and is perceived to exist between any therapist and any patient. Elaboration and exploration of the reality of this differential may provide an important means of access to the transference. My argument is that we have to manage this fourth position if we are to get to the place I think we need to be—that is, through to the point where the issue is not an issue.

Note

An earlier version of this chapter was first published in the *BAP Journal*, No. 34, Vol. 3, January 1998.

CHAPTER FOUR

Is it coz I'm white?

David Morgan

> "Never again shall a single story be told as though it were the only one."
>
> John Berger (2008)

I come from a rather non-diverse background. Indeed, in the rural area I grew up in, the closest I ever came to racial diversity was via the *Black and White Minstrel Show*, the film *The Blackboard Jungle* with Sydney Poitier, B. B. King, Miles Davis, Cassius Clay, and from there to an appreciation of jazz and blues. In fact, it was many years later that I found out that much of the music I was playing on records during my youth was derivative from, or had roots in, black American and Afro-Caribbean culture.

When I trained as a clinical psychologist, psychotherapist, and psychoanalyst, almost all my fellow trainees were white like me, and the trainings at that time hardly touched upon diversity in the clinical setting. This was something I only gradually became aware of as I encountered patients, and, later, supervisees, who confronted me with the confusing experience of difference. This included both sexual orientation and ethnicity. My own analysis and training had not prepared me as much as I thought to encounter this difference, and my patients now made me aware of my own defensive strategies, which I used to manage this confusion. It is perhaps questionable whether these courses represent tokenism and box-ticking genuflections to a politically correct world, or the beginning of a real change. I think prejudice should be embraced, acknowledged, and explored rather than airbrushed away through well-meaning politically correct conscious-raising exercises.

I did remember hearing about Masud Khan, a psychoanalyst from Pakistan who had a complex reputation. I often wondered whether the difficulties he enacted could have been, at least in part, the result of being the only black person in the analytic village. I wondered how much his analysis had been able to explore this while he was in training. This has since become a question in my mind with other aspects of human diversity: race, sexuality, class, and gender.

At university, many of my colleagues had come from differing backgrounds, which in itself felt like enough of a culture clash for me to manage. This was more a class issue, involving discovering that others had attended private schools and even, to my astonishment, public boarding schools. This was my first exposure to the English upper-middle class, which seemed very foreign to me and owed more in my imagination to the fictional worlds of Jennings (a precursor of Harry Potter without the magic) than to anything I had ever experienced. My own world resembled more a "Just William" story of rather ordinary secondary schools with the odd smattering of "Swallows and Amazons", a sheltered experience undisturbed by any awareness of racial or ethnic difference. As already indicated, during my own psychoanalytic training, race or culture in particular were never really addressed. I knew that my analyst was Jewish and old enough to have been in the shadow of the Holocaust. And I was aware that my own Welsh background, which was important to me, with roots in the South Wales coal-mining industry and North Wales agriculture, seemed at odds with the urban and urbane world of psychoanalysis in London.

So, not having the benefit of any preparation to work with diversity, or even basic equal-opportunities training, I discovered differences through exposure to my patients, travel, and living in a culturally diverse area in London. I also supervised a number of therapists from ethnic and cultural backgrounds that were quite different from my own. I must acknowledge that I have struggled to manage and think about diversity, and at times this was a painful experience as it exposed prejudice, which I had not anticipated, in areas in myself and in the analytic milieu. To illustrate the struggles I faced and how I grappled to work with them analytically, below are a few reflections of some work with patients from different cultural backgrounds to myself.

Mr A

Mr A was young man who had been in analysis for a few years. He came from a relatively orthodox Jewish family. His original reason for seeking treatment was his inability to make and sustain relationships with women, any women. He was 33 years of age and had not managed any sexual relationships. There was a strong ethical prohibition on sex before marriage from his religious orthodoxy, and Mr A seemed locked into a powerful oedipal dilemma, unable to separate from what seemed to be a rather infantilizing mother. She still cooked his dinners and did his washing although he had at least physically left home and was living in a flat with a friend.

He used to wish that his parents would help him select a wife for him as many of his friends' parents had done for their sons. But he also somehow felt he should be able to do this for himself, something he put down to his ethnically diverse school and the influence of his peers. The idea of arranged marriages was anathema to me, as I imagined with horror the woman my own mother might have chosen for me. In his background up, until his generation, it had been the norm for parents or matchmakers to do the arranging. While it is something I have encountered with several patients from ethnically diverse cultures, to me this is an antiquated idea, one of a number of cultural practices that I struggle with. For instance, a young Sikh woman decided to have her daughter at her mother's home in Birmingham, leaving her British husband in London for the birth and for an indefinite time afterwards. It is difficult for me not to be judgemental at these times. However, in so doing I recognize the need to be open to thinking about the views of those who may have a different perspective. Where is the feminism? Aren't these cultures regressive, using religion and tradition to coerce the next generation for economic and/or social advantages? I could frame a context in which these religious and cultural ideas might have been regarded as reasonable strategies in difficult times when survival was paramount, but I viewed them as no longer practically necessary in twentieth-century London. But this ethnocentric outlook did not inspire confidence, and I had to recognize that my black-and-white (paranoid-schizoid) thinking was sometimes a way of avoiding other, just as valid, perspectives on the matter.

As Mr A's treatment progressed, he began to meet women via an ethnically focused dating site. He explored his sexuality and eventually met his wife independently. She was someone who was not from an orthodox background but, rather, attended a liberal synagogue and was from a family who seemed more interested in the symbolic manifestations of their rich Jewish heritage than the more concrete, more fundamental interpretation of the Torah.

Looking back, I do wonder how much my unconscious influence, with my ostensibly liberal values and non-religious background, may have influenced my patient's subsequent development.

This conflict between different value systems, his wife's and maybe his analyst's, came to a head later on in his treatment. He married this more liberal Jewish girlfriend, and within a year they gave birth to a male baby. In his analysis, he explored the issue of being a father and how much he wanted his son to adopt his religious and ethnic background. He had by this time—in fact, from the first month, when I betrayed my ignorance of Jewish holy days—realized that I was not of Jewish descent. We had explored throughout his analysis how my ignorance of his ethnicity (religion and culture?) was both a hindrance and in some less obvious ways an advantage. Indeed, I have observed that many Orthodox Jewish patients prefer a "non-frum" analyst to someone who is Jewish.

It inevitably came to pass that the question of circumcision became prominent. He was in no doubt that he would follow tradition and would have his son circumcised. However, his wife was very concerned about the procedure, as she knew of a friend whose son had had complications following the ceremony. In my countertransference, I struggled with my own views—for example, that it was an anachronism, from desert cultures, a position I felt legitimized by Jewish friends, mainly psychoanalysts, who had foregone this procedure. I therefore wondered why anyone should go along unthinkingly with the words of the prophets. However, other friends told me of the dis-identification from the father that non-circumcision represented and how non-circumcised boys often

felt alienated. One story, probably apocryphal, told of children trying to perform their own ritual, so desperate were they to fit in. The
immense need to belong, and fear of punishment for forsaking the
father, seem to discourage rebellion. I now no longer simply think
"why do you listen to the words of the old prophets"—I also think
about the real price to be paid by those who do not.

Helping the patient think for himself was threatened by my own
prejudices, however rational I thought I was being. My supervisor,
who was Jewish, surprised me by stating that there was no issue—
because of course the circumcision should be performed. This surprised me, as until then everything had been transference-based in
this supervision, but this issue seemed to be beyond psychoanalytic
theorizing. I have always been surprised how a number of my
colleagues have maintained strong religious beliefs during their
training and careers, a testimony, perhaps, to the enduring nature of
these ancient regimes or to the importance of ethnicity and cultural
belonging over thought and unconscious understanding.

With Mr A, a number of issues soon came into the analysis when
he helpfully brought a dream. In the dream, he was standing on a
station platform and two trains arrived simultaneously; one was
going to Hendon and the other to Hampstead. His associations
were that Hendon clearly represented his orthodoxy and Hampstead the home of psychoanalysis. He felt that he was "on the horns
of a dilemma" in that he both wanted to be liberal-minded and
follow his conscience in relation to his ethnic traditions.

I interpreted that it was important for him that I was able to help
him think about decisions like his son's circumcision. The question
he posed was, am I able to help him have a mind of his own rather
than feel he has to obey orthodoxies, including mine? Of course,
this interpretation was redolent with my own belief system, but, as
an analyst, how could it not be? Did it enable my patient simply
to think for himself, or was it promoting the idea that his having
a mind of his own was more important than his rootedness in the
ancient value systems based on his ethnic traditional values?

The very practice of analysis flies in the face of orthodoxies and
fundamentalist thinking, yet clearly it can become dominated by
certainties itself. For instance, within analytic institutions there has
been a great deal of psychoanalytic orthodoxy, with each theoretical
group having its own leaders and disciples, impeding the processes
of creative debate.

When, after a few weeks, the patient decided that he would go ahead with the religious celebration of circumcision, I did feel that the religious value system had exerted its power over him, and yet it was right for this patient to submit, as I saw it, and to assert his right to pursue his own direction independent of me, as he saw it. In the exploration of the dream, I felt there was a struggle for shared ground where two minds and ideas could be considered. The station at least represented a place where choices could be made, and it represented a shift in the patient's previously paralysed condition. It is of interest to note that at the actual ceremony he had been able to contain his mother, who, in an attempt to upstage proceedings and rival the baby, got into an argument with the other mother-in-law. The patient was able to stand up to his mother, pointing out her upstaging of proceedings in a way that she was able to respond too. I felt our exploration of mutual space had allowed something new to happen in the family dynamic.

In my countertransference, I would have to admit that I found the idea of circumcising a small baby disturbing. Yet I had to struggle with, and help my patient feel, that there was space to think with me. I therefore had to struggle with my orthodoxy based on my experience rather than impose it on him. I think this exploration allowed him to decide for himself, his autonomy here being expressed in his ability to stand up to his mother's domination.

Ms B

Ms B was in her forties and was single, with two children. She was from an African background and had come to England ten years previously. Her presenting problem was a need to control her anger, particularly towards Caucasian men. In one case, she had "frighteningly lost control" by attacking a taxi after its driver had mistaken her for a prostitute while walking in the north London suburb where she lived. On the one hand this reprisal on her part seemed reasonable, but on the other her preoccupation and sense of grievance with this tendency in some racist British men left her concerned that one day she would get herself hurt. She was referred to me because I had some experience of working with violent patients.

From the beginning, Ms B criticized me for being a white male. Being Welsh did not in any way mean that I did not represent that British colonialism that had enslaved her country of origin. How could I, she said, hope to understand her experience when our experiences, in terms of both race and gender, were so opposite. I said that I thought she was right to explore with me what sort of analyst I was and whether I had any equipment that could be used to understand her. It was possible that I did not; indeed, she doubted any white man's capacity to truly understand. I said it remained to be seen whether she should continue her analysis or end it because I might be a bigoted racist analyst. She seemed thoughtful about my apparent willingness to be thought about as such an unattractive figure. Clearly the analytic vehicle I was using so far did not deserve the same fate as the taxi her abuser was driving.

She stayed in analytic therapy with me. It transpired that there was a great deal that I did not understand. She hardly knew her parents and had been brought up by her extended family. She seemed to have many aunts and uncles who looked after her. The lack of any real parental couple meant that it felt, at least to me, that a lot of the usual reference points from her past were lost. Did this mean that the childrearing practices of the ethnic group to which she belonged left children without a clear sense of a parental couple, or was I pathologizing a culture just because it was different from my own? In the countertransference I experienced a great deal of confusion as to who I was in relation to the patient. To begin with, it was easy to believe that this represented the patient's own confusion from her extended-family experience—her lack of reference points marking the absence of her parents as primary caregivers. In fact it transpired that with these beliefs, based on a simplistic countertransference response, I nearly missed the subtler message, which was: "Can you, the analyst, bear the confusion in your usual reference points—the couple, the oedipal relationship—without reinforcing your position by pushing your idea of normality back into me?"

I saw her for many years, and her tendency to get into fights reduced, as did my wish to impose my belief system onto her. I came to think that it was this exploration of my fear of loss of purpose, the fear of losing my rootedness in the therapeutic process, as

I understood it, which allowed something other than recrimination to develop. This seemed to be what was required, rather than my need to reinforce those of my own preconceptions that were being challenged by her cultural background. It was hard at times to be made aware of my own judgemental stance.

I have understood this struggle as akin to the power of nationalism, in that when we are under threat we often look for flags that we can stand under to protect our identity from fragmentation. Psychoanalytic theory can also be used this way when patients bring "foreign" experiences into the consulting room; it functions as a form of protection to the analyst whose own normative experiences are put to the test.

In these cases, it is enormously important for the analyst to be discovered as someone who might be able to think about his or her own restricted experience without using psychoanalytic theory defensively, as a psychic retreat. This defensive retreat can include the reduction of ethnic beliefs to psychotic mechanisms, the issue of sexual difference to failures in oedipal development, as well as other forms of reductionism. However, at the same time as bearing all this in mind, it is also extremely important that the analyst, as well as having the ability to be open-minded, is not so open-minded that his brains fall out. This is a difficult task, but it may be the only experience some of our patients have ever had of engaging with diverse thinking. It seems vital, if this process is to have a therapeutic outcome, for the analyst to be aware of the initial impulses in the countertransference to repudiate and pathologize alien experiences. This helps maintain our sense of equilibrium, rather than giving the patient the experience of someone whose theories are less important than he or she is.

Ms C

Ms C, a 25-year-old woman from Nigeria, was admitted to the hospital where I acted as a supervisor of nursing and other clinical staff. Her presenting symptom was a desire to run up to complete strangers in the street and embrace them in a large bear hug. She often chose old women who appeared lonely, and who were then obviously traumatized by this unprovoked gesture of familiarity. Ms C's history was that she had been studying law with the intent of earning her living as a lawyer. She had, however, failed her exams and been expelled from her course. Her family had hoped that she would be able to send money home after she qualified, and it seemed that they had been very disappointed. Ms C felt ashamed and expelled from her family. It seemed clear to me that she was reversing her own painful experience of failure and rejection by projecting them into the aged women that she embraced, as if they were indeed her long-lost relatives who she believed had excommunicated her. I was able to share this with staff, who found this explanation of her symptoms helpful. However, unfortunately, I forgot to underline how important it was that this thinking was something to be kept in mind rather than directly communicated to the patient. A staff member shared this interpretation with Ms C, and at the time it appeared that she had been helped by the link it made to her own feelings of loss—loss of family, loss of country, and loss of career. That night she managed to break into a senior hospital manager's house in the grounds of the hospital. He woke up to find her standing over him, just looking at him. Of course, he was extremely shocked by this night apparition. I realized that the patient had also been shocked by a clinical insight that she was unprepared to receive. She had fallen back on her previous ways of managing by projecting her feelings into someone else, and it was they who were to be shocked by her breaking into their homes.

Clearly my failing was to underestimate the importance of ensuring that Ms C's homelessness and alienation was addressed before any understanding could occur. It was a reasonable manic defence that she employed to overcome her own homeless position by choosing to see others as having need of her company. Since then, I have been able to appreciate how difficult it is for those managing in foreign environments to feel safe enough to do analytic work. I might not have any insight into how frightening it is to be in a foreign culture, as I am relatively at home here. The importance with patients from other cultures of appreciating what it might feel like to be in their shoes is therefore of enormous importance. As I have learnt, it is only this appreciation that can begin to allow patients from different backgrounds to feel that they are at first listened to by someone who may have the ability to stand aside, however much prejudice intervenes, from their own experience and be put in touch with something new and unfamiliar.

Psychoanalysis has provided us with an understanding of how we can use the "other"—in particular, their difference—to contain our own anxieties about ourselves. It is important that we recognize that we all have our prejudices, and our patients need to explore our capacities to bear recognizing these in ourselves, if they are to feel understood. We have to be careful in our practice to bear the challenge to our norms that differences confront us with. This includes idealizing difference, which can be as much a defence as pathologizing it.

CHAPTER FIVE

Being "black" in the transference: working under the spectre of racism

Jonathan Bradley

The issue of "racism" looms large in psychoanalytic work, particularly where there is a difference of ethnicity between therapist and patient. I have used the term "spectre" in the title to capture the sense of an unpleasant and dangerous presence, whether real or imagined. After exploring in this chapter some issues that arise in clinical work, and particularly where the "racial other" is very much part of the clinical scene, I explore two clinical situations that, though different from each other in many ways, posed great technical problems and issues to do with my capacity as a therapist to understand what was happening.

Farhad Dalal (2012) likens racism to parasites:

> Parasites mutate and evolve to mimic the functioning of the host in order to fool the host into thinking that the parasite is a good and healthy part of itself. This leads to the parasite dropping "below the radar" of the defence systems of the host in order to sneak into its body. Once ensconced the parasite leeches on the resources of the host, depleting and weakening it. [p. 3]

Dalal uses this dramatic imagery to draw attention to what he feels is a crisis in the world of equality. His concern is that what he describes as processes of marginalization present themselves in a manner that enables them to be taken on and encouraged. He names the "celebrating diversity" movement as a chief culprit, for while its central belief of respecting difference looks decent, it is far from it: "It is insidious because it has fooled the host (democratic liberal society) into switching off its immune system, this being the capacity to think" (p. 4).

There is something compelling in the way Dalal draws attention to the perseverance of racism and to the ways it can survive in hard-to-discern ways. It seems that his thesis is ultimately based on the fear that pressure for change, particularly in the highly contested area of racial discrimination, will demand movement on either side of the spectrum, necessitating mutual re-evaluation but without critical judgment:

> What I am against is an indiscriminate respect and tolerance that requires the tolerator to disengage from their own discriminatory processes. In doing so, they would be abandoning their own humanity as they suspended living according to the claims of their own ethics. On this basis, the price for allowing the other their "authenticity" is being paid by abandoning one's own authenticity. . . . My argument is that in order to exercise the faculty of respect. . . . I have to discriminate. . . . If I cease discriminating then I cease to be human. [Dalal, 2012, p. 246]

I have spent some time on Dalal's viewpoint because although it is controversial and can be contested, it is an argument about authenticity and not being swayed beyond one's doubts by populist movements. He gives compelling evidence to show that change in the area of equality is not happening in many areas, despite the language of reconciliation. Although he is speaking to real-world issues in his book, there are clear implications to be drawn for the world of psychotherapy. If racism persists despite a wish to overcome it, then how is the ordinary practitioner, particularly one working with a patient of a different ethnicity, to be aware of his or her own discriminatory processes and to avoid imposing them on the patient?

Inevitably questions about technique are connected to the debate on the fundamental stance of the therapist. In an important paper, "Normal Counter-Transference and Some of Its Deviations", Roger Money-Kyrle (1956) reflected on Freud's description of the therapist's correct or normal attitude to the patient as "benevolent neutrality":

By this I take to imply that the analyst is concerned for the welfare of his patient, without becoming emotionally involved in his conflicts, It also implies, I think, that the analyst, in virtue of his understanding of psychic determinism, has a certain kind of tolerance which is the opposite of condemnation, and yet by no means the same as indulgence or indifference. [pp. 330–331]

In what seems to be an anticipation of the modern debate about "the blank screen therapist" (Yi, 1998), Money-Kyrle considers the issue of concern for the patient's welfare, which he feels comes from the fusion of two basic drives, the reparative and the parental. It is the reparative drive that "counteracts the latent destructiveness in all of us" (Money-Kyrle, 1956, p. 331). He suggests that the patient must stand for "the damaged objects of the analyst's own unconscious phantasy, which are still endangered by aggression and still in need of care and reparation" (p 331). Money-Kyrle also considers the way in which the analyst is able to analyse the patient only inasmuch as he can recognize his own early self. Empathy and insight (crucial elements in psychoanalytic work), as distinct from theoretical insight on its own (which by implication can be cold and detached), depend on this partial identification with the patient.

The world—in particular, the world of race and ethnicity—has moved on at a pace since Money-Kyrle's comments, and I shall consider this shortly. However, before doing so, I would like to comment briefly on one aspect of his statement, which seems particularly relevant.

It is clear that in 1956 Money-Kyrle is assuming the necessity of personal analysis, to ensure that the therapist is able to give undivided attention to the patient's needs rather than confuse them with his or her own. However, he is not assuming that being or having been in analysis guarantees that the patient will be understood. In fact, within the context of the whole paper he assumes that there will, almost as a "given", be periods of a breakdown of understanding, and the therapist will need to adapt to this situation until a sense of attunement with the patient has been regained. The process of reconnecting with the patient will inevitably involve a journey into the therapist's own defences against failing to understand the patient.

This description of the vulnerability of the therapeutic position seems very relevant to work within the area or racism. More recently, Dorothy Evans Holmes (2006) has raised the issue of the preparedness of therapists to work in the area of race and ethnicity as a pressing concern. She argues that while didactic learning and supervision are necessary tools towards competence, they of themselves are not sufficient: "only the therapist's own treatment attuned to racial meanings, *and for therapists of all ethnicities and races*, can help a therapist master his or her own racially related issues" (p. 65). The aim will be to "bear and decipher the representation of race within ourselves and in our patients—going to whatever abyssal places we must in the process" (p. 66).

In recent years, the presumption among authors has been that the term "benevolent neutrality" is, to paraphrase Dalal, itself host to the parasite of racism. Given the clear evidence that so many factors can influence one's opinions, and that patients can find it difficult to mention issues such as race, there is scepticism as to whether the therapist's "neutrality" is what it purports to be, and whether neutrality is too passive a concept, allowing prejudices to remain in place. A number of authors have explored the unacknowledged prejudices that can accompany the therapist into the consulting room. Kris Yi (1998) summarizes the literature on the question of whether the racial difference between the analyst and the patient served as a facilitator or as a deterrent against development of true transference, referring to Goldberg, Myers, and Zeifman (1974) and Schacter and Butts (1971). Some replies by white analysts noted transferential guilt relating to the social injustice suffered by black patients. Yi suggests that the literature indicated the presence of race-based stereotypes, such as alleging that black patients were aggressive, impulsive, and lacking insight. Other issues centred on feelings of superiority and hostility towards black patients.

There is also debate about how to work within an area of racial conflict. A number of writers are critical about Kleinian approaches. According to Yi (1998), the Kleinian viewpoint is "limited in its strong tendency to consider negative transference as defensive projection on the part of the patient, a defensive manoeuvre to dump unwanted mental contents to the racial other" (p. 87). Yi confirms her negative view of an interpretation of projective identification as leaving no space for a developmental view—it is simply a way of transferring guilt onto the patient. Gibbs (2009) seems in sympathy with the view that reliance on projective identification "leads the therapist to assume that his/her negative reaction to the patient is caused by the patient's destructive impulses" (p. 119).

Something crucial is being missed here. The importance of sensitivity, of identification with the pain of the patient (Bion, 1980), the search for non-inflammatory language, all seem important in this debate. It seems important to clarify whether these authors are saying that the concept of projective identification is itself faulty, or that when used in an unfeeling way it can project a feeling of guilt on to the patient.

In recent years, Davids (2011) has made an important contribution to the debate by his original thinking about the concept of internal racism. When describing the third session of work with a white patient, Davids interpreted an attack as racist. However, in his words, "he had hit the nail too firmly on the head" (p. 28) and was taken by surprise by "an unintended descent into a frankly paranoid transference" (p. 28). He came to see this transference as linked to normal infantile processes—in this case, hastily erected to defend against a catastrophic loss of functioning. His patient was caught between the unthinkable prospect of depending on an analyst (which was unthinkable at the time), and, at the same time, the realization that he desperately needed help. The patient resorted to projection as an attempted way out of the dilemma.

Davids identifies several distinct phases to his patient's defence. First, a real difference between the patient and therapist was identified ("English/native" and "foreign", respectively). Second, that desperate need to find a place of belonging, which is associated with unthinkable suffering in the patient's mind, was located in the therapist, newly perceived as the one who did not belong, while the patient felt free of the anxiety of not belonging. So far, the above is a description of a commonplace occurrence whereby painful experiences are avoided and located elsewhere. However, Davids was struck by the ferocity of the attack on him by the patient and traced it back to his reacting to an interpretation that portrayed him as a *patient in need* (italics in original). At first sight, this reaction by the patient seems to give credence to those who criticize reliance on projective identification, but it seems instead to point to the need for the clinician to be able both to tolerate being projected into and to avoid handing back prematurely what is meant to have been put far away. Michael Rustin describes the idea of race as an empty category, but it is this emptiness that makes it available to be filled with projected fantasies of a primitive nature, which gather momentum from the very process of projection (M. J. Rustin, 1991). Davids noted that following the initial projection into him, a complex internal racist organization was developed to manage the relationship between them. It was as if a kind of status quo could be established to govern the relationship between the patient, now free of his unwanted aspects, and the therapist now carrying them. Interestingly, Davids suggests that the purpose of the template is to disguise the first two steps of the process described above, where racism is more recognizable: "It renders them invisible, and so sanitises the situation" (p. 31). This phrase chillingly recalls the language of Dalal referred to earlier when likening racism to the action of parasites, since it suggests that in dealing with these primitive processes the therapist will be located within, but striving not to be enveloped by, the complex internal racist organization.

Given the primitive nature of the racist organization[1] the question remains as to how best to prepare to work in an area dominated by paranoid splitting followed by projection and projective identification. The need for personal therapy has already been mentioned, but there are two aspects of training that need to be mentioned briefly. The first concerns the primitive feelings experienced in situations of extreme suspicion; the other concerns the type of language used to convey thoughts occurring during the clinical situation.

Margaret Rustin describes the usefulness, within the training context, of an infant observation (M. E. Rustin, 1989). The method of observation within a naturalistic setting, rather than intervention, makes it possible to encounter developmentally early emotional states, as they are expressed by the observed infant within the context of the family, and experienced by the observer, who has to deal with the turbulent environment that is "the stuff" of infant observation. The turbulence comes not only from the observed baby and its environment, but also from within the observer, since it is inevitably the case that early associations to the observer's own infancy and early childhood are stimulated by the process of observation. A process similar to countertransference can be observed as the observer struggles to differentiate what seems to be the baby's experience from his or her own experience and, further, to assess the accuracy and origin of his or her own emotions as they occur in the context of the observation. A further richness is to be gained from identification with the parent (usually mother), particularly in those moments when she is struggling to understand the nature of her contact with her new-born child, the complex world of cries, certainly, but also the communication of near-death terror that visits all babies (and their parents), whatever their upbringing.

I hope the above paragraph will have suggested a number of links with the process of therapy itself, affording insight into both the patient's communication of primitive experiences and the therapist's ability to recognize them for what they are and to contain and interpret them. There is, however, one final point that needs to be mentioned, though not gone into in detail—namely, the search for a non-toxic language, as far as possible, when communicating in the world of infantile processes.[2]

In this section, I have emphasized the pernicious nature of racism, locating it within infantile structures. I have explored issues concerning the therapeutic stance of the therapist and also looked at issues about technique. I have also noted Money-Kyrle's emphasis on empathy and Bion's concern that the pain of the patient should be of paramount importance to the therapist. The emphasis on the need for sensitivity seems more appropriate than a general "ban" on approaches using a Kleinian approach or concepts such as projective identification!

Case material

I now discuss two psychotherapy situations that, at the time, I found very difficult to work with, feeling constrained in terms of technique and of understanding.

The first situation to be described was that of work with a black female parent (Ms D), which took place within a Child and Adolescent Mental Health Service (CAMHS). In this context, it is usual for child psychotherapists to work with parents, and a number of roles are possible. My sense of unease in the situation arose from the client's reluctance to become involved in any way in the ordinary procedures that form an important part of a referral to CAMHS (more so today than when I saw this parent). Additionally I realized that from the beginning of work I had to operate in an atmosphere of great mistrust yet, paradoxically, obvious need.

I was very much aware of the ethical difference between the client and myself, but it rarely felt possible to address this situation directly. I describe the setting in more detail later.

The second situation took place during the long-term psychotherapy of a white female patient. During a particularly difficult part of therapy, when she was trying to resolve issues of care relating to her early years and was feeling that I did not understand about these matters, she had a series of dreams that were a radical departure from usual dreams. They featured black figures in a central role for the first time in the therapy, and, for reasons that I will explain later, it was clear that I was to be "black" in the transference. I found myself initially resisting the images that were being presented to me; however, over time much progress was in fact made due to this initiative by the patient.

The CAMHS setting allows a multi-disciplinary team to be gathered, which provides a range of short- and long-term treatments covering a range of modalities. Appointments would ordinarily be made by letter, though in the particular setting I am describing, self-referral was still possible. In all cases, including self-referrals, a team discussion would be held before an appointment in order to discuss how best to proceed.

Margaret Rustin gives a full picture of the range of work done by child psychotherapists with parents (M. E. Rustin, 2009). The traditional provision of consultation to parents on an occasional basis is commonly found. So, too, is individual work with parents, and, of course, this can be directed towards specific issues such as bereavement, divorce, and crises of confidence in parents as they feel they are losing touch. A great deal of attention has been given to the question of who should work with whom in therapy and by what theoretical approach. The CAMHS clinic in which I worked with Ms D was set in a multi-cultural and multi-ethnic area. At the time of her self-referral, I had had experience of working with adults and children from very different cultural and racial backgrounds, who, as a whole, formed the majority of referrals.

Clinical material: Ms D

Ms D's first contact with the CAMHS clinic took place late on a Friday afternoon. I was asked to come to reception by a distraught administrator who had felt verbally attacked. Ms D was very emotional and angry, declaring that she would not leave until she had seen a clinician. The situation could have developed into a procedural issue (since she had reacted to the white administrator's resistance with screaming and verbal abuse), but after a brief delay it was possible to give attention to her obvious distress. She was quite clear that she had not come to talk but wanted "actions, not words". She wanted a nursery place for her youngest daughter, Dawn, and she felt that she was at the end of her tether. I said her request was a difficult one for me. I would like to help and that it would be important to find out more about her situation. I refer to an account I wrote up after the first meeting:

> She was very suspicious but eventually she entered the room. She was on edge, perched on the edge of the chair, her coat very firmly on. She wore thick men's shoes and socks that gave an ungainly appearance. Incongruous colours completed the scene, particularly a headscarf of bright scarlet. I was struck by how many carrier bags (four at least) were under the buggy. Three were crammed with files, the other seemed to have spare sweaters, a Thermos flask, and what seemed like a food box. The belongings were not confined to the bottom of the buggy—somehow, although the mother kept herself wrapped up, she still managed to spread into the room: the buggy was placed more or less in the centre, taking over available space, and I suppose blocking my route to the door. In addition, toys fell off it, and a blanket ended up on the floor. Her baby had clearly "pooed", but she seemed to have no energy to notice her. Within 2–3 minutes I felt as if the whole room and all my available attention had been completely taken over. I was very struck by her lacklustre eyes, not at all sure that she could manage to give much to the children. I would have liked to refer her to either her GP or Social Services, but it became clear that she felt that that would be tantamount to dismissal, and I felt I would not see her again. I agreed to explore the possibility of a nursery place, but when I asked for her name her reaction was immediate: "What do you want to know that for? Are you trying to psychoanalyse me?" Eventually the information was given, but rather than arrange another meeting she said she would ring the clinic to see what progress had been made.

Afterwards, I felt exhausted and quite astonished that within an hour I had taken on such a huge burden. It took several days for me to realize that Ms D's desperation was such that I had not mattered at all to her but had been thoroughly taken over by her needs, while she had assumed the position of someone who would call in to see how the task was proceeding! Something of Ms D's desperate situation must have flowed through me to various agencies, because a nursery place, funded by the local authority, had been arranged within a week—quite unprecedented in my experience.

Despite the awkwardness of that first meeting, Ms D did engage with me provided that I did not stray from the task of monitoring Dawn's introduction to the nursery. She was, however, very suspicious about leaving any trace of her presence in the service and was adamant that she would deal only with me. Within this restricted brief (about which there was some negotiation), she relaxed slightly and for the first time told me about her situation, particularly about Victoria, her elder daughter, who had a serious skin problem necessitating the application of oils for hours each day. The more I heard about this, the more concerned I felt since it seemed that local agencies felt that Ms D might be the reason that Victoria's skin condition deteriorated between stays in hospital.

After a few months, I was feeling that work about the original nursery brief had run its course. I explained this and told her that I thought she should bring Victoria to the clinic for joint work since Ms D was clearly worried about her. It was a step too far. She stood up impulsively, saying that she would not be back. I said that I would like her to reflect on this and explained how she might get back in touch. However, I was not able to prevent her from leaving.

After almost six months, she did contact me, agreeing to fortnightly joint meetings for herself and Victoria.

Joint work

My role within the context of joint work quickly became the task of trying to act as a "buffer" between Ms D and Victoria. It seemed as if the irritated skin at which Victoria scratched constantly characterized a relationship that saw the two of them colliding into each other, without any hope of respected individual space. The

following brief account after six months of joint meetings describes
the emergence of a more positive relationship eventually.

They both came in, Ms D clearly angry and Victoria looking
grimly at the floor. Ms D sat opposite me. Victoria was at the
table beside me. She turned towards me, showing her legs,
and started to rub and pick at the skin, completely engrossed
in the task. Very quickly there were traces left by the nails as
she slowly pulled them up and down. Ms D was clearly furi-
ous: "It doesn't matter what you do, I'm not going to change
my mind." No answer from Victoria, who, if anything, scowled
more and continued to attack. I asked Ms D to explain what the
issue was. "It's about a rice cake." She had made two, one for
each of them. Victoria had had hers and she couldn't have the
other; Ms D would not give way, would not allow herself to be
bullied by skin-picking. Victoria kept up the attack. There was
now a growing mound of white dust. I felt trapped between
the two of them.

I had noticed that at the beginning of the session Victoria had
glanced at the paper I had given her, as if she was about to use it,
and then quickly looked away. Usually I gave her smooth white
paper, but I had been in a hurry and had given her some that
was slightly yellowing and had wood specks in it! I mentioned
this, and Victoria nodded, saying that she wanted what she usually had. I found some and she started to draw. Interestingly,
while continuing to rub with the other hand, she became more
engrossed in the drawing, gradually attacking herself less. The
space that this provided seemed to allow Ms D to think. We
talked about these two rice cakes, and she was able to be less
preoccupied about her share, eventually commenting that at
least Victoria liked her cooking.

The drawing gradually took over, and the attack on the skin
stopped. It was a drawing based on an abstract of colours, sometimes merging, sometimes separate. The colours were drawn on
tissue and attached to the top of the other sheet of paper with
Sellotape. I said it seemed to be a picture about skin. I noted that
there were three colours and talked about how difficult it was
for the three of us to talk at the beginning. Now there seemed
more peace. We could be together without a fight, and the three

colours told the story of this. Ms D brought me back to earth with a quick "now you're trying to psychoanalyse us". I was prepared for the worst, but to my surprise she said she liked it.

I noted the following immediately after the session:

I am very struck by the issue of space in the room. It seems as if there is no space between them. They collide against each other as if there is no personal space, no sense of where one begins the other ends. Victoria's scratching, which is being brought into the room, seems to represent a vicious determination not to hold herself together. It is really puzzling why she turns at herself in the way she does. Is it the skin she received from mother she is attacking?

There were other sessions, however, that gave rare glimpses from the beginning of a more cooperative attitude between them. One session in particular comes to mind when they described in a conspiratorial way how they had cleared lots of rubbish from the flat. Altogether they had filled twenty rubbish bags and carried them late at night to an empty skip they had noticed outside a neighbour's house. There was a sense of glee that they had cleared space in this way, and part of the shared delight was that someone else would have to deal with the rubbish instead of them.

Individual work with Ms D

A separate part of the contact came after 18 months, with the decision that Victoria needed individual therapy. Increasingly she was becoming uncommunicative at school and was beginning to earn a reputation for being awkward. At home, she was very tearful, very jealous of her sister, and more convinced than ever of never having been loved. Paradoxically, this made her more "clingy", something that Ms D found to be intolerable. Strikingly, Victoria had stopped attacking her skin, but her world was becoming increasingly populated by hostile figures, and even objects such as trees with peeling bark repelled her, to such an extent that she could no longer walk through a rather beautiful park on the way to the clinic.

The individual work with Victoria lasted a number of years, and she made a successful recovery. Not only was this a helpful decision for her, it was also opportune as far as work with Ms D was concerned. She had started to recover memories from childhood, in a painful way, and on one occasion this happened during a joint session, to her obvious distress. Individual work continued for a further three years, but I am confining my comments to the first 18 months of this and will focus on three dreams, since, as far as she could remember, she had never dreamt before.

Although I had to discipline myself to be led by Ms D's own material, and careful too not to generalize too quickly, I felt that there was an easier attitude in the room during this time. Interestingly, it was only at this point that she started to tell me "her individual story", though it became apparent that she had difficulty remembering details, such as how many brothers and sisters she had, their names, when was she sent to England, what school she had attended. All of this needed to be reclaimed painstakingly from her memory. It was excruciatingly painful to witness, and I felt myself becoming most indignant on her behalf.

Dream 1

Three months after starting individual work she said that she had had a dream. She was surprised since it was a "picture" rather than a "story". She was excited because it was the first dream she could remember having:

> *There was a glass with lots of toothbrushes, nine or ten, she thought, and a sink. She did not know which brush was hers when she went to brush her teeth.* That was all.

She was sceptical when I suggested a link between toothbrushes and her large number of brothers and sisters. She pointed out that due to a difference in ages, they weren't all at home together. Therefore, there couldn't have been nine or ten toothbrushes in a glass!

There was much that could have been made of the dream with the help of Ms D's associations, but it was clear that this dream, the first she had ever had (or, more probably, had ever remembered), had come too early. I learnt that when faced with this kind of objection, it was best not to pursue the matter. Subsequently, concerns about brothers and sisters, and family matters generally, came more into the room. It was as if the dream had floated out of nowhere, had to be put back in its place very quickly, but its effects rumbled on.

Dream 2

The second dream took place a year after the first. Following the first dream she had started to organize the flat and had enrolled herself on a course that would enable her to become a lawyer eventually. Accompanying these positive moves were setbacks, including a very difficult break when she was hospitalized (psychiatric care) over the summer break, and the children put into temporary care. The day before she returned, she had the following dream, which she said she needed to talk about because it was so vivid:

> It took place in her home. The social workers came, and they said they were going to take her to hospital. One of them put it in a quiet but determined voice that she needed help because she had become "unhinged". She remembered vividly that this took place in the left-hand room as you entered the house. She was very frightened—they said they had straitjackets with them but wouldn't use them if she came quietly. She asked permission to tell her children where she would be going, and they gave her a few minutes to do so. The children were in the right-hand room, and she went to tell them. They were very upset and did not want her to go.

It is difficult to describe the impact of a dream like this, coming into the room as it did within a climate where every single interpretation has to be thought about carefully before delivery. I tried to link it with the events of the summer and asked her whether she recognized in the dream something of what had happened to her over the summer. She did but seemed strangely haunted by it, and I was left feeling that despite my efforts to think in a broad way and at the same time to keep the dream available for thought, she very much wanted to be rid of it.

I was not prepared for the dramatic way in which the possibility of continuing to work with the dream was avoided. We received a message to say that Victoria was in hospital and they would not be back for several weeks. She had had a violent stomach pain, and Ms D had taken her to the hospital. There was great concern about how ill she was. They had to operate quickly, fearing a ruptured appendix. One of the surgeons was puzzled, saying she wasn't in enough pain for it to be appendicitis. Nevertheless, the decision to operate was taken. Victoria's appendix was removed and was only subsequently found not to be diseased. They thought instead that it was probably a virus. Subsequently, it became clear that Victoria had been suffering from acute period pains.

Dream 3

Soon after this there followed another dream:

She was going to a house. It had a large door at the entrance and a broad stairway. She walked up and noticed that there was a man with her. It wasn't anyone she recognized but she thought he was a doctor. When you got to the top of the stairway you had to go through a door ahead, you had no option. However, although she didn't take another path, she knew that you could, once inside the room, go to the left where there was a comfy place. In the dream, you had to walk straight forward through the door. You kept on and there was a window and you had to go outside. You either walked on to a balcony or you fell over and you didn't know which. The doctor went first and she tried to warn him. She suddenly realized he would fall. Too late! She rushed to the top and saw him down below lying on the ground surrounded by an angry crowd who had attacked him. They poured petrol on him to set him alight. She somehow climbed down the outside of the building, went to him, tried to beat them off and rescue him. She realized at that moment that he must be very important to her. Somehow that scene faded away and she found herself going through the same process of going up the stairs and so on, without the doctor, unable to stop herself going round and round without end.

Afterwards, she was on edge but also fascinated: "What makes a dream?"

There was much that was not accessible, but it was possible to think of a journey involving me and her. She focused first on the "treadmill", a powerful feature of this dream. This was linked first to the external world with her increasing determination and search for qualifications that would allow her to break out of a frustrating cycle of dependency that made her a slave to events. She did not want this any more. She wanted to take more control.

It was also a shattering experience to have had a dream where she cared for someone. She was not sure who the man was but then gave a picture of thinning hair that was unmistakeable. We laughed about this, but she was also troubled. Why was it so savage? Why fire? Why so much harm to someone who had helped her?

I felt I had to restrain myself. This was not a time for attempted answers; rather, I was grateful that for the first time she could ask questions of herself in my presence and feel that I was with her, thinking alongside her.

Reflection

I would like to focus first on the clear contradiction that was presented through my work with Ms D. On the one hand, there was the unconscious appeal for help by the downtrodden, helpless victim. It was an appeal for help that did lead to a calculated risk in the way I set out to help her. But once I had been invited in—or so I thought—the trap sprang shut: "Why do you want my name?" It was as if she was telling me not to expect permission to pay attention to the issue of chaos and disorder that she had presented. Instead, I was to do something practical: "Find me a nursery place!" It is, I believe, a situation that very frequently presents itself in our work. An apparently open invitation to work in the area where we feel most happy—that is, within the infantile structure of the individual—turns out to be a very restricted space indeed. We run the risk of becoming impotent if we do not act and of losing contact with the patient altogether if we tire of the game of patience and speak to the unconsciously presented infantile part without first having received "formal" permission from the other aspects of the personality.

Troublingly, my work with Ms D highlighted the fact that flight from insight can place others in danger. Consider, for example, the dream describing the visit of the social workers and the fear of madness. This dream was connected, it seems to me, to what happened subsequently to Victoria. It is difficult to resist the thought that the mental suffering that would have been associated with reflecting on the dream was avoided so comprehensively that the experience was evacuated and, in the days before the next session, became located in Victoria. This was expressed psychosomatically by Victoria as an unknown pain, and apparently medical opinion decided that her appendix was on the point of bursting. One surgeon expressed doubt that the pain was severe enough for appendicitis, but despite this the appendix (and, I would add, the unwanted and unwelcome hostile visitor "insight") was surgically removed from the right-hand place (where the children were in the dream).

I realize that I have focused on only one contributing factor to a complex scenario, but it was very noticeable when Ms D returned after a fortnight that she had no recollection of the dream itself, only a worried memory that there had been one. It will be remembered that the third dream occurred soon after her return, and it was possibly buoyed by anxiety to bring some understanding to what had happened.

What to do in such a situation, therefore, when the "innocent" may suffer? Should we press on with haste to try to bring about greater insight, or try to avoid raising anything that cannot be resolved within the parameters of the session? Inevitably, the search for some position within these options does lead to a feeling of insecurity within technique as we struggle with the issue of whether we have said too much or dared too little. With the introduction opening paragraphs of this chapter in mind, I would say that my constrained role made it possible for work to be maintained. I decided that I would only comment within an area already broached by Ms D, nor did I ask direct questions, which I felt would be too intrusive. When I needed to raise an issue I did so, but even then I would make sure that the issue was already in the room at that moment, at least in broad context. It was very difficult to maintain a working position such as this. I was very moved, for example, by Ms D's description of a childhood spent with remote relatives and of being sent to this country for the first time at 9 years of age to meet and then stay with her father. I felt outraged on her behalf, but my effort to express sympathy was felt by her as an attack on her (idealized) parents. Similarly, it felt important not to offer encouragement: "out of the blue", she said that she was tired of being locked into the benefits system (of which she was an expert) and had thought she would like to be a solicitor or "something like that". While acknowledging this, I had to dampen my enthusiasm. It was six months before the issue came up again, but when it did, she could be clear that from the beginning it had been her idea, hers alone, and not influenced by me. Pleasingly, after a number of years of work she did achieve her ambition of leaving the benefits system, achieving qualifications, and working in the legal system.

The issue of "restraint" in interpretive work was famously mentioned by Bion (1980). He was asked some questions about how to approach a dying patient. He relates the question to that of his broader understanding of how we are all in a terminally ill condition (!), and the problem is how to learn to best use the unpredictable time that we have available:

> What is your assessment of the job of the psychoanalyst? I have already suggested that it would not be much use being invited to tell various forms of agreeable lies, nor would I want to terrify anybody by telling him frightening stories about his possibly having a fatal disease. Although it may seem theoretical, or even philosophical, I find it easier to fall back on the feeling that I am called upon to make the person familiar with a particular aspect of truth. [p. 126]

The issue seems particularly apposite to the work with Ms D. There is clearly a world of difference when viewed dispassionately between various forms of agreeable lies and frightening stories about a fatal disease. However, in an atmosphere of great suspicion, the compromise of a particular aspect of truth can be hard to find.

Second case: Ms S

The focal point of the second situation I would like to consider is a series of dreams that took place within the psychoanalytic therapy of a white female patient in her twenties whom I have called Ms S. A key issue that emerged in the first two years of therapy included a picture of an unwanted baby affected by her mother's depression, and, it seemed, put out to care by a succession of carers. The overt reaction to the carers was, overall, one of gratitude. After all, they had provided some care, unlike the mother who had been absent.

Outwardly Ms S worked very perseveringly on the relationship with her mother, and despite her difficult beginning she had developed into a person of flair and talent. There was a residual annoyance at having had to do this on her own.

A difficult period preceded the sequence of dreams. Within this period, two main themes developed. First, an acute sense of early deprivation and loss entered the therapy room, particularly before an analytic break. Typically dreams (which were brought assiduously) would describe journeys to airports with her firmly strapped into the back seat with no control over the destination. Second, a sense of dissatisfaction with me, as a therapist, came into the room. Many complaints were small matters to do with the details of the room, but others were on a grand scale, wondering whether I had sufficient talent to work with her and to understand her. Although they were considered individually, it became apparent that the real message was not about individual instances but a determined effort to get me to see that she was doomed to be looked after in a way that could never answer her needs. She seemed to be saying that whatever the intention might have been at the beginning of therapy, I needed to understand that it was a botched job.

It was at this point that a dramatic association intervened. At a moment during a session in which she had been very much in touch with early deprivation, there was a vivid picture. There was a white baby lying back, face gazing upwards. The baby was held from behind, and across the front of the baby were a pair of black, crossed hands. It was an unexpected image. She was silenced by the picture, but without noticing what she was doing she adjusted her position to be like the baby, though her own hands were crossed over her front, unlike in the dream. When the associations started, they were bitter. The black hands reminded her of being left in the care of a hired help, a nanny. The level of care was to keep alive, not nurture. Someone was simply doing a job for which they were paid, but care would be withdrawn if the money were to be withdrawn. The implication was that professional care, whether it be nannying or therapy, was simply to provide the lowest form of care, to keep alive, no more, and most certainly not nurture. My care was felt to be the equivalent of the black nanny's care. When the link was made, despite the clarity of the image there was a protest from a deeply concerned and grateful part of her: this would imply that she was racist, whereas she felt that her nanny had provided care for her where her mother had not. Why would she criticize therapy when it was clear that it was helping her?

At another level, through dreams and associations, the imagery of the baby held by crossed black hands continued to appear in the form of a repeated mute scenario, but more and more linked to evidence in the therapy room of an increasing dissonance between the unquestioned assumption that she was beyond help, had not been provided with the care she had needed from birth, and the increasing evidence that a part of her felt understood and was able to bring about changes both in her relationships with key figures externally and in her capacity to bear intimacy. As an indicator of this, the oft-repeated "black hands" scenario ceased to appear in sessions, almost as if it had fulfilled its role and was no longer required.

The image of "blackness" persisted in another way, as a later dream will indicate:

> She was wheeling a bike across wasteland. The entire frame had been hollowed out and filled with drugs. A teenager appeared in front of her, and she realized that the figure had my face. I was friendly, wanting to talk to her. She wanted to respond to me, but did not dare to. She was on her way to a handover to drug barons (later identified as "black"), and she knew that they would be watching the whole scene from a block of flats in the distance. They would be thinking that there was a double-cross. She and I would both die. In the dream she felt sorry for me because she didn't want me to die. At the same time she felt cross that my enthusiasm and naïvety had got us both into this. It had never occurred to her that she would lose her life.

When we worked on the dream, it became apparent that once again the villains of the piece were the black gang leaders who were prepared to kill to maintain their trade. However, I had moved away from a black identity, as portrayed in the nanny scene, to become an idealistic adolescent (she had discovered my link to the Adolescent Department at the Tavistock Clinic) willing to help, but rather naïve. Did I not realize what I was stumbling upon? While a part of her could respond to my greeting, there were evil and deadly forces at work. It seemed that the frame that was filled with drugs did not really seem to connect to occasional recreational drug use, but was much more connected to a sense of having been taken over by a black gang structure intent on taking over the whole frame. There seemed to be a sense of despair, a feeling that there is something unbelievable about the notion that such forces can ever be overcome. In the dream, she was pleased to see me, but also overcome by great anxiety about the outcome. She realized that she was embedded in a "gang" structure. A disturbing picture emerged of what such membership entailed. She had become a "mule", and in return for a basic level of care, she had lost all freedom, any sort of independent action. While there may have been stirrings of rebellion against such a tyrannical system, the stark realization had set in that you don't escape such tyrannical systems without dire consequences. I am, of course, referring to an internal structure. Externally she could take decisive and thoughtful action, and she showed great reliability within her professional career.

Reflection

In my work with Ms S, I felt I needed to allow myself, first, to respond to the image of the black nanny and, later, to be associated with the unwitting victim of the black gang. The image of the black nanny was a compelling one, and the difficulty about it did not come from doubts about its relevance as a powerful unconscious summary of a transference situation, in which I was viewed, through associations to the image, as an unsatisfactory substitute, a paid help not capable of responding to the deepest needs of my client. Rather, it came from the nature of the image itself, which had all the hallmarks of a racist image. Although she had had an early experience of being looked after by a black carer, what was striking about the image is that it was a caricature rather than a description of a person, identifiable only by the presence and colour of the hands, and generalized. It was therefore a racist image, which linked the role of black nanny to surliness, a grudging attitude to service, linked only to pay, with scant regard for the baby across whom the hands were crossed.

My feelings were complex. In accepting the image, I was agreeing to work with the experience of being projected into, to being seen as a "black nanny". But what does it mean to "accept" such an image? Much of my earlier experience had been very much connected to being very much aware of difference—that is, holding on to what I was not, in terms of culture and race, and putting myself in the position of needing to be informed by the client, particularly when these issues seemed to be inexplicably absent from the setting, or when they were present to a persecutory degree. In this instance, however, I was being asked to fulfil a number of roles. I was meant to provide an excuse (if not a reason) for an explosion of rage at hired but inadequate help and also make a link in a general way between the inadequacies of black nannies and the "scurrilous" profession of therapy. I was being invited to "be in the stocks". It was therefore, a complex image and not simply a matter of rage. I felt that part of the scenario was a need for me to feel resentment at this patient on whom I was felt to be dependent for income, just as a baby from a privileged family might be envied for having more privileges and wealth than the nanny.

Technically, it seemed important for me to work within the constraints of the image provided for me. This enabled me to continue to reflect on why the image was affecting me so powerfully. I assumed that there was felt to be a match between the nanny and how I was being perceived by the patient's unconscious. What I was dealing with was not a description from a black person but a projection into the black-nanny population by a part of the patient. The image faded from sessions as it became possible to acknowledge the emotional price she had had to pay in terms of "nannying" and the actual price in terms of therapy to address this early neglect.

On later reflection, when the image had faded from sessions, I understood that the real issue in the scenario, and the link between the nanny and me, was that we both seem to have been present to take the attacks from a disillusioned and distraught baby-part of the patient. The intended target for her fury was the idealized mother, the one who could fuel the need for perfect mothering but was instead not around to carry out the more mundane occupation of mothering due to a self-preoccupation that made her unavailable. In the case of Ms S, however, this was not the end of the matter. Distressingly the fury was not only directed at individuals, but became generalized and racist, both acknowledging the care given by the crossed hands and using it to make a mockery of the care given, portraying it as "typical black care, only interested in the money". My discomfort at working with the image was, I think, linked to the thought that unerringly the image was meant to engage a racist part of myself in order to attack me but also to enrol me as a guilty accomplice.

There is one other aspect to this episode within long-term work which was troubling at the time but, on reflection, might be helpful: why did it take so long for the image to be understood and the racism to be exposed? It seems to me that an important factor was what might be called the over-perseverance of a sense of "sameness", a clinging together as whites against blacks. I feel that this failure of perception might be generalized to suggest that a similar conspiracy against the facts can apply to therapeutic situations where the race of therapist and patient are the same, whether white or black. This is also indicated, I think, by the earlier quotation above by Dorothy Evans Holmes (2006, p. 65).

Summary and conclusion

At the start of this chapter, I made reference to Kris Yi, who researched the question relating to the impact of racial difference between analyst and patient. My feelings for a long time in my work with Ms D were that I was working in the mental equivalent of a minefield, where an incautious comment would lead to a catastrophic ending. Frequently, I had to absorb what was said and pass back a comment that was very much reflected on, rather than being a spontaneous reflection on what was passed to me. Over time the situation became more relaxed, but it was never comfortable. To a large extent this was bound up with Ms D's state of mind, and I was frequently mindful of her memory that on reaching this country she was held together, she felt, by school, which had lots of polished wood. When she felt alone, she would touch the wood. The image is one of strength and support, but also of distance. In some ways, this was what was needed in the therapeutic situation. Although work was slow, and the beginning unorthodox, it eventually bore fruit. It was very important that long, patient work could take place within CAMHS.

It was also the case that my approach to her lacked the familiarity of understanding her world prior to her arrival at the clinic. The relatively small number of black psychotherapists was an anomaly, and in a practical way this has been a concern for me since that work. It is an issue that has been taken up in CAMHS generally.

It will have been noticed that the concept of projective identification very much helped me in my work with both patients. As I said earlier, many commentators feel that working in this way has no place within the area of race and ethnicity. This is not my experience, though interpretive work has to be carried out with sensitivity in "highly protected areas".

There is a final point to make. It seemed important in the work described for me to continually strive to find a perspective from which I could observe what was happening in the room, not simply be immersed in it. It seems necessary, therefore, to hold onto a distinction based on the different roles of therapist and patient. It is understandable that Yi should worry that the distance from the therapist may become "self-serving", creating a scenario in which "there is no room for the therapist's own pre-existing vulnerabilities to cause unpleasant and painful feelings in the therapist" (Yi, 1998, p. 77). However Money-Kyrle's picture of "benevolent neutrality" linked to empathy fuelled by reparative and parental drives, and a consistent attention by the therapist to the damaged objects of the therapist's own unconscious phantasy, is very much relevant to this debate.

Notes

1. Davids (2011, p. 29) explains that this conceptualization of racist phenomena (i.e., its primitive quality) is particularly found in Britain.

2. Rustin and Bradley (2009) describe the provision of work-discussion seminars for professionals and for those preparing for training in psychotherapy. The two-year seminars help the search for an accurate but non-toxic way of describing thoughts to clients and, in the setting being described, take place alongside a two-year infant observation and a one-year young child observation.

CHAPTER SIX

The complexity of cultural competence

Inga-Britt Krause

There is a tension that is pervasive throughout the social sciences and psychotherapy.[1] This tension is simplistic, but also powerful, perhaps because of its simplicity. This is the tension between the view, the attitude, the argument, or the experience that, on the one hand, we, us human beings, are all the same and have little trouble understanding each other. There might be some superficial differences, but fundamentally all human beings share the same psychological make-up. The other view emphasizes that we are different, that even though there are similarities, the differences between us are crucial and in some circumstances make understanding between us difficult, in extreme cases even impossible. We may refer to the first view as "universalism" and the second as "relativism". The tension between these two views underpins all work and research in anthropology, cultural studies, psychology, sociology, and philosophy and derives from the fact that we must use ourselves to access, explain, and connect with the world around us, including other persons. This tension therefore also pervades all thinking about race and culture, but it is rarely highlighted as fundamental in how to approach what currently is referred to as "cultural competence" (DoH, 2005; see also Bhui, Warfa, Edonya, McKenzie, & Bhugra, 2007; Papadopoulos, Tilki, & Lees, 2004; Singh & Dutta, 2010).

Of course, both universalist and relativist positions can be racist and discriminating. For example, many of us psychotherapists are familiar with the assumption that theories derived from and constructed within the context of our own cultures (in the past referred to as civilizations) apply cross-culturally without us stopping to think about whether this is actually so. These ideas have roots in the Enlightenment and in Social Darwinism in which the rational thought and technological advances of Western cultures were seen to be the pinnacle of civilization towards which all other cultures strive. Those whose cultures and ideas were different were seen to be naturally "less fit to survive" and even "primitive" (as in the writings of Herbert Spencer, the nineteenth-century philosopher, who was an important influence on the early development of sociology as a discipline) (Rattansi, 2007). On the other hand, the institutional and collective assertion of the idea that only those who are similar (most often defined in terms of isolated characteristics) can understand each other and communicate may equally lead to discrimination. Think, for example, of the tendency in the UK National Health Service to address service delivery to minority populations only in the shape of ethnically and culturally matched services. There is no clear evidence that matching of the race, culture, or ethnicity of the clinician with those of the patient produce better outcomes (Bhugra & Bhui, 2006); however, this has been and still is a powerful tendency in thinking about cross-cultural provision and communication. What is clear is that if used as a general policy, this has often been seen by health providers as a way of circumventing the dilemmas and tensions of the cross-cultural debate. Over time, such a policy may have the effect of exempting majority professionals and teams from thinking about and addressing how race and cultural processes enter clinical encounters. Patients and clients from minority backgrounds may then get less choice than others, less access to generic services; in addition, specialist teams staffed by professionals who are themselves minorities may be employed at lower grades and receive lower salaries (Krause & Miller, 1995).

Why are these two positions so pervasive throughout the field, both in policy and complex theorizing and in our own experiences and our reactions to these? Why does the tension between them seem to induce us into a capricious vacillation between one and the other? And why does most cultural competency training avoid addressing these processes? In this chapter, I address these questions. I connect the polarity just described with questions about categorization and about the linking of internal processes and external context. This will allow me to present a window onto the complexity of cross-cultural psychotherapeutic practice with the help of two examples: the first is anthropological, to show the role of cultural norms and expectations in the developing attachment and relationship between an Inuit toddler and her mother and sister (Briggs, 1998); the second is clinical, to show the way culture and social structure are implicated in other aspects of therapy. I suggest that there is no way out of this complexity other than keeping it in mind and working through it.[2]

The third position

There is, of course, a third view. This is the view that to some extent we, us humans, are the same and to some extent we are different and that what is required are not categories for us and them, for ourselves and "the others", but, rather, a process of reflection and thought about our differences and similarities (see Bion, 1962). There is no doubt that we are capable of such a process. Thus, much of psychoanalytic writing, such as that of Klein, Bion, Winnicott, Britton, and Benjamin as well as others, discusses how infants, children, and adults acquire the capacity for this third position and what this position entails.

> A third position [then] comes into existence from which object relationships can be observed. Given this, we can also envisage being observed. This provides us with a capacity for seeing ourselves in interaction with others and for entertaining another point of view whilst retaining our own, for reflecting on ourselves while being ourselves. [Britton, 1989, p. 87]

Developmentally, the third position is achieved when a relationship between the other and a third party can be tolerated (by the child) and may not be achieved without a process of destruction, in this way opening up the possibility of recognizing the other as external to oneself (Winnicott, 1971). Acquiring this capacity also involves a process of symbolization, which for Winnicott is anchored in a subject's relationship with transitional objects and incorporates cultural material. Winnicott wrote: "I am assuming that cultural experiences are in direct continuity with play, the play of those who have not yet heard of games" (Winnicott, 1971, p. 100).

Several writers have observed the parallel between the self/ other dynamic in intrapsychic and developmental processes and wider social, political, and cultural identity/group processes. Benjamin observed:

> The question of recognition is . . . always the question of whether there will be peace or war, a struggle to triumph and annihilate or a negotiation of difference. The question—Can a subject relate to the other without assimilating the other to the self through identification?—corresponds to the political question, can a community admit the Other without her/him having to already be or become the same? [Benjamin, 1998, p. 94]

Other writes such as Cooper and Lousada (2005), Dalal (2002, 2006), Davids (2010), Khanna (2003), Krause (2011), Layton (2006a), Leary (2006), and Samuels (2006) have pointed to this correspondence and discussed the connection between the two areas of social life. I want to comment on two of the many issues that permeate this debate: categorization/classification, and the linking of internal processes and external, cultural, and political contexts.

Categories

If developmentally most of us, at least some of the time, manage the "third position" vis-à-vis our relationships with intimate others and our fantasies about such relationships, why do racist attitudes to those of different colour, culture, and traditions persist? Why does classificatory practice continue to promote racist categories? Is there, as Amin (2010) has recently argued, something fundamentally human about processes of categorization and sorting, which are preserved through institutional practices, which in this way seem to become historicized and hence naturalized? Certainly "race" is not itself a natural category. The first use of the term "race" is recorded in English in the sixteenth century and referred to "family", "lineage", and "breed" (Rattansi, 2007). The subsequent climate of colonialism and the type of rationality that dominated the Enlightenment in Europe contributed to the shaping of this term, so that "black" conveyed something negative and, at the same time, negativity came to be described as having something "black" about it (Dalal, 2006). This was combined with an emerging scientific tradition in which classification of the natural world became a central tenet. Thus, just as the Linnaean classification was applied to the natural world of fauna and flora, so colonial administrators, travellers, missionaries, and the early anthropologists applied such classifications to the populations they encountered in the territories they explored (Rivers, 1910). The categories and the form of these classifications were based on the cultural views of the European middle classes from whom the colonial administrators, travellers, and scientists themselves tended to be drawn. Their own conventions of kinship, pedigree, and genealogy thus had a profound influence on ideas about the relationships of others (Bouquet, 1993; Strathern, 1992) and therefore on the idea of race. This idea, combined with the development of the idea of nation, eventually led to the conflation of nation, race, and citizenship. In addition, the internal political processes of demarcation in a developing class society (Rattansi, 2007) demonstrate how, over time and influenced by a series of social, political, and cultural events, the concept of "race" and the classification upon which it is based—be it physical characteristics or cultural patterns—has come to be historically naturalized. It came to be seen to refer to "essence", either physical or cultural, and in the process all kinds of other relations and aspects of social life and personhood could become racialized.[3] For us, this means that the concept of "race" obscures the complexity upon which it is based.[4]

There is a parallel here with the distinction between phenotype and genotype. The early racism was based on appearances, on phenotype—that is to say, on differences in external appearance such as hair type, skin colour, and facial features. With the introduction of the distinction between phenotype and genotype in the early 1900s has also come the realization that the variation and potential in human populations is best understood in term of genes and that phenotype is superficial and even irrelevant. This suggests a much more complicated way of understanding physical difference. Genes interact with the physical environment in such a way that some genes are never activated whereas others are activated under certain circumstances. In addition, as was made clear with the Human Genome Project, there is no necessary correspondence between populations, or classifications of populations made by us in a census, and the gene pool of this population. Ninety-eight per cent of genes are shared by all of us, and it is not uncommon to find more genes shared between persons from different groups than between persons from the same group (McCann-Mortimer, Augoustinos, & LeCouteur, 2004). This has not prevented a new kind of racism, which, despite scientific explanations having been discredited, conflates culture, genes, and appearance. In such explanations, "culture" has become essentialized—that is to say, differences are explained with reference to the nature of any given culture. In addition, following Foucault (1976), it has been argued that in the modern post-capitalist state,

> . . . biopolitical regimes, with their explicit rules and practices of order based on bodily differentiation and discipline, regulate the state of alert towards the raced body. [Amin, 2010, p. 9]

As Amin also observed (p. 8) this is the process that Fanon (1967) described as the naturalization and internalization of race. No wonder that the academic and everyday debates about race and culture, with which I began this chapter, vacillate between the two poles of universalism and relativism, with similar essentializing results. No wonder, also, that the middle ground, the third position, appears to be difficult to contemplate and achieve even for persons who appear to be emotionally and psychologically mature.

Internal/external links

We have seen how there are many reasons why making assumptions on the basis of appearances has a great pull on us. We may be developmentally and unconsciously predisposed towards such identification, but there are also historical, political, social, and structural reasons why we are predisposed to place a primary importance on the body, on the individual, and on how things appear in the present. On the whole, these circumstances are obscure to us, and this inhibits us in linking what we see to relationships, to history, and to the social context—and even to a developmental trajectory and to the potential of how personhood and relationships unfold. Dehistoricization and decontextualization, together with the developmental difficulties of staying with thought and reflection about the links between internal processes and social context, are ways in which the relationship between emotional forces and social life are unhitched, both in theory and in everyday experience.

However, it was precisely a recognition that culture and collective experiences and expectations are located both inside and outside people that led Winnicott to locate culture in the place that "is at the continuity–contiguity moment, where transitional phenomena originate" (Winnicott, 1971, p. 103). If, as far as child development is concerned, we find this persuasive—and I do—we may turn our attention to how this moment may be played out in mature adult life, in relationships between adults and children, and in general social relationships as well. In other words, this may help us begin to explore further where culture may be located and therefore also what this means for our clinical cross-cultural practice. Here, psychotherapists may find the work of the French sociologist/anthropologist Pierre Bourdieu, and in particular his concept of *habitus*, useful. "Habitus" is the mediating link between the subjective world and the cultural and social world into which the individual is born and which she or he shares with others (Bourdieu, 1977). It is a scheme of dispositions, upon which cultural and social groups draw. These dispositions derive from early relational and tactile experiences and become routinized in repeated performances and in expectations about how such performances should unfold in practice (Bourdieu, 1986). The schemes are outside awareness of persons, functioning "beyond the reach of introspective scrutiny or control by the will" (Bourdieu, 1986, p. 466), and they are instilled in persons in the form of *doxa*, a primary experience of the social world, a kind of knowledge without concepts (pp. 470–471). Doxa are generated by structures of relationships as well as by the mental structures designating these relationships and constitute a kind of "normative unconscious" (Layton, 2006c, p. 62), which both imposes and confronts how things should be done, how we should behave, and how we make sense of the world.

We have, then, two views—that of Winnicott and that of Bourdieu—which complement each other, one from psychoanalysis/psychotherapy, from the inside out as it were, and the other from sociology/anthropology from the outside in. Together these views may give us quite a bit of assistance in how to hold on to the third space, how to hold on to reflecting and thinking (Bion, 1962) in the face of pressures to take universalist and/or relativist positions. The following two case discussions will, I hope, help clarify how therapists may make use of this framework.

The ethnography of an Inuit toddler

We are lucky to have an ethnographic account in which the anthropologist engages with the questions I have been discussing. This
is the excellent ethnography by Jean Briggs from her fieldwork
amongst the Qipisa Inuit of Baffin Island in Eastern Canada (Briggs,
1970, 1998). The research took place in the 1960s and 1970s, and
the group was living in a small year-round camp on Baffin Island
in a small community numbering about 60 individuals. Briggs's
work included many hours of careful observation of the interaction
between Inuit parents and other adults and their children, mainly
toddlers. In particular, for several months she closely observed a
3-year-old girl named Chubby Maata. Briggs was interested in the
way parents teach their children and the way children learn, because
in this reflexive dynamic, cultural processes are accentuated. What
follows is a summary of an episode from Briggs's material (Briggs,
1998, pp. 40–43). In this sequence, a mother, Liila, her sister, Luisa,
who is 19, and her two daughters, Rosi, who is 4, and Chubby Maata,
who is 3, and Jean Briggs herself were present in Briggs's winter tent.
The sequence unfolded as follows.

> The mother and the children came into the room and sat down.
> Rosi sat down between her mother's knees. Chubby Maata was
> used to sitting there, and she responded with a whine, demand-
> ing that her mother move Rosi away. No one responded to this,
> and Chubby Maata repeated her annoyed demand: "Remove
> her!" Her mother did not respond to this demand but, instead,
> began to pull chewing gum in and out of her mouth. Chubby
> Maata took the gum from her mother, and her mother smiled at
> her and began to play a clapping game, encouraging her daugh-
> ter to copy her. Chubby Maata imitated her mother, as did her
> older sister, Rosi. This seemed to have distracted Chubby Maata,
> and she asked "Shall I sit here?" pointing to a spot next to her
> mother. Liila encouraged Chubby Maata to sit and to continue
> making the gestures. At this point, the aunt, Luisa, entered the
> room and joined in with the collective focus on Chubby Maata,
> encouraging her to pretend to be Jean. Chubby Maata mispro-
> nounced Jean's name and was corrected by Rosi. Here I pick up
> Briggs's description:
>
>> Now, it was Liila who intervened. Her tone caressed Chubby
>> Maata and dramatized her affection for her; it was a play-

ful version of the niviiuq-ing voice that Qipisa parents and grandparents often used when speaking to babies and small children in order to teach them that they were loved. What she said was: "Say 'ungaa' (make the cry of a baby) because you're a baby". When Liila said "ungaa" her voice was the voice of a tiny baby crying. And Chubby Maata's voice, when she echoed "ungaa" was a small replica of her mother's. Liila hugged her daughter extravagantly and exclaimed in the same intense, playful niviuq-ing voice, "That darling little one (unakuluk)!"—her arms and voice and words all part of the hug. [Briggs, 1998, p. 41]

Picking up from here, Liila used baby talk and a baby voice dictating the words for "mother", "father", "suck", and "food" to Chubby Mata, ending up giving her another enveloping hug. Briggs describes how this spell was broken by Luisa pushing Chubby Maata's bottom with her shoe and how this gave Rosi the idea of attacking her little sister from behind. Liila explained: "Because you are a baby she's attacking (ugiat-) you" (Briggs, 1998, p. 42) and she also encouraged Chubby Maata to say "ungaa", this time using another term "qia" (cry easily, conveying annoyance) and rescued her. However, the fighting between the two children resumed, with Rosi at one point hiding behind her mother. Again I quote from Briggs's account:

> Liila held out her hand to Rosi, affectionately beckoning her to come. But when Rosi trustfully came towards her, Liila's arm shot out, not to embrace her but to imprison. Holding Rosi down, she said to Chubby Maata, "Hurt (anniq-) her, make her angry (ningngassaarii-); hold your hand on her head so she can't get up. [Briggs, 1998, p. 42]

Briggs herself offers an extensive analysis of the sequence. Here I want to pick up just a few points in order to draw attention to the complexity of this material and the way this implicates cultural expectations and dispositions. There are several interactions here, which I suspect we all recognize. For example, we have our own experiences of sibling rivalry and of a mother's way of handling this. We can tune in to the playful, but benevolent manner in which Liila makes it more bearable for Chubby Maata to accept a seating arrangement, which, for her, is second best. Nor do the repetition of the words "mother", "father", "suck", and "food/game" surprise us. It speaks to the way parents and carers orientate children to the social relations around them as well as to the emotions associated with these relations. But there are also one or two sequences that may puzzle us. What, for example, is Liila's demand that Chubby Maata should "cry like a baby" about? What about the sequence in which Chubby Maata is encouraged to attack her sister? This interaction seems almost cruel, the adults setting the children up to have quite a nasty confrontation. So what is going on here?

The language spoken by the Qipisa Inuit is Inuktitut. Inuktitut is a polysynthetic language, and this means that generally an Inuktitut verb translates as an English sentence (Briggs, 1998, p. 228); the demand for Chubby Maata to cry like a baby is an example of this. The words used by Liila were "ungaalirit" or "say ungaa", which Briggs translates as "cry like a baby". The 3-year-old was being encouraged to cry like a baby several times, but not when she was actually being a baby in the beginning of the sequence, wanting to displace her elder sister. In response, the adults collectively set up a situation in which they and the little girl could play her being a baby, and it is this play that was rewarded with warmth and celebration. Briggs points to the shifts between seriousness and play in the language used by the mother's as well as in her actions.

However, "unga" also has a more general meaning in Inuktitut. To "unga" means to feel "dependent attachment" or "longing" or "to wish or arouse the wish to be with another person" (Briggs, 1998, p. 238). It conveys the reflexivity of an attachment relationship, particularly by an immature partner towards an elder person. From this point of view, when Liila asked her daughter to "ungaalirit" (say "unga") she was asking Chubby Maata to be a baby, but also to show her attachment towards her, and/or evoking in Chubby Maata that she is attached to and longs for her mother as a condition of their relationship (Briggs, 1998). Liila is also conveying something else to both her daughters by her betrayal of Rosi towards the end of the sequence—namely, that a mother will take the side of a baby and if you are not a baby you cannot expect to be protected, and yet perhaps you may not show your anger about this (Briggs, 1970).

There is thus more to this sequence than Liila and Chubby Maata expressing their own private internal feelings, thoughts, and dispositions. Their interactions and communications are social, contextual, and cultural, and they follow rules, etiquette, and concepts of morality, only some of which are within their awareness. They are examples of doxa being transmitted. Liila was both enacting and developing a central concept of Inuit morality in the ungaa- sequence for her youngest daughter and presenting Chubby Maata with the contradiction between being a dependent baby and a growing child who has to look after herself in her relationships. This ontological dilemma between attachment and aggression is something we can recognize, but in the interaction between Liila and her children it cannot be disentangled from the Inuit habitus. Chubby Maata learned that serious baby behaviour is unacceptable, and that it is the playful baby, who is celebrated. These are the first lessons in Inuit morality, in which anger is discouraged, even despised, and control of emotions celebrated.

I think that Briggs offers an excellent example of Winnicott's observation that culture is located in the developmental space of transitional objects and phenomena and that this space is also the space of the habitus. In this way, cultural processes and expectations are both conscious and unconscious, both external as well as internal to individual persons and their relationships. The mother is not wholly conscious, and perhaps not conscious at all, of the extent to which she is enacting, developing, and internalizing cultural codes about Inuit morality and relationships for her daughter, while at the same time addressing universal ontological conditions for child development. Even when Liila may be consciously taking the opportunity to teach Chubby Maata what is right and wrong, she may not be conscious about what it is she is teaching. Equally Chubby Maata may already know something about what to expect from her mother and how to act. Culture then is in the relational process. It is inside the self or the person of Liila and Chubby Maata as aspects of a relational self and in the intersubjective process between them. This does not endorse social determinism. Chubby Maata does not learn or internalize exactly what her mother is trying to get across. She demands engagement and probably feels engaged with through an experience that is only more or less cast in a code about how to interact and communicate. From some points of view, culture can be understood as shared patterns; from others, culture is contested, particularized, and fragmented. And it is the emotional conflict that lends force to the transmittance of doxa and to Chubby Maata's learning (Briggs, 1998; Layton, 2006c).

Psychotherapy with a Tigrayan woman

Habitus or internalized cultural dispositions may also be experienced as oppressive and destructive. I first met Radia, a Tigrayan woman, when she was 24. Radia was referred by her GP because she was depressed, apparently because she could not get pregnant. Radia was a refugee from Tigray, and her husband was a Somali from Ethiopia. As Radia's English was fair and she was able to be creative with language, we managed without an interpreter, which in any case was her choice. In this first meeting, she was evasive about Tigray, telling me only that she had travelled across to Kuwait. She hinted that she had been sexually abused and confessed to being bulimic as well as to scratching her legs until they bled, but I could not connect up the fragments of her story. Instead, she felt it was urgent that she should have tests to find out whether she had gynaecological problems. This fragmented and desperate atmosphere stayed with me, and when Radia came to the second session refusing to say very much, I asked her whether she thought talking was a good idea. She looked at me for a moment, and tears started running down her face. She did not answer, but sobbed for most of the remainder of the session. She came back for further sessions, and this was the beginning of her telling me her story of extreme suffering, abuse, and trauma, which I will only briefly summarize.

> Radia is the eldest daughter of a Tigrayan professional, who was well known in the community and active in the Tigrayan People's Liberation Front.[5] Her mother was the daughter of a well-known land-owning family from Djibouti. Radia has an elder brother, a younger sister, and a younger brother. One day when the family were in their house at midday and her mother was pregnant with her youngest brother, there was a knock on the door. When her father opened it, he was shot by soldiers of the Derg government in such a way that his body was blown to pieces, flying in different directions. This was the end of Radia's childhood. The streets were filled with soldiers and corpses, and a few days later Radia and her family went to live with her mother's family in another town. Shortly after the birth of her youngest brother, Radia watched her mother get on a bus and leave her and her siblings. She had this image imprinted in her mind and referred to it often in the therapy. Now followed two years in her maternal grandmother's house, and this

turned out to be a nightmare. Radia did not know then what she subsequently found out—namely, that she is not the biological daughter of the man she called "father" and that her maternal grandmother strongly disapproved of her daughter's marriage to him. The maternal grandparents had married their daughter to a wealthy family; however, she had had an affair before this and subsequently eloped with her lover. In the meantime, she had had a child, namely Radia, whom she brought into her second relationship. In her maternal grandmother's house, Radia and her siblings were beaten, punished for expressing small and ordinary wishes, neglected, and under strict discipline. As the eldest daughter of this sibling group, she bore the brunt of the abuse and was frequently treated as a servant, beaten if she did not perform household tasks, and confined to outdoor buildings.

Radia's elder brother succeeded in absconding; after trying to run away numerous times, Radia managed to escape with her younger sister, leaving their young brother, who by then was a toddler, behind. A horrendous journey followed during which Radia became separated from her sister. Among other experiences she describes running through minefields and seeing other people's limbs being blown off. She eventually got employment in Kuwait as a servant with a Saudi family, who came to London. This family abused her, and on an outing to Hyde Park, Radia ran away and by chance met a worker from an Ethiopian Community Association, who helped her find a place to live and acquire Permanent Leave to Remain in the UK. By a miracle, her younger sister and elder brother also independently made it to the UK, but her younger brother, who eventually also escaped from his maternal grandmother's house, became a refugee in Kenya. Radia felt terrible about leaving this little boy behind, and in the therapy she often confused this boy with the baby she so wished to have.

During the ten years I have known Radia, there have been periods when I have seen her once a week and other periods when she has attended much less frequently. Her symptoms of overeating, bulimia, scratching her legs, headaches, tightness in body and limbs, and nightmares were severe, and they are consistent with a diagnosis of post-traumatic stress disorder (PTSD).

I do not want to explore PTSD here, suffice to note that in my work with Radia I have addressed these symptoms in terms of their meaning and have therefore come to acknowledge the conceptual problems with the *ICD* and *DSM* diagnoses (Young, 1995) and the cultural dimensions of this kind of suffering (Summerfield, 2004; Zarkowski, 2004). These dimensions cannot be separated from other aspects of Radia's predicament. PTSD is

> neither a natural kind nor a purely socially constructed kind. There is a third possibility. PTSD may count as an interactive kind (Hacking, 1999, pp. 100–124). Unlike natural kinds discovered in nature, interactive kinds are affected by the very process of classification itself. [McNally, 2004, p. 11]

Indeed, I think the case of Radia demonstrates that social and cultural institutions and ideas and the meaning of these are deeply implicated in individual suffering and also in the routes and processes that may lead to recovery.

> Thus, after about six month of therapy, there was a turning point, which happened in the following way. Radia used to go over and over her traumatic experiences, sometimes adding more detail, but equally often repeating the same material. My role was that of bearing witness (Blackwell, 2005). I am not sure how much it was me, or how much it was Radia, who could bear this no longer—perhaps it was both of us. In searching for something good in Radia's life, I had the idea to ask Radia about the house in which she had lived with her father, mother, and siblings before the beginning of the terrible events. Radia responded by describing in great detail the family house, the rooms, the garden, the immediate surroundings, and the view you could see from the windows. She added colours as well as sounds and smells. She described her father's land, the garden, the fruit trees, and the surrounding countryside, the river, and the land you could see in the distance. The description took up the whole session. I asked about details, and we repeated this process in subsequent sessions. After this period, it felt as if Radia had been somewhat released from the endless cycle of repetition of talking about her traumatic experiences and she began to bring her dreams to the sessions and to talk with more compassion about her mother.

Among other issues, this sequence conveys the notion of "belonging" and "home", much written about in refugee work (Blackwell, 2005; Papadopoulos, 2002), and probably reflects a general human predicament in relation to displacement. I can tune into similar notions about my own home country and culture. However, as with "*unga*" it is important not to position oneself in the "universal" camp without first thinking and reflecting about possible differences. Here, I have found the work of Christina Zarkowski useful (Zarkowski, 2000, 2004). Zarkowski is an anthropologists who has worked with Ethiopian Somalis who fled during the Ethiopian–Ogaden war and who, when returning to their land, found that these had been confiscated by the Derg military regime, who subsequently refused to restore rightful ownership. Zarkowski examined how the villagers talked about this experience using the term "*hummad*" meaning "passion", "desire", "yearning", and "fever", specifically when people talked about remembering something about the land, the oranges in their orchards, the loading of camels, and so forth. The term conveys a collective sense of remembering, of survival, and of resistance. Among Zarkowki's informants, this theme was often associated with a theme of loyalty and duty to the lineage and the village and associated with two emotions: "*niyed jab*", meaning "demoralization", "hopelessness", "broken will"; and "*murugo*", meaning "thinking about an insoluble problem or loss", "sadness", "depression". Zarkowski comments:

> The individual experience of "*murugo*" or "*niyed jab*" cannot be understood except by attending to the dynamic connections through which individuals and social networks are mutually constituted. All of the "negative" emotions imply a duty (not always fulfilled) to intervene on the part of the interlocutors, especially close kin or friends, preferably by changing the situation that caused distress. [Zarkowski, 2004, p. 197]

These emotion terms thus commemorate the relationship networks in which an individual person exists rather than the individual person him/herself. Zarkowski argues that the referent of these emotion words and their meanings is a moral community and connects social rupture and injustice with individual suffering. The personal and political axis is a moral outrage lodged in a collective memory, where violence, death, loss, and displacement are not addressed within a psychological framework as we know it, but within a framework that we perhaps may call psychological, but which also is collective, moral, and political, with the aim for the community of standing up for the rights of its members and voicing the injustices done to them. In other words, Zarkowski is describing a habitus, and although I cannot be sure about linguistic similarities, I think that it is at least likely that these themes also resonated with Radia and that the exploration of her childhood home and the locality in the therapy provided a route into this material. However, this was only half the story, the other half concerned Radia's kin and family relationships.

As I have described, Radia was intensely preoccupied with wanting to become pregnant, and although this was not the focus of the first year or so of therapy, she and her husband subsequently received IVF treatment unsuccessfully. To me Radia explained about the significance of children for her husband and his family and that in their eyes she was not considered to be a "proper woman" till she was also a mother, preferably to a son. This is in keeping with patrilineal principles of kinship—that is to say, the principle that kin relations are traced through men to a common male ancestor (Krause, 1998) and that relations that persons can trace through their father receive a different emphasis from relations traced through their mother. In this kind of kinship structure, marriages may be used to emphasize relationship between family groups rather than between two individuals (Lévi-Strauss, 1949). Radia's mother's family had attempted to make such an important political alliance with another family through their daughter, and by eloping with another man Radia's mother thwarted this strategy. This seems to have justified and legitimated the cutting-off of her mother from the family and the inheritance and, by extension, also the maltreatment of Radia and her siblings by her maternal family. A final blow must have been these relatives' accusations towards Radia of witchcraft. A witch is an anti-social force excluded from the protection of a moral community, and Radia explained that this accusation was often levelled against infertile women. In this way, the conventions and expectations articulated in the social structure and in the accompanying habitus dramatically intervened in directing the manner in which suffering and sorrow was understood and expressed by Radia (Das, 1995, 2000). This negation of her personhood and her rightful position in a kinship system haunted her so much that she sometimes in the session with me seemed to believe herself that the reason she could not get pregnant was because she was a witch. This ideology was poisonous to her while at the same time corroborating her own sentiment that the damage she has suffered and her self-respect could only be restored by having a child.

This influence of social structure on the emotional experiences of people was highlighted when Radia felt that she could not go through with IVF again and had begun to think about adoption. Her husband and his family had suggested that he would take a second wife, who then could produce a child for them, reassuring Radia that she would always be the senior (and therefore the most important) wife. At this point, Radia's symptoms returned. In the therapy, we discussed how this solution, being a traditional way of addressing problems of infertility, may not be malice, but also that in view of her previous experiences of being cast out from her social and kinship relationships, this felt to her as a further insult, quite apart from the fact that polygyny is not legal in the UK. I think that Radia's resistance to this traditional solution was a way of escaping the patrilineal discourse and the poisoning effects this discourse had already had on her. Although becoming the senior wife in a household with children would bestow seniority and respect on her, for herself this would further confirm her inadequacy. I consider this resistance as a way of finding a kinship discourse for herself that incorporates elements of, and at the same time reacts against, the patrilineal ideology within which she was brought up. Recently, Radia has become more able to balance her own emotional needs with her needs to be recognized as a social person in the context of her own cultural background, history, and indeed habitus. Reclaiming a piece of land in Ethiopia, which belonged to her now-deceased mother, and actively discussing with her husband the possibility of adopting a child have been pivotal events in this process.

Concluding remarks

Categorization cannot lend much assistance in addressing the complexity discussed in this chapter. Identification and especially self-identification may be a starting point, but any attempt to understand cultural differences must take account of the complex relationship between external social contexts and inner emotional and psychological dispositions. Culture plays a role in both these spheres of existence. For psychotherapists, this means being aware of the universalist and relativist positions and the pull they have politically and emotionally. It also means developing a capacity to hold on to the third position of thinking and reflecting as a continuous process. Although the discussion above has by no means been flawless, I have tried to show what such a position may entail and how it can provide a space where psychotherapy and social science may come together. Bourdieu's idea of habitus provides us with a concept for the space to which Winnicott assigns transitional phenomena, a space where culture and general human dispositions are transmitted together. When such transmissions go well, when the baby experiences continuity, culture, and social structure or habitus without being determining, these are likely to be experienced as containing and enabling. When transmissions are ruptured by trauma, these structures and the meanings associated with them may have the opposite effect. Either way these structures are implicated in general ontological processes and cannot be dismissed. It is this complexity that ought to be central to cultural competence training.

Notes

1. Psychotherapy is no longer considered akin to the physical sciences, as was the case in Freud's days. For an account of the similarities between systemic psychotherapy and social science, see Krause (2002).

2. The concepts of "race" and "culture" are often used interchangeably. Their uses almost coincide when understood to refer to essential characteristics denoting diversity and justifying differential access to power and influence. Alternatively, the concept of "race" refers to categories and classifications, processes that to varying degrees permeate social and political life, whereas the concept of culture is more dynamic and refers to conscious and unconscious outlooks, attitudes, and dispositions, which at the same time provide those who embody them with meaning and are in themselves the products of those meanings.

3. Racialization refers to the process of manufacturing and utilizing the notion of race in any capacity, such as, for example, without regard for the existence of any other ontological or developmental processes.

4. I refer readers to the succinct but comprehensive summary of these aspects of race, racism, and racialization by Rattansi (2007) and to his response to Amin (Rattansi, 2011). On the idea of naturalization see Barthes (1957), Strathern (1992), and Layton (2006a).

5. I have written about this case before: see Krause (2010).

CHAPTER SEVEN

"Class is in you": an exploration of some social class issues in psychotherapeutic work

Joanna Ryan

Class has the potential to evoke extremely charged and difficult emotions; it can be a determining aspect of early experience; some internalized aspects of class experience can be unconscious; and yet there appears to be an absence of frameworks for thought and discussion within the psychotherapy profession. The innovative work of the last two decades on gender, race, and sexuality within the psychoanalytic field has not been matched by any equivalent attention to class, although Altman (1995) does provide an account of class dynamics in psychotherapeutic work from a relational psychoanalytic perspective. This chapter attempts to open up for discussion some concerns about class within psychoanalytic psychotherapy. It describes a small exploratory qualitative study in which experienced psychoanalytic psychotherapists from different class backgrounds were interviewed about aspects of their own biographical experiences of class, and their perceptions of class-related issues in their clinical work with differently classed patients and within the profession of psychotherapy, as they experienced this.

The main concern of this research was with how class and class difference can enter into and contribute to the structuring of the transference–countertransference matrix and how this is perceived, thought about, and worked with by the interviewees. The focus was not primarily about access to psychotherapy, and how class may influence this, significant as this always has been and is, but, rather, with how class can enter into the ongoing psychotherapy relationship. It is probable, however, that classed features of the psychotherapy relationship will be among the many factors influencing access and uptake.

Some of the background and assumptions of this research need first to be briefly indicated. Psychotherapists from a range of class backgrounds were included since, following Elias (1994), it was thought important to study class as a whole figuration. There are many debates within sociology about the criteria for social class definitions. For the purposes of this research, the interviewees' self-definitions of their class positions were used, both as regards families of origin and present positionings. A range of criteria were invoked by the interviewees in their self-descriptions, including income, wealth, education, cultural values, and occupational status. Responses to the initial request for self-definition showed how complex, ambivalent, and charged the emotions surrounding class could be, especially for those who had experienced considerable class mobility in their lives and who saw themselves with mixed class identities.

Another starting point was my supposition that there is a wealth of unformulated knowledge and experience about class on the part of many psychotherapists that seldom gets reflected in more formal discussions or papers. Canestri (1999) argues that the logic of knowledge production common to supervision, which involves a reflective third position, can be a valuable research tool. I therefore used as my main research method the supervision model of facilitated discussion of clinical work.

The research was partly biographical in its framing, in order to provide a possible context for the psychotherapists' accounts of their clinical work, and also to yield information about salient early experiences of class difference, as well as professional ones. The decision to investigate these (necessarily limited) aspects of biography was influenced by a perusal of some of the relevant psychosocial and autobiographical literature, which indicated the life-long effects of class origins, even in the face of later social mobility (e.g., Sennett & Cobb, 1972; Zmroczek & Mahoney, 1999). It was also consonant with my assumption that it is most fruitful to consider the questions about how to think psychoanalytically about class in conjunction with an understanding of the class practices, and therefore experiences, of the very discipline and profession within which such thinking is produced and takes place. Blackwell (2002) and Craib (2002) describe some of the barriers to recognition of specific working-class experiences within a psychotherapeutic framework, and Layton (2004b) emphasizes the central role of anxieties of various kinds, for both working- and middle-class people, in what she calls the "internalization of class relations".

Lastly, the research was envisaged as part of a broader interest in psycho-social theorizing and specifically with a concern for how these two terms, "psyche" and "social", can be thought about together within a psychoanalytic perspective.

Description of research

The 13 subjects were obtained by networking and by approaching psychotherapy organizations and clinics. They were all experienced psychoanalytic psychotherapists with a range of theoretical orientations. They worked in a variety of public sector, voluntary, and private locations. According to their own definitions as regards family of origin, there were 6 from working-class backgrounds, 2 from lower-middle-class ones, and 5 from middle or upper-middle-class ones. Five were men, and 8 were women. I did not pre-select subjects according to class, but asked prospective subjects if they would be interested in being interviewed with social class as a focus. An assurance of confidentiality and anonymity was given as regards any eventual publication. Permission for this publication was obtained from the interviewees quoted below.

The interviews were semi-structured,[1] moving in the first part from self-definitions of class positions, to memories of early awareness of class difference, and then to interviewees' own experiences in therapy as patients and in training. In the second part of the interview, they were asked to describe in some detail their clinical work with two patients, one working class, and one middle class, as this was perceived by the therapist and / or in accordance with patients' self-ascriptions where these were present. They were asked to select cases where they were aware there were class issues, either for their patients or for themselves in relation to these patients, or both. It became apparent that prior preparation for this part of the interview was advantageous, and I sent guidelines to all subsequent interviewees outlining possible topic areas and questions.[2] This is unusual in qualitative research but reflects the reality that to ask therapists to talk in detail about their clinical work does entail thought and preparation on their part. They were asked to provide some general background to their descriptions of their work with each patient, their understandings of class issues for that patient, and any class-related aspects of the transference–countertransference. As the interviewer, I would at times ask for more elaboration or attempt to explore some material further, or sometimes suggest links to other parts of the interview, if appropriate. The interviews were tape-recorded and were then sent for transcription.

Consonant with the exploratory nature of this research, a grounded theory approach was taken to the analysis of the transcripts.[3] The categories of analysis were generated from the transcripts, by identifying themes that could be compared across interviewees and also links and threads within any one interview. I attempted to avoid too much fragmentation of the data for the purpose of such qualitative analysis, in order to preserve as much as possible of the holistic nature of each interview, and of the multiplicity of levels of thinking, the ambiguities and complexities that characterize descriptions of clinical work. What follows is a selective summary of much more extensive material (Ryan, 2004)

Class and clinical work

Most interviewees readily located examples from their practices where they felt class was an issue of some kind. There was only one exception to this, but it is possible that with a differently selected sample, less ready identification of class issues would have emerged.

One interviewee, D, asked in the course of the interview: "Does the social class appear in the transference, and how would the analyst hear it?" The research suggests some provisional thoughts about this and indicates ways in which the class background of the therapist can be a significant factor in how class is heard and responded to.

In what follows, the data from the interviewees from lower-middle-class backgrounds is combined with that from those from working-class backgrounds, as much of their material, both biographical and professional, contained similar concerns and were together distinctively different from that of the middle-class inter-viewees. This and the structure of the research meant that for the purpose of the research analysis there were four possible pairings of therapist and patient as regards class: two with a class difference and two with a similarity. Class issues of many different kinds were reported in all combinations; however, with the middle-class therapist–middle-class patient pairing, there was less ready identification of class issues and less distinctiveness of themes, although ease of understanding and ready identification were men-tioned. This can arguably be understood as reflecting the taken-for-granted hegemonic nature of middle-class positionings and values within the profession and its discourses. With the two pairings where there were differences—working- and lower-middle-class therapist and middle-class patient, and middle-class therapist with working-class patient—there were some distinctive themes, and there was almost no overlap in the reported issues as far as these interviews go. There is not space here to report on the pairings of working-class therapists and patients, although many class issues and insights did surface in this. A more extended discussion is to be found in Ryan (2004).

Working-class and lower-middle-class therapists with middle-class patients

Several interviewees described middle-class patients' apparent con-tempt, disparagement, and arrogance, "being put in your place", which either overtly were, or were felt by the therapist to be, class related. Attacks and negative transferences can happen in any ther-apy, focused on many seeming issues: the specificity here relates to these particular constellations of class when questions about class are asked. For several of these therapists, this created especially difficult class-related countertransferential resonances, as did their perception of their patients' relative wealth and seemingly class-based confidence.

The following examples illustrate these themes. One therapist, A, said of her patient, whose mother owned a very successful busi-ness in the ex-colonial country she had come from:

> She was part of the elite, she spoke in this incredibly posh way, and was very, very aware of class. I started to feel uncomfortable

with her early on, and I was aware of it being all my stuff about class, and she said to me in the second or third session: "I don't know, I have to say this because it's bothering me, I'm wondering if you are going to be any good, because you sound quite working-class." . . . It was awful, it felt like she's got right under my skin . . . It set off these feeling of "am I good enough?" . . . "can I be a good therapist because I don't speak in the right way?" and a sort of anger towards her. I thought, "Who does she think she is?" I'm very very aware that I mustn't retaliate, but what I felt then was "I've got to work harder to show her I'm good", . . . "I've got to see behind all this and not get caught up in my own stuff and see what it's about for her. . . . Which I was able to do, but only by going back into therapy myself . . . because nobody had actually said that to me before . . . and it confirmed my worst fears. . . . I managed with her to turn it around, so I was able to get her to see that she was projecting on to me her own feelings of inadequacy, that although she was posh, she was still black, and that in England she still felt she didn't belong . . . and we did some very good work . . . based on that she was always trying so hard to prove herself.

This also illustrates one of the many complex intertwinings of racism and class that surfaced in other accounts. Further exploration suggested what "working-class" signified for this patient:

It meant for her to be black, very black, both metaphorically and in reality. . . . To be working class was to have no culture. . . . The rejected . . . she was desperately trying to be the kind of person her mother had said she should be but all the time she actually felt like the disparaged people that her mother would talk about, those ordinary black people, "not like us", so it's all sort of mixed up there with race.

In response to further questions about how she addressed this:

It was a real struggle because it all could have failed because I could have got very retaliatory and then it just wouldn't have worked out . . . or/and I could actually have become totally inadequate and become the useless working-class therapist that she thought I was going to be. . . . I'm aware of it when I see other patients . . . and again it's always the accent I go for, and I feel I have to prove myself a little bit more, because I don't speak the same way as them, and that they will pick this up and think: "Well, is she any good, is she educated?"

In this example, the explicitly class-related attacks had the potential to retraumatize the therapist, something that is suggestive of how deep and injurious the impact of class can be. One source of this injury is the class-constructed sense of self, the enduring reverberations that social inequalities can have on a sense of personal worth, the ways in which, as Sennett and Cobb (1972) show in their classic study, "social differences can now appear as questions of character, of moral resolve, of will and competence" (p. 256).

Other therapists articulated feelings of classed-based inadequacy. F said in describing her early awareness of class difference:

> The demarcation was very very marked . . . we were just different . . . there was them up there and us down here . . . and it felt like, you knew you were inferior. . . .

F, while very positive overall as to her own analyst's ability to understand her, identified her feelings about her working-class background as the sole area where she didn't feel heard. Her analyst she identified as middle class:

> So it was right in the room for me. . . . He'd got that public schoolboy, sort of charming, polite, blah de blah. . . . I actually raised how I felt about being working class and those feelings of inferiority and shame, and I felt it was one of those areas he didn't quite understand because he'd hooked into the "you're all equal sort of thing, and I really need to value myself". . . . He couldn't identify with the place where it was painful, or the shame. So I told him that. . . . He was a little bit defensive about it that made me feel . . . there's something about this you can't hear.

This is an example where a seemingly class-blind ideology, put forward with the best of egalitarian intentions, can obscure or serve to deny the far-reaching psychic pain of inequality. The enduring nature of this was expressed by F as:

> Politically, emotionally, and rationally, I think everybody's equal but there's a sort of residue that goes right back to childhood, so it's quite hard to get rid of . . . I can see when it's operating,

because I am aware of it, so I can challenge myself, but it's still there.

F also described an experience of contempt with a patient from an upper-middle-class background, who:

> . . . as she got better . . . she regained her capacity to use her background, some of her attitudes surfaced as well . . . she had a rather grandiose aspect to her . . . I actually think she had a lot of contempt for me when things changed for her . . . it was in her attitude and some acting out she did, it wasn't just contempt, it related to class . . . implied in things she said about her own lifestyle, . . . and I said, "That's very different from what you can see of my lifestyle" . . . I don't think this therapy was very successful, there were a lot of issues that didn't get resolved in terms of envy and contempt. . . .

Asked about how she approached this:

> I think I have struggled with my own prejudices, to be aware of them and not let them colour my judgement . . . it's probably my own values and beliefs about human beings and equality that ground me when I'm struggling with how little she's been paying for years and years and how much she's now earning now she's going . . . I have to challenge these things in myself and I was thinking, "I've helped you for peanuts" . . . partly you realize through the work everybody whatever their class is human . . . her family was just hell . . . that modifies all those fantasies about how wealth would just make life easier . . .

Another therapist, E, also described a complex set of countertransferential reactions, involving feelings in the inferiority/superiority dimension that for her had many uncomfortable implicit references to and resonances of class:

> I'm very aware of her class position, she's articulate, she's clever, she's very confident in many ways . . . she's constantly in competition with me, putting down what I say, . . . I'm usually in the category of doing it wrong.

The class positioning involved in this therapeutic pair made it especially hard for E to muster the resources and understandings with which to work with a very attacking transference. However, her eventual perception that the patient was largely "full of bluster", coupled with her own struggle to find her own sense of confidence in working with her, did allow her to stay with her own analytic position.

The power, within the psychotherapeutic situation, for such feelings of class-related inferiority to be countertransferentially stimulated is also illustrated by B. Faced with a woman with a very high professional status and a wealthy prestigious husband, he said:

> I felt instantly crushingly inadequate. . . . She placed me instantly, she knew exactly like Henry Higgins just where I came from, what my wealth was, . . . this came out later. She complained about the chairs, wrote to the manager about the smell in the room, we moved to a different room. This was a measure of the command she felt she had.

He also felt huge envy of her wealth, but also reflected how he'd had to live quite a long time to understand that money can't buy love:

> I felt genuinely valued but as someone from below stairs . . . just the intimacy and sadness about divisions between people that she genuinely felt.

Like F, B also used his view that wealth cannot ensure happiness to overcome his feelings of envy and resentment. This appears to be an assertion of a value system independent of that which is perceived to be the prevailing one, to overcome the power of what Sennett (2003) calls "invidious comparisons". F used as a resource her sense that she had something of intrinsic value in her own belief system and in what she could give the patient. Her appeal to a sense of common humanity was also used by several other working-class therapists as a way of retaining their commitment to working with patients whose wealth aroused considerable envy, or who exhibited class contempt. It is different from the more usual psychoanalytic notion of the equality of individuals, occurring as it does in the context of an acute awareness of the significance of class difference, rather than from a denial of, or blindness to, this.

E also commented on how she felt that working- and middle-class people take up confidence differently, and she compared a confidence that comes from within, that is full of pride, not just bluster, with a false confidence that can readily turn to arrogance and contempt. Several other working-class therapists also pointed to what they saw as middle-class bluff and bluster, a false confidence. D said:

> Middle-class people sometimes seem a bit naïve, take things for granted easily, which seems a bit silly. . . . I take it that confidence is on the side of the ego some place, and it can be strangely oddly very fragile . . . it seems self-confident but not as clever as it seems.

G said of what she had learned about middle-class upbringings:

> . . . a sense of entitlement, that you are here for them . . . if they want an extra session they can have one, because they've got the money. . . . They have a particular accent, they know how to operate in social milieux, which although it may be quite false, because underneath they may feel like nothing, it gets them through some situations.

While confidence or lack of it is an attribute that can manifest itself on the part of anyone of any class, the above quotations suggest ways in which perceptions and expressions of this can have significant class meanings and class effects, as well as deriving from class-based experience.

Middle-class therapists with working-class patients

Several middle-class therapists reported class-related issues of a different kind with their working-class patients, and also considerable stuckness in attempting to address these dynamics within the transference–countertransference matrix. A recurrent theme was guilt and fear of attack.

N's account illustrates some of these issues. She described the beginning of a long therapy with a woman from a working-class background:

> She immediately made me feel guilty about my privilege, not only my privilege but also my friends' privilege.

N had many struggles both with the perceived differences between them, and the transference–countertransference dynamic:

> I had to work with my feelings that if she's different then I don't understand her. What I realized was that being a patient felt humiliating and dangerous to her. My readiness to feel guilt colluded with her denial of her patient status in a very unfortunate way: I was much more able to work with her condemnation of me as masculine; there I was able to see the projections as well as own the reality. . . . My guilt has meant that I am constantly aware of not wanting to denigrate them [the patient's family] . . . even now I hesitate to describe them as a disturbed family.

N felt that she hadn't been able to sufficiently confront the patient's defences against shame and humiliation, the way in which the patient's anger and envy was expressed as political disapproval:

> She can't bear the powerlessness of being a patient, I can't bear my class privilege and the power of being a psychotherapist, and I think my insights have been limited by this. . . . I do think the class difference has been there, all through the work.

As well as the inhibition stemming from her own class guilt, and from the fear of enacting some class-based denigration, N came to realize that she had idealized the patient in some ways and also identified with her sense of powerlessness, all of which lead to a stuckness in the therapy. N's efforts to resolve her conflicts about her privilege echo much of the discussion in Maher (1999).

Other middle-class therapists also felt that they had not been able to sufficiently take up aspects of transferences that might have included class issues, and especially class-based anger. J described a man in a skilled manual occupation from a working-class family. She felt that she had helped him put into words his angry feelings:

> . . . all related to his bosses who earn lots of money, had big cars, and used him as a skivvy. You could see he resented being in the position he was, violently, . . . he was in a sort of conflict situation with them, which of course repeated some of his earlier experience, and also repeated something in the therapy with me,

because there I was, middle class, with a little warm consulting room, . . . I think it was very difficult for him to articulate anything about my position, I couldn't help him do that . . . I mean it was there in the transference, obviously, but you wondered whether with this man you should be trying to pursue or open this up. It might have been because there was a very violent part to him, and in the countertransference I think I knew that. . . . I never did feel fear with him, . . . it's possible that there was more around than I was able to deal with. He was talking all about these men with big cars, and mine isn't a big car, but that must have been there.

Earlier J had spoken about one of the examples of her own class embarrassment as having a fairly posh car, which sometimes she had felt impelled to hide.

J went on to describe how she felt the therapy had been successful as regards many of the presenting symptoms, but she was still left with a sense of untouchable areas:

He had a grievance about his upbringing, but he wanted to hang on to that . . . there was so much grievance because it had all been so bad . . . there was so much reality factor that it was difficult to go into it, there was very little to work on. . . . I don't know if there was a countertransference that made me feel nervous of doing that, because of what might have been an outcome . . . I felt there was something a bit untouchable.

M also felt inhibited in taking up some aspects of a working-class, upwardly mobile patient's transference. This patient would describe himself using a character from a well-known novel primarily concerned with class differentiation and social injustice. For this patient, M said:

There is clearly a very ingrained sort of class issue for him and power differential and things like that. . . . There's a sense that anybody in the upper class has more power and can afford to be ill, and I'm sure that includes me in the transference. . . . Taking up anything with him in the transference is a prickly area actually, because he can have quite a strong tendency to believe that you are criticizing him.

M said that at times he would make reference to the perceived differences in their status. M wondered whether his hesitation in taking up some of this was to do with his perception of the patient's paranoia and having to be especially careful of what he said to him, or whether it was

> a class thing, a kind of reversed snobbery. . . . It is difficult to challenge him, because of the sense that he would perceive it as dismissing his realities. . . . I'd really like to say: "Look, of all the things he has achieved, . . . what's going on that kind of holds him?" . . . I suppose in the countertransference, I'd like to challenge him . . . I don't think it would be very helpful head on, but sometimes I feel like if only he could see the world a bit differently. . . . I don't think it's all about class, but you could see him stuck in that sort of grudge, he's very much stuck there.

The inhibition felt by these middle-class therapists and the limitation of their analytic work as a consequence is part of the anxiety about crossing the boundary of inequality from a position of social advantage within a therapeutic context. These excerpts illustrate Sennett's (2003) description of what he claims happens when "true mutuality" is lacking—namely, silence, caution, and fear of giving offence.

Some of these difficulties were cast by the interviewees in terms of "reality factors" and the opposition that was felt between the acknowledgement of these and an analytic stance. It was as if the therapists' own acute and often anxious awareness of class "realities" prevented them being able to bear and usefully work with being put in the transference in the position of the class oppressor. The biographical connection with actual class position is important here, along with the extent to which adequate analysis for the therapist in relation to this has taken place, as to whether the therapists' own class anxieties limit the work. N, for example, made links between her class-related difficulties with the patient she described and her own early acute awareness of class differences. She had felt that her own analysts had not been at all able to understand or help her with intense shame and guilt about her privilege. From the interview material it would appear that this had a limiting effect on her work. J, by contrast, had felt very helped by her own analysis during training in addressing what she called her "complicated inversion" or "inverted snobbery", and that her unconscious identification with the "do-gooder" and marked guilt about privilege had been effectively understood and challenged. It was still, though, an issue that had enormous resonance for her in some of her clinical work, as the above excerpt shows, illustrating what Sennett (2003) calls " the perverse seductive power of inequality".

These therapists also spoke of "grudges" and "grievances", which is perhaps a significant use of language to allude to stuck anger, reflecting the therapists' sense of frustration at what could not be further worked with in these particular pairings. P, a middle-class mixed-race therapist, did not use these terms in describing his work with a working-class man "who was defiant and proud about it but who was carrying a lot of hatred and envy." Coming from an economically and emotionally very deprived background, he had, P said, "a terrible anger" and a determination never to be so impoverished or out of control of his finances. P was seen both as the "toff" and as the migrant that had made good and who tried to conceal himself with his accent. P described a threat of violence at times during the analysis, which he managed to contain; at the end of a long intensive analysis, the patient "was still as angry and emotional but the language had changed, he had an ability to look at things that would worry him". As well, this patient had made huge changes in his material and professional circumstances.

The interview data suggest that P's ability to work productively with this working-class white patient may well have important links with P's own biographical experience of having to deal with being subject to racism, as well as his reported experience in his own analysis of having felt well understood in relation to issues of "race" and class. It would seem that P could move around issues of class-related anger, of being able to grasp the many intertwinings of social realities with intrapsychic issues, which enabled him to bear the transferential and actual class positioning of himself without guilt or undue fear.

Reflections

My own experience of conducting these interviews was frequently of opening up a hidden subject, about which most of the interviewees had many thoughts and concerns but with little or no framework for articulation or discussion. Such an absence is also described by Craib (2002) and Blackwell (2002). The silences around class reported here underline the unacknowledged embeddedness of its seeming middle-class mores, despite the huge personal, material, and social trajectories that many working- or lower-middle-class therapists had made to enter the profession. The therapists from these backgrounds conveyed an intense awareness of the classed nature of their professional environment (as did several of the middle-class therapists), but they were somewhat isolated in finding their own personal accommodations to this. The absence of any framework for the explicit discussion of class is something it would be fruitful to address in professional contexts, and it would go some way towards defraying the sense, described in relation to the perpetuation of educational inequalities, that " Class is everywhere and class is nowhere" (Walkerdine, Lucey, & Melody, 2001).

Much of the biographical material of the working- and lower-middle-class therapists echoed other writings on the psychic demands of social mobility and the resulting senses of displacement, mixed identities, and lack of confidence in middle-class milieux. The powerful, persistent, and far-reaching psychic effects of class were evident in how many of the therapists understood both themselves and their patients—as one said: "Class is in you." How, psychoanalytically speaking, class is "in" a person is something that this study raises for further research.

As regards clinical work, the distinctiveness of themes for the two main groupings of interviewees is striking, and while this small study can at best be suggestive, this is worthy of further discussion. What does the reporting, by working- and lower-middle-class therapists with middle-class patients, of being the target of contempt mean when questions are asked about class in clinical work? It lays out what is often kept politely or defensively hidden—the attributions of inferiority and superiority—which are part of class. It illustrates aspects of the construction of classed psyches: the working- or lower-middle-class fears of inferiority and humiliation, and the middle-class use of class as a defence, to create an illusion of superiority and false confidence, warding off fears of failure and inadequacy. The intensity of the analytic encounter with differently classed subjects brings to the surface (often instantly) these complex intertwinings of class-based anxieties and projections. The working- and lower-middle-class therapists' countertransference experiences with these middle-class patients appear to have derived from being the recipient of projections of feelings of denied inadequacy, combined with their own vulnerability to this, which in the clinical situation could be powerfully evoked. The rawness and forcefulness of these denigrating projections were for some therapists intensified by their own historical class experiences, which contained descriptions of shame, inferiority, and low self-esteem, intertwined with economic and material inequalities, and also anger in relation to class differences. As illustrated by these reports, these therapists did largely find ways of fruitfully working with these complex dynamics, but the psychic demands of this were considerable.

A salient feature of the reports of some the middle-class therapists was a sense of inhibition in taking up aspects of the transference which involved class-based anger and dealing with the countertransferential aspects of guilt about privilege. It is not hard to see how anxieties about inequality from a more privileged position can lead to fears of attack, but what is striking is the reported stuckness and difficulty in working with this, something that suggests a degree of misperception about the assumed vulnerability and rage of the other, and also unresolved anxieties about privilege. This meant that the necessary projections could not be therapeutically allowed or worked with. It is as if the emotions surrounding inequality could not be faced openly and therapeutic progress became stalled. If such a dynamic is commonly experienced by middle-class therapists working with working-class patients, or even by a few, then it can be seen that inequalities would be perpetuated by this therapeutic inhibition, over and above any other class-related difficulties in access to and uptake of psychoanalytic psychotherapy. This interpersonal class dynamic may also contribute to the common misperception that working-class patients are not so psychically available for psychoanalytic work, as well as to the likelihood of premature endings. Such limitations, as well as many of the other matters raised in this exploratory study, would benefit from further study and discussion and could also be addressed as a matter of training and professional development.

Postscript (2012)

Since this article was first written, there has been some opening-up of arenas for discussion of class within the psychoanalytic field, such as a UK conference in 2009,[4] as well as various publications, and the inclusion of class as a topic on some trainings. These, combined with earlier work not referred to above, have all added to the understanding of how class can operate within clinical practice, and also of the factors that have led to what I have called its elision and disavowal within psychoanalytic theory (Ryan, 2009). The enduring and personally felt nature of class-related experiences suggests a topic of psychoanalytic concern as to how class constructs subjectivity and leaves its marks in and on the psyche. Knowledge of class, as Hartmann (2005) argues, is often unconscious, embodied, reified, and not available for mentalization. I would also argue that class cannot just be understood as "difference". Class has to be addressed within a framework of the economic, material, cultural, and other inequalities that constitute it, and which has hindered access to psychoanalytic therapy and trainings for many from non-middle-class backgrounds. For the practitioner, an understanding of his or her own class positioning is necessary, as an individual, as a worker (see Dimen, 2006), and as a user of a body of theory (psychoanalysis) that has significantly excluded class from its corpus of concepts.

Hartmann (2005) describes how, with particular patients, the realization and acknowledgement of how class was at play in the clinical work lead to a significant deepening of the therapeutic process. Hartmann traces what he calls "the power of [his] class unconscious", as evidenced in some countertransferential enactments with a patient whose demands, seemingly work-related, evoke for Hartmann conflicts and estrangements in his relationship with his working-class father. Hartmann argues that class is conveyed enigmatically to children by the parents' spoken or unspoken attitudes about work, communicated in their bodies, affects, and thoughts. This is an unusual, much needed, incorporation of the materiality and psychic effects of parental employment into psychoanalytic thinking, even if Hartmann's theorization of this as "the class unconscious" begs as many questions as it seeks to answer.

Hartmann's understanding of the vicissitudes of his own class mobility is similar to Blackwell's (2002) reflections on how social mobility can "upend" and complicate the father–son dynamic. Blackwell, like Hartmann, argues for greater psychoanalytic acknowledgement of the losses and conflicts involved in such mobility, so that adequate mourning can take place. The complex psychic demands of upward social mobility were vividly described by many of the interviewees above, the ways in which moving into more middle-class environments exposed them to great challenges as regards their own sense of self-worth and entitlement, along with the resulting sense of dislocation, dividedness, and multiple identities.

Botticelli (2007) argues that the most salient feature of class in many arenas is that its existence is most often denied or minimized. Mitchison (2009) describes the disjunction between its significance in individual lives and its absence from much therapeutic discussion. The ways in which class, race, and gender issues can be entwined and displaced into each other are illustrated in Armitage (2009), as they also are in some of the examples in the research above. In *The Moral Significance of Class,* Sayer (2005) provides a wealth of examples of great psychoanalytic relevance concerning the ambivalences, equivocations, pain, and denials that can surround talk about class, to which inequalities between people are central. This known but not-known quality suggests that, in a clinical situation, class-related issues, where present, are likely to be powerfully evoked, albeit split off, disavowed, and entwined with many other aspects of personality and development.

Botticelli also suggests that some class experiences bear a structural relationship to trauma, insofar as both can engender a tendency to blame the self for the lasting effects of external forces that have inflicted injury. This is strikingly evident in Sennett and Cobb's (1972) classic and extensive work on the internalization of class relations. It is also suggested by some of the accounts in the present research of working-class and lower-middle-class subjects whose early class experiences left powerful legacies of an undermining and conflicted kind, with which they were consciously struggling. One, E, said she was "traumatized by class, my sense of low self-esteem, sense of embarrassment, . . . not feeling that I had something to say. . . . Now I don't feel so raw." Skeggs (1997) describes her extensive ethnographic work with working-class women thus: "it is a study of how social and cultural positioning generates denial, disidentification and dissimulation rather than adjustment. It is a study of doubt, insecurity and unease: the emotional politics of class". For middle-class subjects in my research, the legacies were in some cases unavailable for conscious reflection, in others accompanied by a degree of shame, confusion, and inhibition that could hinder thoughtful clinical practice.

For a more fruitful incorporation of class into psychoanalytic discourse and practice, it is important to understand the theoretical issues at stake. I have argued (Ryan, 2009) that these can be traced to the foundations of psychoanalysis, where Freud's clinical accounts are replete with descriptions of the class-inflected lives of his patients, but where none of this enters either the interpretations offered or the theorizing. This is especially marked in the case of the Wolf Man (Freud, 1918b [1914]). I try to show in some detail how this extrusion of social relations from the theory happens, through a discounting of the significance of conflicted attachments to domestic employees and through a dialogue Freud poses between two alternative understandings. My reading of this concurs with Calvo's (2008) reading of the same text, as regards the elision of both race and class. This underlines the importance, for any more socially orientated psychoanalysis, of understanding how oedipal scenarios and social hierarchies are "intertwining fantasies and sites of dense condensation" (Calvo, 2008), in which powerful social forces and imaginaries are given a dynamic equivalence with intrapsychic processes, in the earliest constitution of the subject.

Much contemporary psycho-social work on class emphasizes its relationality, the ways in which "(C)lass is produced in a complex dynamic between classes with each class being the other's Other" (Reay, 2005, p. 923). While actual class experiences are much more heterogeneous and hybrid than this binary might suggest, nonetheless it underlines the ways in which class divisions and hierarchies can take root and reproduce themselves in and through the psyche and become a fertile ground for the most anxious and fearful projections. Such relationality also underlines the importance of studying middle-class subjectivities, which are as much part of class as the more studied working-class ones. Reay's (2008) distinction between different middle-class attitudes to inequality (within an educational context) and the ways in which these are articulated, defended, and equivocated, have relevance to any understanding of the class inflections of psychoanalysis and its predominantly middle-class positionings.

Notes

This chapter was first published in the *BAP Journal*, No. 34, Vol. 3, Jan. 1998, but has been updated by the author for this publication. I would like to thank the Tavistock Institute of Medical Psychology, London, for its generosity in funding this work. I would also like to thank all the interviewees, quoted or not, for their time, patience, and thoughtfulness and for their willingness to talk openly about aspects of their lives and work. Thanks also to Georgie Parry-Crooke and Vic Seidler for helpful comments and encouragement.

1. The interviews were semi-structured in the sense that while there was a range of topics I hoped to cover and a rough order of questions, I also wanted to create space and time for a freer flow of thoughts and associations in each person's responses.

2. This part of the guidelines is reproduced here:

Please identify in your mind two patients, one working class and one middle/upper class in whatever settings, for whom class issues stand out. This can be either (or both) because of the material/histories that they brought or your own responses to them. If possible, patients whom you have worked with for a substantial period of time.

Possible areas to explore, details depending on particular patient–therapist dyad in question:

Brief account of patient, and how presented self in relation to class, how this emerged within the therapy, in connection with what issues, circumstances, or events. Explore and enlarge on this as appropriate, and how worked with. Possible examples are: money; perception of therapist and setting; material and cultural deprivation/advantage; shame and feelings of inadequacy/superiority, envy, and guilt. As well: language; ways of seeing and expressing emotions; class mobility/dislocation and identity; educational experiences. Gender and race interactions with class. Transference–countertransference issues, if not already covered, including your own feelings and responses in relation to class issues of the patient, how these are understood and dealt with, possible identifications and disidentifications, and associated feelings.

3. By grounded theory is meant an approach in which theory and interpretation emerge from or are generated from the data, rather than using a pre-existent theory or hypothesis. In practice, these different methodological perspectives are often used conjointly to various degrees.

4. The conference, "Class and Psychoanalysis", was sponsored by the Site for Contemporary Psychoanalysis and the Freud Museum, London. The conference papers are in *Sitegeist*, No. 3, 2009.

CHAPTER EIGHT

Psychoanalysis and homosexuality: keeping the discussion moving

Juliet Newbigin

In January 2012, the British Psychoanalytic Council (BPC) agreed a position statement on homosexuality, which began: "The BPC does not accept that a homosexual orientation is evidence of disturbance of the mind or in development." In doing this, they were following the example of the American Psychoanalytic Association, who had first drawn up a statement of their own in 1991. The BPC's initiative was accompanied by a conference entitled "Homosexuality and Psychoanalysis: Moving On". There was a palpable sense of relief among those who attended, and hope was expressed that it marked the beginning of a new era, leaving behind the troubled history of the relationship of British psychoanalysis to homosexuality. The BPC, readying itself to become a body with regulatory responsibilities as part of the Council for Healthcare Regulatory Excellence (CHRE), was seen to be taking an important initiative, bringing it into line with the Equality Act of 2010. This act had introduced "protected characteristics"—to defend the rights of named categories of persons who had been shown to be vulnerable to discrimination by employers and service providers. This Act identified these categories under the following headings: "age, disability, gender reassignment, race, religion or belief, sex, sexual orientation, marriage and civil partnership, and pregnancy and maternity". The Act now extended protection to include cases of indirect discrimination where organizations could be shown to have policies that disadvantaged people in the above categories.

I am aware that the BPC's position statement was not welcomed by everyone. Some said that they felt it infringed on the autonomy of member organizations, the proper sources of authority on psychoanalytic theory. Others complained that it made it sound as if the belief in the pathological nature of homosexuality among members of the BPC was wide-spread, which was not the case. Some therapists felt that to suggest that members of the lesbian, gay, bisexual, and transgendered (LGBT) community fall into a special category as patients was in itself discriminatory, that they have been seen in psychotherapy practices for many years, without this work presenting special challenges. However, this does not account for the enthusiasm that greeted the BPC's conference. In this chapter, I attempt to explore why it has been necessary to draw up this statement.

Whatever the nature of individual members' practice, the founding organizations of the BPC are nevertheless seen as having practised discrimination against members of the LGBT community. It is believed that these are a group who have for many years been barred from training and are thus under-represented in those organizations. In April 1995, the Association for Psychoanalytic Psychotherapy in the NHS invited American psychoanalyst Charles Socarides, who was well known for his view that homosexuality was a pathological condition in need of cure, to give the annual lecture. This provoked considerable protest, and a Letter of Concern was published in a number of psychotherapy journals. Subsequently, there was a period of debate and activity, mainly outside the BPC organizations, on this perceived discriminatory policy. During the last 20 years, there has been a growing literature exploring the attitude of the psychoanalytic profession in Britain to homosexuality and its conservative stance (see, for example, Barden, 2011; C. Denman, 2004; F. Denman, 1993; O'Connor & Ryan, 2003; Shelley, 1998). Little of this discussion, however, has found its way into the scientific life of the founder organizations of the BPC. Since the controversy surrounding the Letter of Concern has died down, the atmosphere within these organizations has been described by Jeremy Clarke of the New Savoy Partnership, which represents psychological therapies in the NHS, as an "uneasy silence" (Clarke & Lemma, 2011). And as far as the sexual orientation of members is concerned, the culture has tended to be one of: "Don't ask; don't tell." Disclosure is not regarded as appropriate for a psychoanalyst or psychotherapist. It seems as if the atmosphere in the BPC is now finally beginning to change, and my title refers explicitly to my hope that discussion of these issues can keep us moving on.

The American Psychoanalytic Association's 1991 Position Statement on Homosexuality was issued to disengage psychoanalysis in the United States from what Mitchell (2002) called "the suggestive–directive approach" to work with gay men and lesbians, intended to "cure" their sexual orientation, seen as a pathological deviation from normal development. British psychoanalysis has not produced crusading analytic figures like Charles Socarides, Irving Bieber, and Lionel Ovesey, who shared the view that homosexuality was the result of a pathological rejection of an innately heterosexual drive. In fact, some analysts adopted a humane and agnostic tone on the subject. Edward Glover gave evidence to the Wolfenden Committee, recommending that homosexuality be decriminalized between consenting adults, and Gillespie (1956) wrote about his homosexual patients in a sympathetic and non-judgemental way. But in the UK, the profession in general theorized homosexuality in their patients as a form of perverse behaviour, designed to defend the fragile personality against overwhelming psychotic anxiety. In spite of the decision in 1973 by the committee in charge of compiling the third edition of the American Psychiatric Association's *Diagnostic and Statistical Manual of Mental Disorders* (*DSM–III*; APA, 1980) to remove it as a pathological condition, these ideas have not been thoroughly reviewed.

The history

How did this come about in a discipline that began with Freud, whose views on sexuality were scandalously liberal? His extended exploration of the nature of human sexuality, written between 1905 and 1920, opened with an exploration of "The Sexual Aberrations". He cited the condition of "inversion" or "having contrary sexual feelings" in order to argue for a thorough-going questioning of our assumptions about the sexual instinct. Although it was popularly believed that sexual desire was "absent in childhood, . . . set in at the time of puberty in the process of coming to maturity", and was "revealed in the manifestations of an irresistible attraction exercised by one sex upon the other", while its aim was "presumed to be sexual union, or at all events actions leading in that direction" (Freud, 1905d, p. 135), Freud set out to unseat this assumption.

A significant group of people existed who were attracted to members of their own sex, a phenomenon that could be "found in people whose efficiency is unimpaired, and who are indeed distinguished by specially high intellectual development and ethical culture" (Freud, 1905d, p. 139). There were many different forms of inversion, some absolute, some contingent, some allowing for a degree of bisexuality. Beyond this lay groups of people whose sexual desire took forms that he designated as perverse, such as fetishists, exhibitionists, and those who found pleasure in inflicting or experiencing pain. These phenomena demonstrated the wide variation found both in the nature of sexual aim and in the sexual object. In fact, Freud stated: "From the point of view of psychoanalysis the exclusive sexual interest felt by men for women is also a problem that needs elucidating and is not a self-evident fact based upon an attraction that is ultimately of a chemical nature" (p. 146 fn.). He adopted an open-minded position on the causes of inversion but argued that "a bisexual disposition is somehow concerned" (p. 143). Inversion did not simply occur in those individuals possessing attributes, mental or physical, associated with the opposite sex. Indeed the characteristics of "masculinity" and "femininity" were terms that were "among the most confused that occur in science" (p. 219 fn.) and, when used to describe personality traits, seemed to be found standing for "activity" and "passivity"—which could be found in some combination in all individuals, regardless of anatomical sex.

Freud upheld this broad-minded attitude to "inversion" in other contexts. As is well known, he wrote a letter in response to a mother who seems to have asked him what hope he could offer of a "cure" for her son's homosexuality. He told her: "Homosexuality is assuredly no advantage but it is nothing to be ashamed of, no vice, no degradation, it cannot be classified as an illness; we consider it to be a variation of the sexual function produced by a certain arrest of sexual development . . ." (quoted in Lewes, 1995, p. 20). He publicly supported Magnus Hirschfeld, an early pioneer of sexual freedom and homosexual rights, and he wrote, along with

Otto Rank, to Ernest Jones, disagreeing with Jones's proposal to exclude homosexuals from analytic training: "We feel that a decision in such cases should depend upon a thorough examination of the other qualities of the candidate" (quoted in Lewes, 1995, p. 21).

However, another current in Freud's writing developed his thinking about homosexuality in a different direction, as many writers have pointed out (e.g., Drescher, 1995; Lewes, 1995; O'Connor & Ryan, 2003; Schafer, 1995). This line of argument led him to the previously quoted description of homosexuality as "produced by a certain arrest of sexual development". Schafer points out that although Freud radically questioned the subjective assumption that sexual desire was innately heterosexual, elsewhere, speaking scientifically, "He viewed the individual as the carrier of the reproductive organs and substances designed to guarantee the survival of the species" (Schafer, 1995, p. 193). When speaking as a neurologist, he could imply that, from an evolutionary perspective, nature required that psychosexual development culminate in reproductive heterosexuality. Therefore, although Freud asserted that homosexuality was a variation of the sexual function, was not an illness, and could be manifested in a person whose "efficiency was unimpaired", he could nevertheless also describe it as "caused by a certain arrest of sexual development". In the third of the *Three Essays* (1905d), he describes how adolescence is dominated by a movement towards genital potency with a heterosexual outcome, in spite of bisexual deviation along the way, and the retention of traces of polymorphous perversity from the early stages of life. Although he makes it clear that an "inverted" sexual orientation may have congenital roots, and that those who do not exist in a state of internal conflict with their nature will not present themselves for analysis, all his descriptions of his work with homosexual patients offer clinical accounts that demonstrate how their homosexual orientation has arisen defensively, having been deflected from an expected heterosexual course of oedipal development. This is true of his monograph on the development of Leonardo (Freud, 1910c), the homosexual phase in the case of "The Wolf Man" (Freud, 1909d), his account of "The Psychogenesis of a Case of Homosexuality in a Woman" (Freud, 1920a), and "Some Neurotic Mechanisms in Jealousy, Paranoia and Homosexuality" (Freud, 1922b).

There are two Freuds: Freud the biologist, who speaks as an objective scientist of the phylogenesis of the species, and Freud the clinician, concerned with the internal world of his patients, attempting to shed light on our subjective experience of what it means to be human. Dana Breen (1993), in her introduction to *The Gender Conundrum*, suggests that Freud chose to maintain this bifocal vision of sexuality or gender identity because he recognized that we could never speak of them without becoming entangled in obscurity. She quotes Freud's comments from "The Psychogenesis of a Case of Homosexuality in a Woman":

> Psycho-analysis cannot elucidate the intrinsic nature of what in conventional or in biological phraseology is termed "masculine" and "feminine": it simply takes over the two concepts and makes them the foundation of its work. When we attempt to reduce them further, we find masculinity vanishing into activity and femininity into passivity, and that does not tell us enough. [Freud, 1920a, p. 171]

Freud wished to convey that although sexuality and gender identity can be thought about in bodily terms—"The Ego is first and foremost a bodily ego" (1923b, p. 26)—they are also bound up with the mental representation of the body, a subjective experience that is ultimately elusive and unknowable in its essence. It is impossible to stand back from our identity as "man" or "woman" and see it from the outside.

Freud's views about the fluidity of sexual desire, and his theory of gender identity as something that emerged from processes of discovery and renunciation, were controversial from the outset. This is most obvious in his account of feminine development in which the experience of subjective discovery is foregrounded (Freud, 1931b; 1933a, Lecture 33). The little girl initially believed herself to be "a little man" and had a masculine understanding of the pleasure-giving potential of her body. Horney, Jones, and others contested Freud's theory of "phallic monism", arguing that girls, like boys, must start out with some knowledge of the biological destiny implied by their anatomy. Klein, too, assumed that there were essential predispositions in boys and girls which shaped a gendered experience of the oedipal stage. As Breen points out, it has been Lacan who elaborated the implications of Freud's account of the Oedipus complex as a process of subjective construction. Lacan (1973) approached Freud by means of a linguistic interpretation. The discovery of the phallus as something that can be missing or lost is not understood in physical terms, but, rather, as a powerful signifier that structures the language of desire and initiates the child into a web of socially constituted meaning, in which she or he must find a place. The fluidity of polymorphous perversity and the incestuous assumption that one can be the fulfilment of the desire of one's primary object belong to territory that is foreclosed; indeed the only trace of its ever having existed is to be found in an after-echo—the individual's insatiable longing for a state of complete fulfilment which will never be fully satisfied. Jacqueline Rose explains Lacan's position thus:

> Sexuality belongs in this area of instability played out in the register of demand and desire, each sex coming to stand, mythically and exclusively, for that which could satisfy and complete the other. It is when the categories "male" and "female" are seen to represent an absolute and complementary division that they fall prey to a mystification in which the difficulty of sexuality instantly disappears. [Mitchell & Rose, 1982, p. 33]

Breen demonstrates how this "difficulty of sexuality" has divided schools around the world. Indeed, Freud himself did not always keep in mind the slippage and ambiguity involved in naming gender categories. In spite of his assertion that the terms, masculine and feminine, were "amongst the most confused that occur in science", and having uncovered the complex process by which he believed a little girl came to recognize her femininity, he nevertheless fell into "absolute and complementary divisions" of a dominant heterosexuality when thinking about the positive and negative Oedipus complex. It seemed to him that, whereas the "positive" version of the complex is gendered and results in a sexual identification aligned with anatomy, in the grip of the "negative" complex, the position has become "cross-gendered"—"feminine" in the case of a man and "masculine" in the case of a woman. Although every individual may recognize in him/herself the negative position, this oedipal matrix seems to suggest that the choice of love object, under the ascendancy of the negative complex, implies a repudiation of the body's biological reproductive capacity and thus a retreat from "normal" development. In the third of the *Three Essays*, "The Transformations of Puberty", Freud tells us that "The sexual instinct is now subordinated to the reproductive function; it becomes, so to say, altruistic" (1905d, p. 207). In spite of the opening passages of the first essay, here the foundational expectation is of development in the "positive" direction—that, if one is a woman, a normal developmental line will lead to desire for a man, and vice versa. If this is so, then a mature genital love cannot be imagined for an object of the same sex, except from an internal position of the opposite gender. "You cannot *be* what you desire, you cannot *desire* what you wish to be", as O'Connor and Ryan (2003, p. 239) put it, quoting from John Fletcher (1989).

Thinking about this theory of gender "identification", Judith Butler (1995) reflects on Freud's use of the term in *The Ego and the Id*, where he says identification "may be . . . the sole condition under which the id can give up its objects . . .". Here Freud goes on to say: "It makes it possible to suppose that the character of the ego is a precipitate of abandoned object-cathexes and that it contains the history of those object choices" (1923b, p. 29). Referring to his insight in "Mourning and Melancholia" (1917e), Butler suggests that, in gender identification, the loss of the same-sex object remains unacknowledged and unmourned:

> It seems clear that the positions of "masculine" and "feminine" which Freud (1905d) understood as the effects of laborious and uncertain accomplishment, are established in part through prohibitions that *demand* the loss of certain sexual attachments and demand as well that those losses *not* be avowed and *not* be grieved. If the assumption of femininity and the assumption of masculinity proceed through the accomplishment of always tenuous heterosexuality, we might understand the force of this accomplishment as the mandating of the abandonment of homosexual attachments or, perhaps more trenchantly, the *pre-emption* of the possibility of homosexual attachment, a certain foreclosure of possibility that produces a domain of homosexuality understood as unliveable passion and ungrievable loss. [1995, p. 168]

Butler argues that this accounts for the anxiety that sexual uncertainty provokes:

> Hence, the fear of homosexual desire in a woman may induce a panic that she is losing her femininity; that she is not a woman, that she is no longer a proper woman; that, if she is not quite a man, she is like one and hence monstrous in some way. Or in a man, the terror over homosexual desire may well lead to the terror over being construed as feminine, feminized; of no longer being properly a man or of being a "failed" man. . . . [p. 168]

From Butler's reading of Freud, it could be argued that homophobia is a psychic retreat from the confusion that we would feel, confronted by evidence that our settled categories are less settled than we would like. Indeed, this is one of the central difficulties that must be confronted by a young person growing up gay or lesbian, surrounded by peers who are grappling with their own anxieties about sexuality, and perhaps becoming the target of their projections in a bullying way. We will expect to find traces of this anxiety both in ourselves and in our homosexual patients. Perhaps it can only be named now when the demarcation line between traditional gender roles is breaking down, allowing the possibility for a more fluid sense of these binary distinctions to come into view. In societies that preserve more absolute differences between men and women, defences against this anxiety may result in harsh punishment of homosexuality, particularly when threatened by liberalizing pressures from without.

Gender and sexual identity are inextricably involved with one another. And the history of psychoanalysis shows how difficult it has been to build on Freud's more tolerant attitude towards these obscurities. After two world wars, psychoanalysts, concerned to establish the credentials of their discipline within the institutions of the time, sought a more settled definition of sexual "normality", which "naturalized" a heterosexual view of gender difference. Writing in the United States in 1940, Rado drew a clear line under Freud's ideas: "It is imperative to supplant the deceptive concept of bisexuality with a psychological theory based on firmer biological foundations" (1940, p. 464).

Extending one aspect of Freud's thinking, homosexuality became generally accepted as evidence of a developmental retreat, even as a fixation at the oral stage of relating. As an identity founded on rejection of the reproductive "reality" of the body, it was seen as a borderline condition, and an individual who did not regard it as a serious problem to be cured was understood to be maintaining a perverse denial of their pathology. Same-sex object-choice was narcissistic and led to the formation of unstable patterns of relating. With the disappearance of any complexity or uncertainty in theoretical thinking about sexuality, the unconscious prejudices of the analyst could freely be expressed through generalizations about homosexuals, particularly men, as a marginalized group. Some male analysts did not hold back:

I have no bias against homosexuality . . . [but] homosexuals
are essentially disagreeable people, regardless of their pleasant
or unpleasant manner . . . [which contains] a mixture of super-
ciliousness, false aggression, and whimpering. . . . [They are]
subservient when confronted by a stronger person, merciless
when in power, unscrupulous about trampling on a weaker
person. . . . [Bergler, 1956, quoted in Lewes, 1995, p. 3]

The homosexual "is ill, in much the same way that a dwarf is
ill—because he has never developed" [Allen, 1958, quoted in
Lewes, 1995, p. 137]

In 1962, Irving Bieber published an influential monograph, entitled
Homosexuality: A Psychoanalytic Study of Male Homosexuals (Bieber
et al., 1962), reviewing the work of nine clinicians with homosexual patients over a ten-year period. This became the standard reference text for the psychoanalytic view of homosexuality
as pathology. Details were presented of the family background of
patients to support aetiological theories. This study is one of the
main sources for the idea that homosexuality in men arises in
families where there are close, seductive mothers and cold, distant
fathers. All the participants in the study were analytic patients,
and many had been diagnosed with serious problems, including
schizophrenia. Ninety per cent of them had described themselves
as unhappy with their sexual orientation. As Lewes (1995) puts
it: "Thus, beginning with the assumption that all homosexuals
were disturbed and using a preselected disturbed sample, [Bie-
ber] found that indeed all homosexuals were disturbed" (p. 198).
Throughout his long career, Charles Socarides defined homosexuality as indicative of serious pathology. He stridently opposed the
removal of homosexuality from the mental disorders listed in the
DSM in 1973 and continued to argue this position until his death
in 2005:

The obligatory homosexual has been unable to make the pro-
gression from the mother–child unity of earliest infancy to
individuation. As a result there exists a fixation, with the con-
comitant tendency to regression, to the earliest mother–child
relationship. This is manifested as a threat of personal annihilation, loss of ego boundaries and a sense of fragmentation.
[1968, p. 30]

In the UK, there has been a lack of direct focus on the subject of homosexuality in recent years. At the 2012 BPC conference, Marilyn Lawrence (2012) suggested that the reluctance in British psychoanalysis to revisit theories of sexual-identity formation might be a legacy of the Controversial Discussions (King & Steiner, 1991). Fear of re-opening arguments about the nature and timing of the Oedipus complex has led to a shift of focus towards pre-oedipal phenomena in clinical work.

However, British psychoanalysis assumed homosexuality to be categorized as a perversion, and the exclusion, on this basis, of gay men and lesbians from psychoanalytic trainings has inevitably led to ignorance among clinicians of the realities of the LGBT community. The tone in which many psychoanalytic papers about homosexual men and women have been written positions them clearly as objects of study rather than as potential colleagues, making generalized statements about "the homosexual" as a clinical phenomenon. The deference that trainings within the BPC display towards earlier theorists can result in papers like this being offered to current trainees without comment or criticism. Here are examples from papers that are still used in training seminars:

> The homosexual syndrome, as it has been described in relation to certain clinical types, is seen as part of a defensive movement directed at lessening anxiety or at creating barriers against eruption of unbearable conflicts, and quite often simply at ensuring survival. . . . It follows that the homosexual solution is a defence which, when encountered, should be treated with the utmost caution, especially in those cases where its removal is under consideration. [Limentani, 1977, quoted in Rosen, 1979, p. 224]

> Most of my [lesbian] patients were conscious of an intense feeling of having triumphed over the mother, and a wish that she would feel abandoned and punished. . . . There is a large measure of triumph over the father also, since the homosexual solution implies the denial of the father's phallic role and genital existence, and the proof that a woman does not need either a man or a penis for sexual completion. [McDougall, 1990, pp. 128–129]

Although they may accurately describe their patients as individuals, these analysts are generalizing from particular cases. They take no account of the part that social stigmatization plays in the stress that these patients are under; they assume that sexual orientation accounts for their patients' pathology. The attitudes of these analysts and those like them simply reflected their belief in the normativity of heterosexuality as a biological given, to which psychoanalysis had reverted after Freud's more questioning approach. Clinical literature of this kind should no longer be offered to trainees uncritically. Nancy Chodorow has said: "We psychoanalysts embed conscious and preconscious, unthought and unnoticed, pre-theoretical cultural assumptions . . . in our theories and thus shape what we see and hear clinically" (1999, p. 99). This has been an attitude that has affected us all, gay or straight, and until recently it is likely that homosexual patients would expect to meet it in a therapist whom they assumed to be heterosexual. But now that the LGBT community has raised awareness in society at large, and gay men and lesbians have begun to train in analytic therapy, the biases demonstrated by such clinical commentary can no longer go unnoticed (see Domenici & Lesser, 1995; O'Connor & Ryan, 2003; Shelley, 1998).

Changing views of the clinical relationship

We are more aware now that patients such as those described above are likely to be members of a vulnerable group, who might indeed be responsive to the idea that their sexual orientation was the cause of their distress and persuaded that they should convert to a "healthier" heterosexuality. Having internalized homophobic attitudes and struggling to come to terms with their sexuality, they could be in conflict with their identity, feeling depressed and finding relationships difficult. Richard Isay (1996) has written movingly about how hard he worked to fulfil his analyst's aspiration that he would overcome his homosexuality and embark on married life, a role that he later realized made him feel as if he was living a lie. Although our society is becoming more open to the complexity of sexual orientation, we know that the incidence of depression, suicidal feelings, and self-harm is considerably higher among members of the LGBT community than among heterosexuals (Chakraborty, McManus, Brugha, Bebbington, & King, 2011). Both the British Council for Psychotherapy and Counselling and the United Kingdom Council for Psychotherapy have recently condemned as unethical the clinical practice of therapists who claim to "remove unwanted same-sex attraction", often motivated by their own religious beliefs.

Practitioners in the British tradition are trained to think of themselves as aspiring to a neutral, reserved stance. The task is one of reflective listening, providing "containment" in the model of Bion, or Winnicottian "holding", with the ultimate intention of contributing to the patient's deeper understanding of themselves. The infant–caregiver dyad has been a powerful organizing metaphor for interaction in the clinical setting, whether we invoke a developmental history model or focus on the here-and-now transference. In search of a deeper understanding of the patient's communication, the therapist consults his or her countertransference to see what it might have to say about the patient's use of projective identification. This metaphor privileges the interpretive authority of the therapist, whose job it is to promote the patient's awareness of him/herself. Without the confidence of that authority, the therapist would find it difficult to maintain an attitude of steadiness which allows the patient the freedom of a secure setting to explore emotional reactions, associations, and memories which he or she has previously been unable to recognize. Although, increasingly, we acknowledge our potential to be drawn into enactment and see it as a therapeutic tool—as in Sandler's (1976) role-responsiveness model, for instance—we see our task as that of holding the therapeutic frame and perhaps in the process idealize our capacity for objective understanding.

However, the impact of post-modern cultural theory has meant that psychotherapists and psychoanalysts are increasingly aware of the psychological dynamics of prejudice and the stigmatization of difference. This introduces the idea that the therapist, like the patient, cannot be a neutral partner in the therapeutic relationship. Recently, writers have drawn attention to the impact that cultural difference, and particularly colour difference, can have in the clinical setting (e.g., Dalal, 2002; Davids, 2011; Lowe, 2008; Morgan, 2002). These therapists argue that colour difference is a potent category for the white therapist, arousing unconscious anxiety which can provoke a stereotyping response. Cognitive psychologists call this "spread" (Dembo, Leviton, & Wright, 1975), referring to "the organizing power of a single characteristic to evoke inferences about a person" (Wright, 1983, p. 32, quoted in Olkin, 1995, p. 55).

"Homosexual" is a characteristic with the power to produce "spread". And, in recognizing the bias that has crept into psychoanalytic thinking about homosexuality, we can identify it in all theorizing that claims to understand "the homosexual", "the homosexual solution", "the homosexual syndrome", etc., which singles out same-sex love as the central, organizing characteristic of an individual. If we see the distorted nature of this assumption, it becomes clear that it is the attitude of other people in the patient's life towards his or her sexual orientation which makes it appear problematic—attitudes that the patient may indeed have come to internalize. We must ask ourselves how this dynamic might affect the clinical relationship. Steven Flower (2007) describes how he had to process his own emotional response to his homosexual patients' sexual orientation, and he sensitively shows how this influenced his work:

> I did not immediately recognize my own countertransference hurt and jealousy that it was my brother and not me (in the dream) he engaged with sexually. He needed me, I think, to feel the pain of being sexually excluded but, to receive this projection fully, I would have to allow myself to want to engage with him sexually. [2007, pp. 435–436]

Ryan (1998) and Frommer (1995) have both noted how rare it is to find a discussion such as Flower's of the therapist's countertransference in clinical accounts where a straight therapist is meeting a gay or lesbian patient. Frommer, speaking of a male therapeutic dyad, attributes this to the fact that both patient and therapist may share difficult feelings towards the sexuality of the gay man. Even though he may regard himself as liberal in his attitude towards homosexuality, this discomfort may inhibit the therapist's willingness to explore the patient's internalized homophobia, fearing his own response to the patient's potential erotic transference:

> In order for the analyst to make contact with the patient's child self and attend to, unmask, and analyse the critical dynamics involved in the child's developmental experience which can lead to shame and self-hate, the analyst must be able to consider fully the psychic consequences of growing up gay in a social context which stigmatizes the same-sex desire and marginalizes those individuals who do not preserve the culture's mandated

relationship between biological sex, gender and sexual orientation. In order to do this, he must first be able in his own mind to
undo a prescriptive relationship between gender and sexuality.
. . . This aspect of the work ultimately entails the identifying
and working through of introjects—something analysts do all
the time. In this case, however, the analyst's ability to do this
with the patient requires that he is first able to do it with himself.
[Frommer, 1995, p. 80]

Frommer's argument here assumes the existence of diverse perspectives on sexuality and gender. He takes for granted that therapist and
patient may not see things in the same way, and thus the therapist
can no longer be confident in falling back on traditional theories to
understand the patient's sexuality. This work requires the therapist
to be aware of how she or he may appear to the patient and of where
ignorance or preconceptions might undermine the patient's trust.
A relational model of therapy takes for granted that subjectivity
is culturally constructed and understands the dyadic therapeutic
relationship as interactively and intersubjectively constituted. In
the United States, following the influence of Mitchell, Ogden, and
Schafer, much contemporary clinical work is of this kind. Donnel
Stern (2010) suggests that all meaning made in clinical work "is not
predetermined but created in dialogue" (p. 7). Ogden (1999) speaks
of the participants' need to create an "Analytic Third" anew in each
encounter:

> The art of analysis is an art form that requires not only that we
> struggle with the problem of creating a place where analyst and
> analysand might live, but also requires that we develop a use
> of language adequate to giving voice to our experience of what
> life feels like in that ever shifting place. [p. 11]

Work with gay and lesbian individuals demands a reappraisal of
those aspects of psychoanalytic theory that suggest a fixed hetero-
normative view of gender-identity formation. Leaving aside the
issue of gender reassignment, which deserves separate consideration beyond what can be discussed here, most therapists today
would recognize that, however stable the *field* of gender categorization appears, the individual patient in therapy does not experience
him/herself as discretely defined within a settled "identification".
Although core gender identity is assigned to a child at birth or even

before, each one of us develops a sense of our gender as a form of *habitus*, using Bourdieu's (1980) term: as ongoing, lived experience, inevitably in internal dialogue with the images of masculinity and femininity we encounter in our formative relationships, and affected by stereotypes we see reflected in the external world. Butler (1990) suggests, even more radically, that gender could be considered "as *a corporeal style*, an 'act' as it were, which is both intentional and performative, where *'performative'* suggests a dramatic and contingent construction of meaning" (p. 190, italics in original).

Although it may be only certain individuals who experience their gender identity as "performance" in the way Butler suggests, we need to be aware of our susceptibility to binary stereotypes that prevent us from remaining open to psychoanalysis' original insight that there is no settled way to be a man or a woman. It is tempting to find ourselves thinking about the apparent "feminine passivity" of gay men or the "masculinity" of a lesbian. Issues of space and confidentiality prevent me from exploring more fully how important I have found it to question my own countertransference assumptions in clinical work with lesbian patients, but I illustrate it with two brief vignettes.

> One woman, who dresses in casual clothes and never wears a skirt, turns out to wish, not to be masculine, but to be "invisible". She wishes to stay below the radar, disliking her feminine body for its vulnerability, but not wanting to be seen as "butch". She feels very frightened of being stereotyped as a "dyke" and secretly longs to dress up and be glamorous, in a safe context.

> Another lesbian patient described how difficult she had found it to believe in her own sexual experience, and to "come out", to herself, let alone the outside world. Although gay men's sexuality had been criminalized, she pointed out that a lesbian's had not been considered to exist—how could she admit to herself her own active and passionate sexual desire for another woman? Having described to me how she sometimes wanted "to tear the clothes off" a woman she was attracted to, she was then very upset by a dream in which she had a penis. We explored the possibility that telling me about this exposed her to the fear that I would reject her desire, seeing it as unnatural, and leave her with feelings of shame and confusion about herself.

Adolescent awakening to sexual attraction towards the same sex can be confusing and shameful. E. M. Forster's novel, *Maurice*, was written in 1914, but did not appear until 1971, eighteen months after his death. Forster, who is supremely good at capturing the vague and confusing nature of internal experience, describes here the feelings of his hero, a somewhat unimaginative, middle-class boy, not yet fully sexually awake, on settling into life in his Cambridge college:

> Once inside college, his discoveries multiplied. People turned out to be alive. Hitherto he had supposed that they *were* what he *pretended* to be—flat pieces of cardboard stamped with a conventional design—but as he strolled about the courts at night and saw through the windows some men singing and others arguing and others at their books, there came by no process of reason a conviction that they were human beings with feelings akin to his own. He had never lived frankly since Mr. Abraham's school . . . but he saw that while deceiving others he had been deceived, and mistaken them for the empty creatures he wanted them to think he was. No, they too had insides. "But, O Lord, not such an inside as mine." As soon as he thought about other people as real, Maurice became modest and conscious of sin: in all creation there could be no one as vile as himself. No wonder he pretended to be a piece of cardboard; if being known as he was, he would be hounded out of the world. [Forster, 1971, p. 23]

We must recognize the crucial importance of this experience of self-discovery for someone who senses that his or her sexual desires are different from those of peers. Psychoanalysis is only beginning to recognize the deep impact of internalized homophobia and a gay man or lesbian's continuing experience of being different. Drescher describes how, even as a gay man, he can by surprised by this:

> Gay men and women, who are otherwise reasonably adjusted, often display enduring feelings of intolerance for their own homosexuality. Lesbians and gay men must continuously decide who or what they will tell and will not tell all about themselves. Should one say "I" or "we", speak as a single person or as a couple? Should one let people know which neighbourhood, resort, movie, play or club they attended over the weekend? Life is a daily accretion of these experiences and coming out

is a process that never ends. This results from a combination of internalised fears and criticisms, external realities and hard experience. Antihomosexuality in the culture forces gay people to constantly think about "their" proper place. [1996, p. 233]

In the United States, where it is possible for gay and lesbian analytic therapists to be more open about their sexual orientation, these issues can receive more attention, including the controversial question of the therapist's disclosure discussed courageously by Isay (1996). In the UK most BPC organizations have not reached this point, and it is to be hoped that gay and lesbian candidates in training are able to find sufficiently supportive contexts, where they can reflect on how issues of sexuality are raised in seminars, and how these differences impact on their clinical work with both gay and straight patients.

Drescher has pointed out that we commonly speak of "a homosexual lifestyle" rather than simply "a life", and one of the most powerful stereotypes of gay male sexual behaviour is that of the "cruising homosexual", who does not look for a settled partnership but lives in a world of shifting, addictive part-object relatedness, possibly sado-masochistic. Therapists, when faced with a gay or lesbian patient who is not in a settled relationship, might be inclined to wish for a "healthy" therapeutic outcome where the patient becomes part of a committed, monogamous couple. At a symbolic level, we speak of the developmental achievement of an internal image of the parents in creative intercourse. But this is not an image that necessarily maps onto the experience of gay and lesbian relationships, which, until recently, had no means of achieving collective recognition and sanction. When meeting an individual, gay or straight, who does not practise monogamy, perhaps we should first ask what such behaviour actually means to him or her. This area can become difficult to explore if the patient fears the moralistic judgement of the therapist and becomes either ashamed or completely silent about the details of his or her intimate sexual life.

Similarly, we have heard reports of analytic condemnation of lesbian couples who want to have a family, and have their babies by donor insemination, not to mention reactions to those gay men who become parents through the use of surrogates. The traditional analytic view has been that a child needs a parent of each sex in order to develop a balanced internal world (e.g., Rose, 1990). However, the evidence so far suggests that same-sex couples need not bring up damaged children (Fitzgerald, 1999; Patterson, 1997). But this can feel like uncharted territory in which a therapist, with no previous exposure to such issues, may feel at sea.

The challenge that work with lesbian or gay patients presents to the psychoanalytic psychotherapist is to recognize how different things may look from where each partner in the relationship is standing. A crucial requirement in a collaboration that allows the therapist to attend to unconscious communication is that of finding the capacity for "orientation" (Di Ceglie, 2013) towards the patient's perspective, without which the therapy cannot be experienced as containing. The impact that the external world may have had must be acknowledged, before an exploration of the internal world becomes possible.

I hope to have shown that psychoanalysis has in the past developed a theoretical bias that has distorted its view of the experience of lesbians and gay men and, in detecting and questioning this bias, we have an opportunity to make our discipline more open and responsive to the complex society we live in. We should return to the open-minded curiosity and self-questioning that Schafer (1995) points out goes best with being consistently analytic.

CHAPTER NINE

Paradoxes and blind spots: an exploration of Irish identity in British organizations and society

Aideen Lucey

> "The romantic writer says: there is an essential Ireland to
> be served and a definitive Irish mind to be described. The
> modernist rejoins: there is no single Ireland, but a field of
> force subject to constant renegotiations; and no Irish mind, but
> Irish minds shaped by a predicament which produces some
> common characteristics in those caught up in it."
>
> Kiberd (1992, p. lxxvii)

I subscribe to the modernist view that there are many Irish minds, experiences, and versions of reality, as I believe there are for all peoples. However, in this chapter I want to look at something specific—the projections that the Irish can be on the receiving end of in Britain and in British institutions. By doing so, I want to acknowledge that I am addressing just one element of Irish experience.

This chapter is written from my perspective as an Irish organizational consultant working in Britain. It aims to clarify thinking about Irish identity in order to inform consultancy practice as well as to open up a more general discussion about the way in which Irish identity may be used unconsciously in British institutions and society.

The starting point for the chapter was actually a realization that in the past I had given very little attention to my Irish identity in my work. As a consultant working psychodynamically, I had to ask myself why I had neglected something that could potentially be an important factor in the transference and thus a source of valuable information and meaning.

What came to mind were some of the paradoxes associated with being Irish in Britain. How could I draw attention to uncomfortable issues to do with what an Irish person might represent in Britain at the same time as making a good living and home here? And, perhaps more uncomfortably, how could I square up feeling at one level proud of my Irish identity while at another recognizing that in leaving Ireland there were parts of my Irishness that I wanted to leave behind? In addition, despite feeling very different when I first came to London, I was surprised to find that Irish identity did not seem to be considered very significant in dialogues about difference in the organizations I was part of. On exploring these issues, I came to the conclusion that there are many internal and external pressures for the Irish in Britain to underplay or hide their identity. So this chapter is addressing the question of why certain aspects of Irish identity seem so difficult to look at.

This chapter is therefore the result of my attempt to resist the pressures not to think about the experience of being Irish in Britain. In so doing I have sought to understand why the issue of Irish identity in Britain seems so difficult to look at.

Theoretically, the ideas in this chapter were inspired by the work of a colleague, Frank Lowe, in a paper called "Colonial Object Relations" (Lowe, 2008). He uses the concept of colonial object relations to explore the psychic relationship between black and white people in Britain. Lowe, whose work draws strongly on Fanon (1967), highlights the psychic legacy of colonialism, where "Black and White are both part objects and constitute a destructive type of object relation inherited from the history of slavery, colonisation and empire" (Lowe, 2008, p. 20).

Drawing on Lowe's work, here I look at the way the Irish could be seen to be a part-object in relation to the British. I consider the particular projections that I think the Irish can be on the receiving end of in Britain, and I link these to specific social, political, and religious impacts of colonialism in Ireland. I argue that it is the identification with certain negative projections that makes it difficult for

Irish people to speak out about their experience and, furthermore, that there is a psychological investment for others in keeping it this way. As with all forms of splitting, this leads to impoverished relations for people on both sides of the split.

I explore an example from my consultancy practice where I felt issues to do with my identity as an Irish consultant were probably more present in the transference than I recognized at the time. I also consider what I may have represented for the client and how, if recognized earlier, this could potentially have been used in the service of the work.

Colonialism in Ireland

Ireland was colonized by the British for eight hundred years until partition of the island and the formation of the Irish Free State in 1921. Colonialism took many forms over the centuries, a few key events of which are highlighted here. Initially the colonization was partial, but in the sixteenth century England seized control of the whole island. Cromwell consolidated this in 1649. Under Cromwell, the native Irish were driven off their land, and it was divided into large estates where settlers from Britain were planted. Cromwell was exceedingly brutal in Ireland (Churchill, 1957; Ó Siochrú, 2008); as well as driving people off the land, he led massacres of men, women, and children, but despite this he is still very much seen as a heroic leader in Britain today.

After Cromwell, the Penal Laws were introduced in the late 1600s. This policy was like a form of apartheid directed at religion rather than race: "the essential purpose of the penal laws . . . [was not] to destroy Roman Catholicism, but to make sure that its adherents were kept in a position of social, economic and political inferiority" (Beckett, 1981, p. 159).

Catholics were prohibited from voting, from acquiring land, from receiving education, and from practising their religion freely. The Penal Laws had the impact of reducing the majority of Irish Catholics to an underclass, resulting in poverty and lack of education. One can see, therefore, where the stereotypes of laziness, stupidity, and the fighting Irish originate.

Following the Penal Laws, much of the land in Ireland was held by absentee Anglo-Irish landlords who rented tiny plots to

Irish peasants. Destitute tenants worked for their rent by producing cash crops for export to Britain while relying on the potato for their own consumption. This led to a highly distorted economy, which served the interests of the British economy and Anglo-Irish landlords. It also led to overdependence on the potato by Irish tenants. When a potato blight struck in Ireland in 1845, it destroyed the only means of subsistence for the majority of the population and resulted in famine.

During the famine, one million people died of starvation and two million people emigrated (Donnelly, 2002). The response by the British government was very inadequate. While people in Ireland were starving, large quantities of crops and livestock continued to be exported to Britain (Woodham-Smith, 1991). Some writers have even argued that British response to the famine was deliberately inadequate in order to consolidate land and maintain power in Ireland (Kinealy, 1995). Despite British colonization being a significant contributor, if not the cause, of the famine in Ireland, it came to be seen in Britain as the fault of the Irish and confirmation of a view of the Irish as racially inferior.

Oppression (and starvation) leaves its mark on the collective psyche in numerous ways. So when the British colonized Ireland, as elsewhere, they were perpetrating not only a political act but also a psychological one. Colonialism resulted in a "psychology of self-doubt and dependency among the Irish linked to the loss of economic and political power but also the decline of the native language and culture" (Kiberd, 1996, p. 6).

The Irish language almost disappeared under colonialism. It is not too difficult to see that losing one's language and having to adopt the language of the oppressor will have had a very eroding effect on the Irish psyche. In Joyce's *Portrait of the Artist as a Young Man*, the character Stephen Dedalus during a conversation with an Englishman says, "The language in which we are speaking is his before it is mine. How different are the words 'home', 'Christ', 'ale', 'master', on his lips and on mine! I cannot speak or write these words without unrest of spirit. His language, so familiar and so foreign, will always be for me an acquired speech" (Joyce, 1916, p. 210; quoted in Kiberd, 1992, p. xxxvii).

Colonialism, based on forcibly occupying another people's land and the notion of racial and cultural superiority, consigned the colonized to an inferior position, which has been so well written about by Edward Said (1993) and others. In his book, *Black Skin, White Masks*, Franz Fanon (1967) very passionately and painfully makes the point that the impact of oppression is that oppressed persons come to feel inferior and, in order to deal with that unbearable state of affairs, they end up wanting to be not like themselves but like their superiors—that is, the oppressor. In other words, by adopting a superior position, the colonizer projects feelings of inferiority into the colonized and the colonized comes to experience themselves as inferior. You can see then why there is a need to get rid of this through identifying with the oppressor and why, consciously or unconsciously, one may play down or hide one's identity.

Paradoxes and blind spots

To turn to the question of why Irish identity in Britain seems so difficult to look at (blind spots), the paradoxes mentioned earlier offer a useful platform to explore the issues because they not only conceal but also potentially reveal something of what is being turned away from. The paradoxes are that:

» Despite feeling different in Britain, the Irish are treated on the surface as if they are the same as the British. This is primarily a British blind spot.
» As well as there being pride among the Irish in Britain, there can also be a (less visible) wish to leave part of their heritage behind. This is an Irish blind spot.
» Despite the negative impact of colonialism, many Irish people make a good living in the land of the colonizer. This is both a British and an Irish blind spot.

I use these paradoxes to examine what is being turned away from and to show how this turning of a blind eye (Steiner, 1985) takes place in both the Irish and the British.

Being the same but different

Most Irish people are white and generally look quite similar to the majority of the population in Britain, but our history is very different. In many ways, Irish people have more in common with people from India, Africa, and the Caribbean than with people from Britain. When I first came to live in London, I felt very different. I was very conscious of having an Irish accent. This was in the 1980s. I was very aware that people's association with my accent would be the IRA bombings in Britain. Yet the dialogue that was going on around difference in British institutions at the time was very much in terms of black/white issues. It is not that discrimination against black people should not be an important focus of attention, but equal opportunity initiatives have had a rigidity about them that leaves little room for the complexities of discrimination to be understood. This I see as one way that a blind eye is turned on issues to do with Irish identity in Britain.

I think there is a big investment for British people not to look at the Irish experience, because it protects them from guilt and ultimately taking back what has been projected into the Irish. One unconscious solution to this is to treat Irish people as if they are the same as British people. This is even enshrined in the 1948 British Nationality Act, which gave Irish people the same rights as the British, unlike any other colonized group. This was largely a way of dealing with complications posed by the partition of Ireland (Garrett, 2002), but it also allows a psychological manoeuvre that puts us in the impossible position of being the same but different.

When we are treated as if we are the same as British people, it causes confusion about the colonial relationship: the British can act as if they never colonized Ireland, and the Irish are left holding the stereotypes and the projections. I think this was very evident in the discourse in Britain about Northern Ireland during "the Troubles". It was as if it was Ireland's war not Britain's—"Those uncivilized Irish people warring over there"—whereas "the Troubles" were the result of centuries of unresolved conflict between Catholics and Protestants arising directly from British colonization. This kind of splitting is encouraged by the British educational system. The British school curriculum covers very little Irish history, so the population is socialized to see "the Irish problem" as Irish as opposed to a British/Irish problem.

The experience of Irish people in Britain is very different from that of British people. We may no longer be subject to the overt discrimination of the "no blacks, no Irish, no dogs" days, but like black people we still experience prejudice. When it is subtle and unacknowledged, it can feel particularly disturbing because you may be treated on the surface as if you are the same, but somewhere not so far beneath the surface you are receiving a very different and much more aggressive kind of communication. The covert nature of this kind of discrimination, and the way that it distorts reality, makes it very difficult to address.

Fintan O'Toole (2009), writing about sexual abuse and the economic crisis in Ireland, talks about the "unknown known", referring to circumstances surrounding these events that were at some level known but that at another level denied. I believe that there is a similar kind of "unknown known" at play in Britain in the paradox of being the same but different. Because of the lack of the visible difference of skin colour, discrimination can be denied while at the same time one can have the distinct feeling of being treated as "less white" than others (Dyer, 1997; Garrett, 2002). Lack of visibility of the Irish in Britain, and denial of anti-Irish racism, has been highlighted by a number of writers in the last couple of decades (Garrett, 2002; Greenslade, 1992; Hickman & Walter, 1995; Rossiter, 1993). There has, subsequently, been some increased awareness about the specificity of the Irish experience—for example, recognition of the disproportionate rates of mental illness (Bracken, 1998; Care Quality Commission, 2011; Greenslade, 1992) among the Irish in Britain.[1] However, I am arguing that in many ways the Irish person's different experience remains an "unknown known", and I provide an example later of how this plays out in an organizational consultancy setting. At a psychic level, this leaves the Irish person to continue to carry the projections of inferiority and protects British people from their own feelings of inferiority as well as guilt and shame associated with the past. This, I am arguing, is the investment for British people not to look too closely at issues to do with Irish identity.

Irish pride vs. the wish to leave part of one's heritage behind

I now want to address the issue of why someone might be proud of their Irish identity but, at the same time, feel a need to leave part of his or her heritage behind, whether metaphorically or literally through emigration. This is where some of the Irish blind spots come in.

Emigration is a well-known aspect of Irish history connected with colonization, famine, and unemployment. Emigration from Ireland is generally seen as an economic phenomenon. On the face of it, this, of course, is true, but if you dig a bit deeper you discover a number of other layers. The Ireland that I left in the 1980s was a small country still reeling from centuries of colonization, nowhere more evident than in the conflict that continued to rage in Northern Ireland. To look at the reasons for emigration as purely economic is reductionist, but it may also perform the useful function of protecting people from seeing some of the more hidden reasons. One of the hidden factors, as I see it, has to do with an oppressive atmosphere linked to our colonial history. An Irish friend and colleague I talked to in researching this chapter said she left Ireland so that her soul could breathe, and she quoted the following lines from a Yeats poem.

> Out of Ireland have we come.
> Great hatred, little room,
> Maimed us at the start.
> I carry from my mother's womb
> A fanatic heart.
>
> [Yeats, 1933, p. 288]

I grew up in the Republic of Ireland post–Irish Independence in the 1960s and 1970s. One of the most striking things, which I can now see but which was not evident to me at the time, is that many of us in the Republic of Ireland distanced ourselves from Northern Ireland. Perhaps that was necessary for the development of the new state, but it had a high cost. For a start, it left people in the North of Ireland with the actual burden of how to bridge the divide between Catholics and Protestants based on centuries of conflict. It also left them with a psychological burden—the stereotype of the fighting Irish while the rest of Ireland could try to clean up its act. This is part of the Irish blind spot—a wish to forget history, and the shame and guilt associated with it.

What I think now was a significant contributor to the oppressive atmosphere in the Ireland I grew up in was a great anxiety about our aggression. I believe aggression, while frequently a source of discomfort for people, is particularly so for many Irish people because it still too closely connected with actual violence associated with colonization and, as Yeats acknowledges in the poem above, our own hateful reaction to that.

The Catholic Church has also played a major role in the creation of the oppressive atmosphere. I believe that a certain number of Irish emigrants and women in particular have felt a need to get away from a society and culture that was so dominated by this patriarchal institution. The Catholic Church in Ireland has had an unhealthy and unusual amount of influence on the state. In the last decade, the extent of sexual abuse within Irish Catholic institutions has come to light. What has never been mentioned, however, in these disturbing disclosures, is that the power of the Catholic Church in Ireland is directly related to colonization. Because British colonialism in Ireland was essentially about the subordination of Irish Catholics, identification with religion became a matter of survival for Catholics and blind faith was placed in the Church. The Church could not be questioned, and this, I believe, is one of the main reasons that so much denial and cover up about abuse in Irish Catholic institutions was possible for so long even when the evidence was beyond doubt. One could also see the sadism within the Irish Catholic institutions, at least to some extent, as identification with the colonizer in the form of aggression turned against the self. The extent of and abuse of power by the Catholic Church in Ireland could be seen as a kind of internal colonization mirroring that of actual colonization. Much could be added about the history of the Catholic Church in Ireland, but that is beyond the reach of this chapter.

The last couple of decades in Ireland have seen great change, and I am sure the experience of recent generations is quite different to mine. The Church has lost its credibility and much of its influence, even to the point of where it has come to be seen as almost entirely bad. It seems easy now to forget that the Catholic Church played an important role in developing the tradition of scholarship in Ireland, recalled by the expression "The Land of Saints and Scholars". But what I am concerned with here is the psychic legacy of our history, which I think, does not change so easily.

A novel called *The Secret Scripture* by Sebastian Barry (2008) captures something about Ireland's disturbing history. It is set in Ireland in the early 1920s, just after Irish independence and at the time of the civil war. It is about a woman who ends up in a psychiatric hospital and who is telling her story at the end of her life. One important theme is the alienation, humiliation, and degradation this woman is subjected to because of allegations of infidelity and an illegitimate baby. For her "crime", she is consigned to a psychiatric hospital for the rest of her life, as, in reality, was the fate of many Irish women who were seen to have breached the sexual norms of the Catholic Church. It would almost have been an unbearable read except that, despite all her misfortune, the character does not actually lose her mind and manages to tell her story with a truly wonderful voice.

The book was a big success inside and outside Ireland. Yet often when I try to talk to family or friends in Ireland about our disturbing history, I feel I get a message that goes something like this: "Why are you going on about this? That's all in the past." This is important because it links with one of the main points of this chapter—a feeling that there is something we are not meant to talk about. The fact that such subjects can be addressed in fiction tells me that there is a wish to know about and engage with our history despite there also being a real wish to forget it. What I think we wish to forget is the overwhelming feelings of pain and shame associated with such a past.

Emigration, I am arguing, as well as serving an economic purpose also serves the purpose of evacuation. By leaving Ireland, the emigrant themselves may be trying to leave part of their experience behind, which despite best efforts is usually not possible. The collective leaving of emigrants could then be seen as an evacuation from Ireland of experiences and feelings that are intolerable.

This is how Hilary Mantel, 2009 Booker Prize winner, who is a second-generation Irish Catholic in Britain, describes the impact of Irish Catholicism on her:

> You grow up believing that you're wrong and bad. And for me, because I took what I was told really seriously, it bred a very intense habit of introspection and self-examination and a terrible severity with myself. So that nothing was ever good enough. [Mantel, 2009]

I see this self-blame that Hilary Mantel talks about as an internalized projection. One feels "I am inherently bad". Of course, this kind of self-blame is not necessarily the experience of all Irish people, but I think it is common enough to be seen to be one of the characteristics of the colonized mind.

The current disastrous economic situation in Ireland speaks loudly of the ways in which the colonized mind lives on. The economic crisis in Ireland is part of a wider phenomenon linked to global capitalism, but how it has played out in Ireland could be seen to be related to our history. Because of colonization, economic development in Ireland was delayed in comparison to most other Western countries until a couple of decades ago. When opportunities for development arose through globalization and membership of the European Union, Ireland went from relative impoverishment to wealth overnight. Prior to its collapse, the booming economy (colloquially known as the Celtic Tiger) enabled the Irish to shake off some of the shackles from the past, but it also involved a kind of greediness that was like the feast after the famine. The Celtic Tiger allowed the Irish to get in touch with their own agency, creativity, and a sense of pride after centuries of deprivation, but it also allowed them to get very cut off from the past. With the benefit of hindsight, the economic boom in Ireland could be seen to have been based on an omnipotent delusion, a manic defence against the pain of the past. It is no coincidence that Ireland's Celtic Tiger and its subsequent collapse was a drama that took place around the land. It was overinflated property prices together with collusive and corrupt relationships between the politicians and the bankers that led to the boom and subsequent collapse. This, of course, was supported by the general population's desire for wealth. The height of the boom saw behaviour that was clearly triumphant.

When the artificial "island of England" off the coast of Dubai—aptly enough built on sand—was sold in 2008, it was predictable that it would be bought by Irish property developers who outbid British investors. The pleasure of owning England was worth the extra money (O'Toole, 2009, p. 99). This is one of many examples given by O'Toole where Irish property developers paid overinflated prices to outbid British investors. According to O'Toole, "Property development was the new armed struggle, the war of independence by other means" (2009, p. 98). This, we now know, had a very tragic ending in the shape of one of the most serious economic crises in history, with the country having to be bailed out by the EU and the IMF—Ireland's most recent owners. If this is not a return of the repressed, what is? Ireland could be seen to be once again colonized, and the repressed feelings of rage, shame, self-blame, and inferiority come back to haunt us. In Europe, Ireland is blamed for its reckless lending and spending. The European institutions, which recklessly lent to Irish banks, see this, admittedly extreme version of a global economic phenomenon, as "an Irish problem", and once again Ireland can be the receptacle for projections of inferiority. What is important here is the link with history. As we know from Freud (1914g,) when we deny history we are destined to repeat it.

By making these links, I am not seeking to blame Britain or to exempt Ireland from its responsibility. I am making the case for remembering history and understanding the psychic legacy of colonialism so that it can be worked through rather than re-enacted over further generations.

The economic crisis has resulted in another generation of Irish people having to emigrate. However much they wish to be rid of the legacy of history, they will no doubt take their share of shame and self-blame with them.

Why this is important for the Irish in Britain is that this legacy makes us very vulnerable to negative projections, and if we identify with those projections then, of course, we can't speak out about our experience because we just feel bad and guilty.

Making a good life in the land of the colonizer

The final paradox is that by choosing to live in Britain the Irish person is choosing, like many of the children of the British Empire, to live in the land of the colonizer. When an Irish person emigrates from Ireland to Britain, he or she may, on the one hand, be trying to get away from the negative impacts of colonialism (whether material or psychic) while, on the other, making him/herself dependent on the very agent that has created the problems from which the person wished to escape in the first place. This presents one with an inner conflict that is uncomfortable and easier to avoid. When the Irish have a good experience of living in Britain, there is even more of an incentive to avoid looking at this paradox. How can one draw attention to what one might represent as an Irish person in Britain while at the same time making a good living here? There is also an incentive for the British not to look at this paradox, as they may not want to be reminded of their colonial history and the reasons that the Irish have turned up on British shores in the first place. However, this blind spot not only covers up something uncomfortable, it also potentially exposes something hopeful. That an Irish person is able to make a good life in Britain is testament to another side of the story—that the British are capable of reparation and the Irish are not inevitably consigned to the position of an underclass. Emigration to Britain from the colonies had its exploitative side—the provision of cheap labour—but it also provided opportunities and asylum for many people.

Emigrants from Ireland have ended up all over the globe, but a significant number have ended up in Britain, and it is interesting to ask "why Britain?" Britain is geographically closer to Ireland, but in all sorts of other ways Britain is also closer to Ireland. As well as dividing us, our history also connects us.

Kiberd says: "If Ireland had never existed the English would have invented it" (1996, p. 9). He also says: "If England had never existed the Irish would have been rather lonely. Each nation badly needed the other for the purpose of defining itself" (1996, p. 2). I find these statements refreshing because they capture something about the way that we need each other, and not only for destructive purposes but also to make sense of who we are.

One of the more positive stereotypes of Irish people is that of creativity and a rich literary and cultural tradition, and this is also in some ways linked to our colonial history. According to Kiberd, in the process of colonization, Ireland became England's unconscious. In the mind of the colonizer, they were the civilized ones whereas the colony was uncivilized, "a place where unbridled instincts ran wild" (1996, p. 18). Even several centuries ago, the Irish themselves were aware of a kind of splitting involved in this kind of thinking; when such notions were conveyed in British writing, the Irish wrote back—even if covertly—their own version of the story, and so Irish literature was born. Kiberd (1992) points out that, in their work, Joyce, Wilde, and Shaw all created male characters who were in touch with their feminine sides, and these were seen to represent an alternative to the dominant male hero of colonialism. The British, missing the parts of themselves that were projected into the

Irish, were very welcoming of Irish writing and culture, even if it sometimes got reconstructed as British.

For the Irish immigrant in Britain, there can also be the finding of a part of oneself that is felt to be missing. Not all Irish people in Ireland or Britain live up to the stereotype of the free-spirited spontaneous Celt, and some of us find a more serious, reflective part of us validated in this country. Living in multicultural Britain reminds us that we do not have a monopoly on the role of the oppressed, and we are, if we are open to it, also challenged to face up to the oppressor within ourselves. Britain then can be seen not just as the oppressor but also a place where previously split-off parts can be brought together.

When we deny our different identity and the way that this can disadvantage us, we also do not see clearly the other side of the story. Millions of Irish people have immigrated to Britain over the years, and many of them have been able to make a good life for themselves here and have contributed to what it means to be British today. This is only possible because of a generosity that is also part of British culture. Another paradox is that people fleeing some of the indirect impacts of colonialism, such as women who suffered at the hands of the oppressive Catholic culture or people who were mentally distressed, have turned to England as an escape. They have not always been welcomed with open arms, but many have found asylum and support here.

The Irish peace process, despite the setbacks, is a hugely significant development in recent times and shows that split-off parts to do with the past can be brought together. The Queen's historic visit to Ireland in 2011 also marks an important symbolic moment in the repair of Irish–British relationships. These developments speak to me of the possibilities of whole-object relating.

Case study

This case study relates to consultancy work I did for a university a number of years ago. I believe it demonstrates the way in which the Irish can be at the receiving end of negative projections. I think it captures some of the issues I have outlined earlier about how difficult it seems to be, both for us and for others, to look at Irish identity in the work. I think it also demonstrates the disabling effect of the colonized mind and the way that this can be used in British institutions.

The work took place in a department of a university. The Head of Department asked for an intervention to help him and his senior colleagues to work more effectively as a management group. There were increasing pressures on the department to respond to management and administrative demands from the wider university. The Head felt that he had to carry most of the burden of these demands and that the rest of the team acted as if it was not really part of their responsibility. They would acknowledge the issues in meetings but in reality did little to move things forward. Initially I visited the department for an exploratory meeting with the Head and the team. I remember feeling most uncomfortable as soon as I walked into the building. It had a rather old-fashioned grandeur that felt quite intimidating to me. Mostly the team members were polite, but there was a level of formality and superficiality that I found very disconcerting. It felt to me as if everyone was acting, and it was very difficult to make any real contact with them. Most of the team members seemed puzzled by my presence, as if they couldn't work out why I was there and how I could possibly help them. I had a feeling of being humoured. A couple of the team members who had worked in the department a long time were quite contemptuous. In answer to the question "Could tell me a bit about your work? one brushed me off with "Have you not read the documents that were sent to you in advance?" When I went on to say I was hoping to hear from them something about their experience of the work, he pretended not to understand me. It felt most hostile, and I felt like a student who was being told off for not doing her homework.

Despite the ominous start, they agreed for me to run a number of workshops to help them think about the increasing demands on the department and how they could work more effectively together as a team to respond to them. I asked a colleague, a British woman, to join me in the work, realizing it was going to be complicated. The team responded better to my colleague than they had to me. At first I was relieved, as I thought if she could relate to them then at least it would save the project from failing; however, I also felt it must be something to do with my inadequacy that I couldn't get a better connection with them.

In the subsequent workshops, I often felt inadequate and stupid. When I spoke, I felt as if people didn't understand me. I often had the feeling that I was not being taken seriously, again as if they were humouring me. I discussed my experience up to a point with my colleague, but neither she nor I seemed to find a way of understanding the situation that made any great difference. She did have more success than me with her interventions, but overall our work had a feeling of fragility.

Around the same time, I was doing some work in an international context where I was feeling more authorized, and a colleague of mine was talking about leadership and difference and the importance of using one's difference in leadership. I was hit by the realization that I had been shrinking behind my Irishness in the work with the university. I realized that, as an Irish woman in this setting, I felt very different, and I felt ashamed of my difference. I felt somehow unacceptable. I felt that as an Irish woman I had the wrong profile for this British institution. Note that I felt there was something wrong with me, not with the university. I felt I could not talk about the Irish dimension of my experience with my colleague, not to mention with the client. I had this feeling of illegitimacy that, if I raised it, they would think "What the hell are you talking about?"

My colleague in the international setting had given an example of how, a number of years ago, the Dutch CEO of a British company had used his "Dutchness" to make changes to what was at the time a highly rigid and class-ridden institution. Hearing this reminded me that there were parts of Britain that were still very much like the old British establishment, and it made me see more clearly that my experience at the university may have had as much to do with them as me.

As it happened, I had this realization as we were coming towards the end of our work with them. I remember going back to the university for the last session feeling different in light of this and determined not to take an apologetic stance. I was doing a presentation for the team, and for the first time I felt as if they engaged with me and acted as if they knew what I was talking about. This may have been reparation on their part, as well as a change in my attitude. But what is important is that if I had arrived at the realization earlier that my Irish identity was a factor in the experience, and I had been able to share it with my colleague, we may have been able to respond to them more robustly and use it to link to some of their issues.

The projection that I think I was on the receiving end of here was stupidity. One can see how stupidity is the one thing people may fear most in an educational institution, and I think it was very likely that these feelings were around in relation to one of their issues, which was that it was felt by the Dean of the School that this department was not responsive enough to the changing times. In retrospect, it seems easier to see that behind the contempt and polite formality was probably a lot of fragility to do with being in a rather outdated setup and not wanting or perhaps not knowing how to change. In addition, there would of course have been feelings or fears of stupidity among the student group that the staff would have been asked to contain. In this context, it was, I think, very difficult for them to acknowledge any feelings of inadequacy. I think I represented the stupid parts of themselves that they could disown and get relief from and yet relate to by being contemptuous of me. On checking the etymology of the word "stupid", I discovered that it comes from "the Latin verb *stupere*, for being numb or astonished, and is related to stupor" (Wikipedia). This is fascinating because as well as conveying the more obvious meaning of unintelligent, it also captures the sense of being cut-off that is experienced when we cannot bear to be in touch with difficult feelings, which was relevant here both for myself and for the university department.

I have demonstrated earlier how the Irish became a container for British feelings of inferiority as a result of the Penal Laws, the famine, and other historical events. The projection of stupidity still seems to be a need for the British in certain circumstances, because despite the tradition of scholarship in Ireland and the fact that several decades of Irish emigrants have been highly educated, this is still a stereotype that we encounter. This is not as prevalent as in the past, but clearly it is still alive and well.

That, I think, was their part of the dynamic; my part was that I was so identified with the projection that I was not able to make it available for work with them around these issues. I think one of my overwhelming feelings during this work was shame at feelings so inadequate. I felt the problem was mine. Had I and my colleague been able to address what I represented for this group, we may have been able to help them face up to and tolerate feelings of inferiority and inadequacy associated with the demanding managerial climate of their work so that this could inform their response. As stated earlier, I see my failure to do so as due to a kind of colonization of the mind, and this is what we need to free ourselves from, but in order to do so we first need to recognize it, understand it, and be able to talk about it.

Conclusion

What I have shown here is that Irish identity doesn't get thought about enough in dialogues about difference in the UK, perhaps more widely and particularly in the systems psychodynamic world.

I have argued that there is an investment for ourselves and others in not looking at issues that are both painful and shameful. There is a cost to this especially for the Irish in what they get left to hold, but also for the British in lost opportunities for whole-object relating.

Acknowledgements

I owe a debt of gratitude to Frank Lowe, without whose inspiration I would not have written this chapter. I would also like to thank Jina Barrett, Gabriella Braun, Jean Byrne, Derek Deasy, Rohina Ilyas, Barbara O'Toole, and Jennifer Petriglieri who provided valuable feedback at various stages of its gestation. I am also grateful to all those who engaged with earlier versions of the chapter at Thinking Space and the OPUS conference, for their support and thoughts.

Note

1. Much could be said about the links between oppression and mental illness, and this is an important topic in itself, but I do not have the scope to go into that here.

CHAPTER TEN

Dehumanization, guilt, and large-group dynamics with reference to the West, Israel, and the Palestinians

Martin Kemp

For many years I have been concerned about the course taken by the conflict in Israel/Palestine, in particular at the denial of the rights of the Palestinians, and worried that Western contributions to the conflict in the Middle East have been misconceived and counter-productive. A visit to the occupied Palestinian territories and Israel in November 2008 both deepened and complicated this view. What had previously been for me an abstract political issue was now peopled. As part of a fact-finding tour with a group of medical and mental health specialists, I was meeting individuals from both "sides",[1] all of whose lives seemed to be defined by the conflict. Our encounters with Palestinians were stressful because their daily existence was overshadowed by the profoundly asymmetrical power relations between themselves and the Israeli state. It was distressing to see the uses to which this power was being put—the checkpoints, evictions, house demolitions, the system of military justice, the incursions of religious settlers into Arab towns. A Bedouin village inside Israel was demolished several weeks after we had been shown around its new health centre. The more recent fate of another village in the Negev was reported as follows:

> This summer Israeli bulldozers drove into the unrecognized Negev Bedouin village al-Arakib. As the families who lived

there looked on, the bulldozers razed the entire community leaving some 300 residents, including 200 children, without a home or water at the height of the desert summer.

"I saw the smiles of the policemen and the inspectors who did it," Al-Arakib resident Juma al-Turi told Ha'aretz. "They simply enjoyed it while the children were left without a home. They made victory signs with their hands after the destruction."[2]

The report, by the pro-Israeli, pro-Zionist New Israel Fund, suggests an attitude of—perhaps necessary—indifference to the villagers' fate among those carrying out the destruction. I repeatedly encountered Palestinians, some belonging to our own or related professions, who described a system that made ordinary life impossible and which they perceived as designed to encourage their emigration. What puzzled our informants was the indifference of Europeans and North Americans: they believed their passivity reflected a lack of information and hoped we would contribute to wider understanding of their predicament.

There are indeed grounds for arguing that in Western[3] public discourse the opinions and rights of the Palestinians have not been granted parity with those of the Israelis (Philo & Berry, 2011). A more inclusive picture was presented recently in Peter Kosminsky's 2011 Channel 4 television series *The Promise*, unusual for its interweaving of the major national and colonial currents that have defined the present reality in the Middle East, and also attempting to include diverse voices among both Palestinians and Jewish Israelis. This reflected our group's experience: we were hosted by two Israeli human rights organizations whose analysis largely cohered with those of the Palestinians we talked to. One aim of this chapter, then, is to consider why Kosminsky's diverse and complex coverage of the conflict should be so unusual.

I returned from the Middle East with the intention of sharing my impressions with others. This decision, however, was immediately accompanied by a deep apprehension, a sense of being burdened by an assignment that ran counter to professional and wider social expectations. So, as well as publishing some notes on our visit (Kemp & Pinto, 2009), talking to psychotherapists, and researching psychoanalytic work on the conflict, I also found myself turning to psychoanalysis to understand the emotional ramifications of the visit for myself.

David Black (2011) suggests that deep emotional engagement in an issue is a prerequisite of the formation of values and moral judgements (as an expression of the ego-function of conscience, not of a moralizing superego). For him, the basis of this engagement is sympathy, defined not as the active affect of compassion but, rather, as the "perceptual capacity" to recognize and appreciate the subjecthood of others (pp. 52–53). In changing perceptions towards "historical developments"—he cites slavery and capital punishment—he considers, though, that the operation of sympathy is insufficient: "to arrive at proper values requires a great deal more. . . . Imagination, dialogue and conscious reflection are also required" (pp. 58–59). The problem, as I perceive it, is that as regards Israel/Palestine the conditions for these processes to operate do not exist in the West, and this chapter is an attempt to suggest why this might be so. I begin by arguing that psychoanalytic theories concerning the unconscious element in inter-communal strife are a useful starting point in considering the underlying reasons for this. I then suggest an application of these theories to consider the legacy of history on the development of dynamic features in the collective psychic life of Western and Israeli societies.

The resulting chapter may be read as partisan, as "pro-Palestinian", and in the crude dichotomous language of everyday politics this is accurate. The reality is more nuanced: while it is a given that one identifiable group is in the ascendant over another, the struggle of ideas and ideologies cannot be neatly divided along ethnic or religious lines. My views are as much informed by Israeli (and non-Israeli Jewish) as by Palestinian intellectuals, distinguished by the priority that both give to human rights and democratic values and by their disaffection from ideologies of ethnic nationalism.[4] My focus, however, is on a psychodynamic exploration of emotional linkages in the relationship between Israel and the West which, I believe, have contributed to a gulf between the latter's stated values and its behaviour. I omit anything that is not germane to this topic, including a historical account of the conflict and the part played in it by regional tensions and international power politics.

A final clarification: I am interested in a particular phenomenon, the anxiety and inhibition that attends reflection on Israel/Palestine in particular, that seems to impact upon public discourse in a way that it does not in more private spaces. The terms "public" and "private" are used here descriptively, to convey my experience of moving from locations (informally constituted meetings of psycho-therapists and other professional groups, for example) in which discussion felt weighted towards an interest in understanding and concern, to situations (the responses to publishing an article in *Therapy Today*, for instance) where issues of conformity and the potential for giving offence seemed to take priority (see, for example, Sabbagh, 2009).

Psychoanalytic study of inter-communal conflicts

To address large-group phenomena we need notions such as "cultural complex" (Singer & Kimbles, 2004), "social unconscious" (Dalal, 1998), or Volkan's "large-group psychology".[5] I depend here on Volkan,[6] a writer concerned with exploring connections between aspects of group identity and inter-ethnic conflict. His ideas are relevant to understanding relations between Israel and the Palestinians but are also useful in discussing British/Western responses to that issue.

Volkan disparages a reductive transposition of psychoanalytic paradigms to explain social phenomena; what is required, he says, is a conceptual framework built upon psychoanalytic practice which is then completed in accordance with the particularities of each situation (Volkan, 1998). As far as the unconscious sources of conflict are concerned, he gives pride of place to his notion of the "large-group identity" (Volkan, 2002), a shared or social complex made up of all the internalizations occurring in the process of childhood development, along with other "deposited representations" that convey what it means to be part of the large group, notions of ethnicity, and so on (Volkan, 1996, p. 258). This construction is maintained by what he refers to as the community's "large-group tent", a container that provides safety and cohesion, defines basic values, and differentiates "us" from out-groups (on to whom the rejected "bad" aspects of the self-group can be projected). Personal identity incorporates this group canopy, becoming part of the individual's core self, so that tears in the tent structure are experienced as threats occasioning profound anxiety and states of terror (Volkan, 2002).

Paradoxically, he says, among the most highly cathected elements that might be woven into this binding structure are narratives of societal collapse: some groups unconsciously "select" trauma as a foundation for their identity. When this trauma has been "deliberately inflicted upon a large group by an enemy" the society "besides suffering losses and facing helplessness, also experiences shame, humiliation and an inability to assert itself" (Volkan, 2009). Inhibited mourning leads to the "transgenerational transmission" of these affects, leaving communities vulnerable to what he terms a "time collapse", akin to a collective flashback:

> *Time collapse* may lead to irrational and sadistic or masochistic decision making by the leadership of the large group and in turn members of the large group become psychologically prepared for sadistic or masochistic acts, and in the worst-case scenario, perpetuate otherwise unthinkable cruelty against others. [Volkan, 1998]

A traumatized group locked into "perennial mourning" but defending itself against the shame and humiliation associated with the trauma is susceptible to an "identification with the oppressor" and to ideologies formed around a sense of entitlement (Volkan, 2009; see also Moses-Hrushovski, 1996, pp. 182–186). The articulation of political programmes informed by such unconscious processes he terms "irredentist ideologies", which are often "characterized by the dream of regaining all the lands that the group considered 'lost' and now occupied by others" (Volkan, 2007). "Exaggerated 'entitlement'", he writes, "provides a belief system and a renewed sense of omnipotence that asserts that the large group has a right to own what they wish to have" (Volkan, 2009).

Volkan is alive to the way his theories might be applied to analyse the unconscious drives at play within Israel/Palestine. "I consider", he notes, "the Holocaust still to be a hot trauma on its way toward becoming a chosen trauma",[7] and he includes Zionism among a list of "irredentist" ideologies (Volkan, 2009). Nevertheless, there seems to have been no in-depth "Volkanian" study of the conflict.

Psychoanalytic theories of group formations posit the existence of unconscious structures to which all members of a collective are in some ways subject. Volkan is explicit about this: mental representations of, for example, a social group's "chosen traumas" will be shared by *everyone* who identifies as a member of the group, including those who have no historical connection to the traumatic experience itself (Volkan, 1996).[8] He is clear, however, that people's conscious attitudes are *not* pre-determined. An illustration might be taken from Chasseguet-Smirgel (1990), who proposes that universal unconscious fantasies, impacted upon by specific traumas in German history, had contributed to the forms taken by, and the popular appeal of, National Socialism. There is no suggestion here that "all Germans were Nazis"—far from it. So, when I refer to collective psychic structures, I believe I am referring to something tangible and meaningful, without the implication that any society is monolithic. I hope that this is particularly apparent in my discussions of Israel's "large-group tent", which is drawn essentially from Israeli writers and psychoanalysts.

Dehumanization of the Jews

In encountering narcissistic object relations in the individual, clinicians think in terms of early disturbance. For the newborn, the humanizing of the mother is a developmental achievement to be extended, hopefully, to other family members and beyond, until we understand that—in principle at least—all members of the human family are sensate beings like ourselves. We know that this is a fragile achievement that can be undone, momentarily under stress or systematically in the face of trauma. A line is established between that which is deemed worthy of protection and care and that which is not. The line is not fixed but is subject to variation; it is both individually and socially determined (De Zulueta, 1993, pp. 225–247).

The dehumanization of the Jews and the dehumanization of the Palestinians are historically discrete and the forms they have taken quite distinct. But I believe that both in the Middle East itself and in the collective mind of the West, they have become inseparably linked. This has the consequence that individuals somehow find themselves having to choose between the eradication—from their minds, their concerns—of either one people or the other.

It is virtually impossible, I think, to stay with the human realities that are kept out of as much as brought into mind by the term "Holocaust". Silence seems the only appropriately respectful stance, and I am reluctant to offend those who identify most closely with the victims of European anti-Semitism. Yet I do not think this is helpful. Seventy years on, the Holocaust plays a complicated but profound role in the deadlocked politics of Israel/Palestine and, I believe, in a moral confusion in the face of it.

Post-1945 everyone—in Volkan's terms, each large-group identity—faced the challenge of incorporating knowledge both of the genocide and of the part played by their society in its antecedents. One outcome was to recognize that this genocide was the result of a complex mix of socio-economic and psychological factors that had coalesced in an ideological formation that targeted a particular minority, and that such circumstances could re-occur in any society. Urged on by the work of Raphael Lemkin, in 1948 the United Nations introduced the Convention on the Prevention and Punishment of the Crime of Genocide. In this trajectory, we were and are all potential perpetrators and victims sharing a responsibility to prevent its repetition. This "universalist" interpretation was not the only one, however. An alternative was to view the event as exceptional, and distinctively a Jewish experience. I do not want to suggest that there was nothing unique about the Holocaust, and I would see nothing to be gained in making comparisons with any other historical events. Nor is it at all surprising that Israeli perceptions should be "overdetermined by the memory of real mass-extermination in the twentieth century" (Bunzl & Beit-Hallahmi, 2002, p. xiv; see also Segev, 1991). At the same time, there is a sense in which the claim to the "uniqueness" of the Holocaust—and there is an ongoing debate on this issue—has political ramifications. Simon Schama (2009) states that: "Ultimately, Israel's case is the remedy for atrocity."[9] There are psychological implications too, I argue below, for both Israel and the West.

The Western powers had known what was befalling Germany's Jews during the 1930s, but "In the 1930s the rest of the world considered the persecution of the Jews to be an internal German matter".[10] During the war, as information about the genocide emerged, Allied leaders rejected Jewish requests they bomb the extermination camps. Nothing was done to hinder the progress of the genocide. These failures became a powerful argument in support of Zionism and a rebuke that has ever since haunted the European mind.

The Nazi genocide realized the murderous potential of a racism that had characterized Western culture for over a millennium and, the evidence suggests, rendered anti-Semitism an even more guilt-ridden topic than white-on-black racism. The latter is now widely considered to be a deeply embedded cultural phenomenon needing to be addressed as a question of theory and practice. It is given considerable attention in training, organizational consultancy, and the like. The idea that racist assumptions have been internalized, that these residues can be activated with extreme ease and—for anti-racists—have to be consciously acknowledged and combated, is now broadly accepted. Belatedly, there is a significant psychoanalytic literature on racism, looking at its unconscious determinants as well as its impact clinically and organizationally, an engagement that has, I think, benefited both blacks and whites by making its acknowledgement safer and less persecutory. There is a capacity to retain a clear view of the asymmetrical power relationships that racism sustains and expresses, and an openness to its complex and still anxiety-laden and destructive dynamics.

The same cannot be said for anti-Semitism, a prejudice that was frequently expressed by people at all social levels prior to World War II. Widespread horror met the news of the liberation of the death camps—but did this purge anti-Semitism from Europe and North America, or simply render it a taboo issue?[11] While it would be difficult to believe that any minority—let alone one towards which prejudice has been so ingrained—would not be exposed to racism, in public discourse anti-Semitism has been outlawed, being left to (projected into) those neo-fascist groups responsible for occasional attacks on synagogues and the desecration of Jewish graves. There is widespread concern at the prospect of such groups returning to the political mainstream, particularly in Eastern Europe. Nevertheless, rather than a painful acceptance that we all partake in primitive splitting and utilize socially available— even if scientifically meaningless—categories of race as vehicles for projection, anti-Semitism seems to be regarded as something akin to a repugnant virus that infects only certain types of politically suspect groups of people.

I would suggest that the proximity and nature of the Holocaust led to the splitting-off and projection of European anti-Semitism by mainstream Western society, leaving an ineradicable unconscious link between any negative affect felt towards "Jews" and the horrors of the Nazi genocide. It cannot be worked through even to the extent that we attempt to address other forms of racism. I then wonder if these defences are so fragile that they paralyse thought and leave the West submissive and inarticulate in the face of an Israel strongly identified with the victims and survivors of European anti-Semitism.[12] It is hard, perhaps, to see Israel in terms other than that of victim. I am suggesting that the attempt to offset profound guilt may have led Western countries to concur in Israel's definition of what an ally should be, and that this may have ultimately required acquiescence in the dehumanization of the Palestinians.[13] In this way, our disengagement from one historical tragedy is perpetuated in the failure of our response to another.

The dehumanization of the Palestinians

Retrospective accounts of the formation of Israel identify a number of features that are seen to have left the new society encumbered by unresolved guilt that has itself complicated perceptions of the Palestinians, reinforcing the demonization of the enemy that could be anticipated in any serious conflict.

It is widely agreed that representations of the Jewish character within Zionist literature—as evidenced in Herzl's writings—incorporated an anti-Semitic stereotyping of Jews as feminine, submissive, and degenerate (e.g., Kane, 2005, pp. 941, 943; Witkon, 2008, p. 910; Zureik, 2011). Beit-Hallahmi writes that: "What Zionism was proposing was not only national liberation and human renewal, but a complete physical and psychic changeover . . ." (Bunzl & Beit-Hallahmi, 2002, p. 12). Kane, in a psychoanalytic commentary, suggests that: "Many Jewish Israelis (like most of us) learned to despise what they feared in themselves: weakness, vulnerability, and naiveté" (Kane, 2005, p. 941). Holocaust survivors were for many years marginalized in Israel, perceived as examples of what the "new Jew" was intended to replace. To Zuckerman, this contributed to "the primarily preconscious or unconscious feelings of guilt connected with the cultural or psychological negation of Diaspora Jewry in general and of the Shoah survivors in particular" (Zuckerman, 2002, p. 65).

After 1967, the State increasingly identified itself with the victims of Nazism: there is now an active socialization of Israeli youth into an identity as survivors of the Holocaust.[14] But Kane suggests that this memorialization of the genocide disguises a basic denial of its reality, a denial linked to Israel's behaviour towards the Palestinians. "To transform violence into compassion," she writes, "we must bear the knowledge of how we ourselves were psychically maimed" (Kane, 2005, p. 947). Kane describes a causal connection between a "necessary blindness to the catastrophic impact of the founders' own traumatic past" and a blindness "to the equally catastrophic impact of their treatment of the local Arab population" (Kane, 2005, p. 934).

Eliane Schwager, working with the descendants of both Nazis and their Jewish victims, looks not only at the psychological impact of trauma on individuals, but also at how group responses affect social and political attitudes. The consequence of being preoccupied with "the residues of being a victim or a perpetrator—the hopelessness, lack of worth, shame and guilt" (Schwager, 2004, p. 565) is the adoption of a "dualistic" or "genocidal mentality" that, unresolved, leads to trans-generational re-enactment. Schwager offers a compelling picture of a worldview characterized by the insistence on the distinction between perpetrator and victim, evil and innocent:

> If one can designate what is evil and eliminate it one has a better chance of ensuring one's safety. There is little awareness that it is this clear drawing of lines that in part contributed to the horror. [Schwager, 2004, p. 556]

From its beginnings, political Zionism struggled to accept that the realization of its aspirations was impeded by the fact that another people lived in the land it coveted (Goldberg, 1996, pp. 60, 94–95; for exceptions among early Zionists, see Rose, 2005). Herzl's contribution to the movement—to provide it with a political strategy based on the support of the imperial powers—obviated the need to secure the consent of the existing inhabitants. Instead, what was needed was the acquiescence of the leading powers in upholding the priority of Zionism's claim to the land for the Jewish people. Publicists such as Frankenstein argued that European concern for the indigenous population was misplaced: the local inhabitants were few, parasitic, and cosmopolitan. Their alleged failure to develop the territory deprived them of the right to claim title to it (Frankenstein, 1943, pp. 116–143).[15]

The situation within Palestine required a more realistic assessment, and Zionist groups developed plans for the displacement of long-established Palestinian Arab communities, implemented in the aftermath of the British withdrawal (Pappe, 2006). It is generally acknowledged that myths were disseminated in the years that followed, including the assertion that the perhaps 800,000 people who had fled had made themselves refugees voluntarily or in obedience to instructions from other Arab regimes (Brunner, 2002; Zuckerman, 2002). When from the 1980s Israeli scholars began to publish academic histories of the period that challenged such foundation myths, there was a passionate response (see Glass, 2004). The historians concerned were regarded as traitors by some, for whom "the unmaking of the myths seem[ed] to raise the spectre of national disintegration, fragmentation, and despair" (Brunner, 2002, pp. 119, 121). Using Kohut's concept of a fragile narcissism, Brunner sees in such reactions evidence that Israelis were too vulnerable to have a real mirror held up to themselves (pp. 125–126).

Recognition of the implications of Zionism's success for the Palestinians is still a point of contention within Israel. Ofer Grosbard, an Israeli psychologist who has analysed the conflict from a psychoanalytic perspective, writes: "As long as we do not understand that as far as [the Palestinians] are concerned we landed on them from another world, settled in their land, expelled them from their homes, and ignored their existence, there will not be reconciliation" (Grosbard, 2003, p. 25). Grosbard is hopeful, seeing the obstacles in the way of a settlement as primarily psychological. Another possibility is that the subordination of the Palestinians follows from ideological objectives that have still not been securely achieved: Suleiman has argued that "the marginality of Palestinians as citizens is embedded in the definition of Israel as the State of the Jewish people" (Suleiman, 2002, p. 74).

Zuckerman asserts that there has been a psychic price for political and military success:

> The total demonization of those towards whom one had become fundamentally guilty, the deflection of one's own intolerable guilt, and its projection onto the source of the feeling of guilt, that is the victims. . . . The end of their demonization would necessarily mean dealing with the guilt accrued towards them. . . . [Zuckerman, 2002, p. 66]

Raphael Moses considered that unconscious Israeli guilt emanated from the expulsion of the Palestinians in 1948 and the massacres committed at that time and subsequently, and from the treatment of Palestinian citizens of Israel. "We cannot but have guilt feelings about that because all of these were acts carried out by Israelis in the name of Israel, in our name" (Moses, 2002, p. 97). He suggests that by displacement and projection the guilt is transformed into aggression, and that Israelis search for approval "from the international great powers" for aid in rationalizing their behaviour (pp. 97–99).[16]

A clinical example is given by Rena Moses-Hrushovski, describing a group of Israeli Palestinian and Israeli Jewish teachers:

> When in one session the Israeli Jews ruthlessly accused the Arabs of ingratitude for the benefits that the Israeli State had provided for them, and especially attacked them for violent acts by Arabs throughout the country, I felt that their aggressive assaults served also to defend them against their own guilt and shame; and I said so. It was amazing to realize that for quite some time nobody from the Jewish group had any notion about what they as representatives of Israeli Jews could possibly feel guilty about. It became clear that the guilt and shame relating to the humiliation and atrocities that tragically are carried out in the service of the Israeli occupation could not be owned at that moment. [Moses-Hrushovski, 1996, p. 185]

Grosbard writes that: "To the Jewish public, [Israeli Arabs] are nonentities and even less than human" (2003, p. 49). Central to the defensive ends served by the denigration of the Palestinians is the avoidance of a profound depression that would follow from the acknowledgement of Israel's responsibility for the Naqba (pp. 88, 91). His book is, fundamentally, an exploration of the past necessities and current unconscious defences that, in his view, drive the Israelis to dehumanize the Palestinians, with a commentary on the ways in which breaking with this necessity and embracing their humanity is a requirement for both peace and for Israel's survival. To use Volkan's terminology, he is suggesting that Israel's "large-group tent" is in large part held together by the projection of Israel's profound and unresolved conflicts on to the Palestinians, and that dehumanization of the latter is over-determined and extremely difficult to reverse. One conclusion might be that political Zionism has not offered an escape from the dynamics of oppression, merely a reversal of roles.

Further evidence for the potency of these collective defences can be found in the responses of individual Israelis to being deprived of their comforts, of having to grasp the humanity of the "other".

Chana Ullman writes following her experience of working for Machsom Watch, a group of Israeli women who witness and record what they see at Israeli checkpoints in the Occupied Territories:

> At the checkpoints I am suddenly faced with the concrete human meaning of life without hope, life without any semblance of the autonomy that I completely take for granted. The facts were available to me but I did not imagine the humiliating routine, the helpless submission and fear that this routine breeds in the other; I did not imagine the arbitrariness, numbness, and cruel automatic functioning that it breeds in us. All those become concrete and undeniable at the checkpoints. As in the return of the repressed: I now know that until now I knew nothing. [Ullman, 2006, p. 183]

For her, the consequence is to be consciously aware of "the shame and guilt" that ensues from a fuller understanding of her society's role in traumatizing the Palestinians (p. 196). It could be argued, then, that the circumstances of Israel's birth required that the indigenous population be rendered into a form where their humanity could be compromised and their rights accordingly disregarded, and that the need to defend against the guilt engendered by this requires their continued demonization (see Kane, 2005).[17] This situation, one can see, precipitates a vicious circle, a proclivity to further acts of aggression which all the time add to the burden of guilt that cannot be acknowledged.

Taking this and the previous section together, it could be imagined that the collective psyches of the West and Israel are each grappling with a crippling burden of culpability. I suggest this, and that each engages the other in their efforts to minimize the consequences. The West, aware of the pain that guilt would occasion for itself, achieves distance by reassuring Israel—identified with the fate of "the Jews"—that it has no need to feel guilty. The West has regularly upheld Israel's position that it is the Palestinians who need to make up for something, and that it is their failure to do so that explains the protracted stalemate. For the West to concern itself with the lived experience of the Palestinians would be to challenge an Israeli psyche in part held together by its refusal to acknowledge those realities.[18] I suggest that something of this kind may well be the case and that, as in a defensively constructed coupling, there has been an avoidance of anything that might upset a fragile but rigid *status quo*.[19]

A book that brings out similar and related features in the way two different large-group psychologies interrelate with one another is Erlich, Erlich-Ginor, and Beland's *Fed with Tears—Poisoned with Milk* (2009). The book offers a highly condensed account of the Nazareth Conferences, involving German and Israeli analysts. The Conferences were organized to address the belief that the historical past for each community had inscribed representations of the German or Israeli Other, and a complex of dissimilar but complementary emotional responses to these representations, organized around the issue of responsibility and guilt, that inhibited members of both communities from recognizing each other's basic humanity: encountering the Germans, the Israelis' outlook was characterized by assertiveness and a sense of entitlement; faced by Israelis, the Germans' outlook was affected by anxiety and defensiveness. This provides an illustration, I think, of an entwined dynamic involving two geographically distant group processes. Similarly, I would argue, we are still all subject to the pressures of belonging to our own particular large groups.

A difficult topic within psychoanalysis

That this feeds into the way that the psychotherapy profession has, or has not, thought about the problems in the Middle East is, I think, apparent in the relevant psychoanalytic literature. One can imagine the courage it might take for citizens of Israel, whether Jewish or Palestinian, to challenge consensus assumptions about the conflict. Several Israeli training analysts have described how, some years back, their attempts to step outside the mainstream— highlighting health professionals' silence about the impact of the conflict on Israeli society, participating in training programmes for Palestinian mental health professionals—met a hostile response (Bunzl & Beit-Hallahmi, 2002, pp. 186, 204). Raphael Moses was told that his writing about Israeli guilt towards the Palestinians was anti-Semitic (p. 96).

In February 2010, OFEK—an Israeli organization linked with the Tavistock Institute of Human Relations—held a conference on the topic, "How to Make Peace—Learning from the Example of Others". In the summary of proceedings on the Internet, one Israeli Palestinian participant, Aida Touma-Sliman,[20] "objected to the word 'conflict' and claimed that what was occurring was actually [a] 'conquest'".[21] She was objecting to a word that serves to conceal history and renders unintelligible the nature of the present confrontation between Israel and the Palestinians. In sympathy with this, I suggest that mainstream public discourse, in the West generally, is constructed around framings of the "conflict" that obscure direct human experience—framings that do not enable us to make sense of the destruction of al-Arakib that I referred to at the beginning, for example.

When such framings are challenged far from the conflict zone, outside the clinical context, there is often an inexplicably sensitive response.[22] The point of interest here is not the anger shown by some of Israel's supporters, but the anxiety of those not directly involved in the face of that anger. Dogmatism can, of course, be found on all sides of this as of any contentious problem. But I cannot think of any other topic around which there is an equivalent difficulty in airing dissenting opinions. Wollheim once commented that: "Judiciousness is the appearance not the reality of objectivity" (1987, p. 12). He continues: "I am aware that it is by now a piece of right-thinking that, on the one hand, non-Jews, and, on the other hand, Jews, do not really have the right to speak critically of Israel" (p. 13). He was suggesting that narratives that reflect official Israeli concerns determine the limits of legitimate debate.[23] Although we live in a pluralist society in which one could find every point of view represented, I think that there is truth in this and that its effect can be detected within psychoanalytic discourse.

The heightened emotion that characterizes public discussion of the subject can also be found within psychoanalytic papers: recently, Israelis who support the Palestinians were described in an American psychoanalytic journal as suffering from a range of psychological disorders (Silver, 2008).[24] A "Special Editorial" appeared in the *International Journal of Psychoanalysis* denouncing the call for an academic boycott of Israel (Gabbard & Williams, 2002). My letter urging the need to debate the matter was accepted for publication (Kemp, 2005), but the editors subsequently apologized for overlooking the "partisan hatefulness" it contained and declared that they would "close the discussion" with a response by an American analyst the tenor and content of whose comments, including references to my "incendiary provocations", were quite unlike that characterizing other disputes within the profession (Poland, 2005).

I want to argue, in addition, that the psychological dilemmas aroused by the conflict lead to a diminished affective and moral response to it. Two principles informed the *IJPA*'s "Special Editorial": a defence of academic freedom and a rejection of action taken "in support of one side in the Middle East conflict" (Gabbard & Williams, 2002). No interest was shown in the degree of academic freedom enjoyed by the Palestinians, a point made by Judith Butler some years later (Butler, 2006). There was no consideration of the other issues that might have obtained, where a state had maintained—at that point for 35 years—a military occupation over another people that denied the latter political or civic rights.

References in the psychoanalytic press to the struggles in Israel/Palestine have most frequently appeared within articles devoted to the study of terrorism. Terrorism exists as an observable phenomenon—the violent targeting of civilians in political conflicts—and as a key concept in Western attributions of "goodness" and "badness" in world affairs. According to Edward Said, it has "occasioned a whole new signifying system . . . used . . . to justify everything 'we' do and to delegitimize as well as dehumanize everything 'they' do" (Said, 1984, pp. 254–255). A review of psychoanalytic work in this ideologically fraught area would, I think, suggest the powerful influence of large-group assumptions upon our professional discourse—in implicit definitions of terrorism, in notions of modernity versus fundamentalism, pathologizing alien cultures and overlooking sometimes the beams in our own eyes (see Said, 1997). Emanuel Berman has urged analysts to "work through self-analytically [their] own unavoidable value-judgments": "Current discussions about terrorism", he thought, revealed a "mobilized psychoanalysis" which promoted "splitting and reductionistic divisions where analysts identify with the 'us' and reject the 'them'" (Elmendorf & Ruskin, 2004, p. 985).

What is absent from many psychoanalytic commentaries on terrorism is adequate recognition of what Leopold Nosek has called "the terror in everyday life" for people in peripheral communities experiencing the social dislocation attendant on globalization (Nosek, 2003). George Awad (2003, pp. 155–156) has addressed this matter specifically in relation to the Middle East: "I am writing about [Arab/Palestinian perceptions] because I believe that their voices are often misrepresented and are rarely heard. . . . And the Palestinian resistance movement, which evolved as a struggle against losing their homeland, has been painted in the darkest colours since its inception. Why is this?". Responding to Peter Fonagy's suggestion that we attend to the moment when terrorists decide to "abandon their species decency", Awad writes:

> Less dramatic, but also lethal, is the slow and cumulative aban-donment of a deeply ingrained species decency where there is no defining moment: this can be seen in the increasingly destructive actions of the Israelis against the Palestinians. A powerful oppressor can, more often than not, afford to wait things out and take his time; an occupation or an embargo can slowly yet effectively destroy the soul and the body of "the others". The powerful can kill without dirtying their hands or exposing themselves to imminent danger . . . many Arabs and Muslims, even if they are horrified by the nature of the suicide bomber's attacks on innocent civilians, do not see such attacks as being any more horrible than the slow, methodological killing of *their* innocents by the powerful. [2003, p. 170]

Beginning with the lived experience of the subjects under consid-eration, the perpetrator of violence is seen as typically trapped, unheard and overwhelmed *by something*: the "terrorist" is then perceived as any human being responding in the way humans do respond to exceptional circumstances. This concern with the detail of context and history, I think, accords more closely with psycho-therapeutic approaches to the study of violence in general.

Various socio-political explanations have been advanced to explain the widely perceived bias towards Israel in Western policy in the Middle East (e.g., Chomsky, 1999; Mearsheimer & Walt, 2006; Said, 1997). Here, I am concerned with the psychological factors involved, insofar as discussions about Israel/Palestine raise more complex emotions than other comparable situations. If I were to conclude that, following Touma-Sliman, "conquest" may be a more accurate word than "conflict" to describe current realities, I would still refrain from using such a term, in part because it might alien-ate otherwise interested readers, but most of all out of an anxiety powerful enough to interfere with my wish to be candid. If I take this anxiety seriously I find it contains personal elements—the associations to it are my own, relating to my personal history. But I do not believe that it is in this sense neurotic, some idiosyncratic creation. Rather, it seems to me to relate to a psychological dynamic that is deeply social, and to understand it, I would argue, one has to "take the group seriously" (Dalal, 1998).

Anxiety, rule breaking, and the ethics of psychotherapy

It is into the matrix described above—an interlocking system of defences against guilt—that one steps, I believe, when participating in a consideration of the Israel/Palestine situation at a public level. To speak—to transgress the terms of this social complex—conflicts with the wish to conform and raises anxious questions: how will I be perceived, isn't this breaking the rules? In particular, isn't this contravening the expectations my peers would have of me as a psychotherapist?

One might think that our professional formation would act as an antidote to this anxiety. Our work, after all, specifically involves challenging that which is presented to us as fact. With each new clinical relationship we enter into a co-constructed world whose parameters will be largely determined by the patient's disturbance, and where we shall be under pressure to conform to its rules and taboos. Yet we know we are of use only if we break the rules by making them conscious from a position of respect and independence. To "think the unthinkable" is a meaningless phrase unless it includes a capacity to question received wisdom.

However, according to both Volkan and Dalal, the unconscious is inherently conservative, and the failure of our discipline to grasp this has meant that our theory and clinical practice tend to naturalize the status quo rather than interpret it (Dalal, 2002, pp. 64–66; Volkan, 2004, pp. 7, 11). Dalal, in his work on the racialization of the unconscious, describes how relationships of inequality and subordination are internalized as natural rather than contingent. As well as personal anxiety that may arise when challenging such norms, group responses will come into play: marginalization, stigmatization, the identification of the critic with a rejected outgroup, and the employment of "gossip" to delegitimize criticism (Dalal, 2002, pp. 190–198).[25]

Lack of clarity about the ethical basis of psychotherapeutic work perhaps reflects and reinforces a conformism that undermines clinicians' imaginative capacities. Codes of ethics frame clinical obligations, but the profession has nothing equivalent to the physicians'

Hippocratic Oath, with its imposing absolutes. Instead, by some process, a loosely defined neutrality has come to be regarded as an analytic ideal, perhaps discouraging professional engagement with some of the major social challenges of the last century.[26]

The question of neutrality only arises where less conventional positions are taken. Hanna Segal was worried that if "we . . . can hide behind the shield of neutrality" this could blunt the profession's capacity to engage in issues of moral concern (Segal, 1987, p. 9). Emanuel Berman, an Israeli analyst, attributes psychoanalysts' silence in the face of Nazism to "their illusory 'neutrality', which was really avoidance of the issues" (Berman, 2002, p. 178). He was urging that therapists should abandon such ideas as would impede their need to address issues such as the Israel/Palestine case. The *IJPA* reviewer said of the book in which Berman's comments appeared that: "The nine contributors . . . share a far from neutral point of view. . . . The book portrays a harsh, unflattering portrait, which some might find difficult to accept" (Levy, 2003, p. 1642). What made this book distinctive, I think, was that contributions were based on history rather than myth; moreover, the asymmetrical nature of the conflict was acknowledged, and there was no presumption that the aspirations of one national group trumped the rights of another.

The force of received opinion can be seen where this notion of non-partisanship is advocated, as in the *IJPA*'s "Special Editorial" referred to previously. In this and other instances where "neutrality" is given as a reason not to delve into an issue where the assumptions and beliefs of one perspective clearly predominate, such neutrality could reasonably, although paradoxically, be seen merely as a code designed to preserve the status quo.

But even if "neutrality" was cleansed of partisan content, could it then be an appropriate guide to the profession, can it provide "the basis of responsible commitment" as described by Black (2011, pp. 162–179)? Laplanche and Pontalis call neutrality "one of the defining characteristics of the attitude of the analyst" and quote Freud to the effect that one should not "[behave] like the representative or advocate of some contending party" (Laplanche & Pontalis, 1973, p. 271). This, however, refers to the analyst's clinical function where neutrality is a stance designed to deter the analyst from allying with one psychic structure against another. Clinical neutrality is the *application*, I would argue, of a universalist ethic, appropriate to the clinician's openness to encountering the patient in *all* his or her aspects, thereby promoting psychic health and development. In the clinical sphere, neutrality is subversive, providing optimum conditions for the repressed to find its voice.

Extended beyond the consulting room, neutrality could, however, provide a cover for amorality disguising itself as "fairness" or "impartiality". Dalal is suspicious of any scientific approach that seeks to be above the "dirty" and uncomfortable world of politics. As "power relations are part of the fabric of human existence", he writes, politics is an intrinsic aspect of our psychic lives. "[It] is not the politicization of events that needs to be questioned," he argues, "rather it is the impulse to de-politicize that needs to be examined" (Dalal, 1998, p. 113). Here, the "impulse to de-politicize" becomes an ideological element designed to cover up unequal power dynamics by delegitimizing dialogues at the point where these asymmetries become an object of reflection.

It would be uncontentious to state that adherence to the truth, as far as it can be perceived, and respect for the personality are core psychoanalytic values. No clinician is perfect (or perfectly analysed), and psychotherapists bring into their work a variable mix of personal and social "imperfections". Insofar as these distort perceptions of the other, they contradict and are contrary to the work's core purpose, and it is incumbent upon practitioners to struggle to minimize their impact. Could a key aspect of Freud's achievement be described as the humanization of aspects of our nature that had formerly been dismissed as alien—that mental illness is a meaningful expression of our individuality rather than an indication of hereditary disease or debilitation? Conversely, we are troubled by moments when psychoanalytic writers concur with, rather than interpret, the capacity of Western culture to objectify others as "primitive" and "uncivilized" (Dalal, 1988; Freud, 1912–13).

What I am proposing is that relativism and essentialism have no place in our ethical foundations and that our outlook could be more consciously based on universalist foundations.[27] At its core, universalism is an insistence that no person should be dehumanized. Relativism, essentialism, and particularism all admit the notion that one group might have more value than another. While any group, in its frailty, may tend towards such depravity, it is the responsibility of all collectively to defend and promote a belief in human equality.[28]

After World War II, newly invigorated multinational institutions began the process of clarifying and revising standards of international behaviour.[29] This represented a significant victory for universalism[30] over moral relativism and particularism—the assertion that there are no moral principles applicable across the board. The Declaration of Human Rights was *Universal*; the Covenants on Human Rights "also speak in universal terms: 'everyone' has the right to liberty, 'all persons' are entitled to equal protection, 'no one' shall be subject to torture, 'everyone' has the right to an adequate standard of living" (Steiner & Alston, 2000, p. 367). Lord Alderdice has described "an end to empires, the growth of democracy and the clarification of reasonable and fair law and economic rules" as "a communal equivalent to the search for personal freedom and boundary setting which is familiar to us in the clinical setting" (Covington, Williams, Arundale, & Knox, 2002, p. 6). These developments, surely, would be welcomed by most psychotherapists as consistent with and supportive of the core values of the profession itself. We would want to put our psychic equipment fully at the disposal of our patients' process, something that cannot be possible if we are secretly feeling superior to the patient, or imagining some essential difference in the nature of their and our humanity (David Black, personal communication).

Concluding comments

George Awad, a Canadian psychoanalyst of Palestinian heritage, asked:

> What can we say to those who have been subjected to brutal occupation, reduced to living their lives in subhuman conditions, where there is no future . . .? Why has world opinion tolerated and seemingly supported the extremely desperate situation in Palestine for over half a century? I suspect the answers to these questions, if ever they are to come, will be quite painful to examine. [Awad, 2003, p. 172]

How is it, Awad is surely asking, that we in the West have been so complicit in this situation that we cannot even recognize what we have done? I have argued that part of the explanation lies in an unconscious pact by which Israel and the West, with their distinctive but linked histories of dehumanization—the West towards the Jews, the Israelis towards the Palestinians—have each allotted roles to the other in their large-group ways of thinking (Volkan's "tents") which in turn have enabled them to avoid the profound guilt that otherwise threatens them. In doing this, they have established a kind of couple relationship, the unconscious terms of which have prohibited a relationship emerging between the West and the Palestinians. It has prevented a genuine triangulation between these three entities from taking place. This has led the West, as a whole, into a repetition of the "bystander" position (Cohen, 2001) that characterized its response to fascism two generations ago.

It is unclear how whole societies or cultures mourn their traumas in such a way as to avoid the compulsion to repeat, or how they can be helped to do so, but I am sure that an important contribution is made, one way or the other, at the level of ideology. "The use of defence mechanisms is manifest at the collective level by the development of a system of societal beliefs" (Halperin, Bar-Tal, Sharvit, Rosler, & Raviv, 2010, p. 10). Ideologies carry representations of the past, institutionalize the lessons drawn, organize the emotional lives of their adherents. The reason I emphasize the importance of universalism is that it is a philosophical approach with profound psycho-political consequences,[31] which at least constitutes a bulwark against the blandishments of heavily ideological dominant discourses. The West continues to pay lip-service to universalism, while in practice—and for more reasons than have been adumbrated here—often abandoning it in favour of more ethnocentric approaches.

To maximize our potential to contribute towards a just and peaceful future, I believe we need to make our own "sober assessment" of the situation, as Freud did in 1930,[32] unencumbered by misplaced guilt or misguided notions of neutrality, and informed by an explicit universalist ethic. Awad clearly feels he was writing during an era where this could not happen. I suggest that his frustration relates to coherent and recalcitrant psychic structures that still inhibit our capacity to reflect fully on the conflict. Yet such structures are a product of history and subject to dynamic transformation. The thesis advanced here could have validity for the present, or it may describe a reality that is changing. This chapter itself may be a product of a shift that has already begun.[33]

Notes

This paper was first published in the *British Journal of Psychotherapy*, Volume 27, Number 4, November 2011 (John Wiley & Sons Ltd).

1. The inverted commas here draw attention to the fact that "sides", used to describe as complex a situation as exists in Israel/Palestine, is always a clumsy metaphor. If it suggested that the conflict was one between two national groups, this would both obscure the ideological issues involved and itself suggest a particular ideological interpretation. It could imply two clearly articulated political programmes broadly representative of opinion in each religious or ethnic group, when the spectrum of opinion is broad in each community and there are significant numbers of people on one "side" who support the other—Israelis who support the call for a boycott of Israel, for example (see http://boycottisrael.info). We also know that in a relationship in crisis the development of polarized perceptions of the other, the feeling that the two are divided by fundamentals, is itself an aspect of the problem, and is a factor that makes reconciliation all the more difficult.

2. Source: New Israel Fund (www.nif.org/index.php?option=com_content&view=article&id=537). The event was hardly covered in the British media: see BBC (www.bbc.co.uk/news/world-middle-east-10777040) and the *Guardian* (www.guardian.co.uk/commentisfree/2010/jul/28/ethnic-cleansing-israeli-negev).

3. A search for "Western" on PEP Web produced many thousands of results, suggesting that this is a widely acknowledged conceptual category widely used in public debate. In this, I consider "the West" as operative on many levels—as a culture or group of interlinked cultures, as an aspect of the identity of those belonging to those cultures (not necessarily applying to all those resident in Western countries), and as a concentration of economic and military power. Within this umbrella concept I see many other forms of group identification operating, including national ones—"Israeli" or "British" belong to but can be considered individually or in relation to "the West" as a whole.

4. Ideologies that reinforce perceptions of the conflict as the inevitable expression of the irreconcilable needs of distinct national groups. It seems as though we hear little of the range of initiatives that span the communal divide, offering perhaps models for a shared future based on justice and mutual acknowledgement, among them the Bereaved Families Forum (www.theparentscircle.org), Combatants for Peace (http://cfpeace.org/), Israeli Committee Against House Demolitions (www.icahd.org), and Physicians for Human Rights-Israel (www.phr.org.il/default.asp?PageID=4).

5. Volkan has used his theories to study international conflicts, including those in the Balkans and Cyprus. Alternative schema have been employed by other authors to offer other applied examples of large-group dynamics, e.g. Dalal's (2002) account of the racialization of Western culture and Fletchman Smith's (2000) work on the transgenerational consequences of the Atlantic slave trade.

6. Vamık Volkan: Turkish Cypriot/American psychoanalyst, published widely on aspects of individual psychoanalysis and inter-communal conflict, former Director of Centre for the Study of Mind and Human Interaction. He

has published a selection of his papers online at www.vamikvolkan.com where most of the papers referred to here can be found. The references in this chapter are to the online versions and hence appear without page numbers.

7. For two films that document the role of past traumas in the socialization of young Israelis, see *Defamation* (2009, directed by Yoav Shamir) and *Avenge But One of My Two Eyes* (2005, directed by Avi Mograbi).

8. Regarding Israel, a recent socio-psychological study conveys the same idea: "The degree to which society members adopt ideological and religious beliefs that justify maintaining the occupation may vary, leading to differences in the degree to which they experience psychological difficulties resulting from the occupation. . . . Nevertheless, we maintain that . . . the societal challenges and mechanisms presented below affect a large majority of society members, characterize the group as a whole, and provide an orientation for the group's behaviour in the context of occupation" (Halperin et al., 2010).

9. Schama's words appeared in a critical review of Sand (2009), *The Invention of the Jewish People*, an attempt by an Israeli historian to diminish narcissistic investment in aspects of Israel's large-group identity: to emphasize the mythological status of traumas such as the Exile, to historicize the concept of a "Jewish people", and to distinguish between the fantasy of a "Jewish State" and the reality of the Israeli nation. The latter, he suggests, can only be normalized by an abandonment of its ethnocentric ideology.

10. This sentence appears on the wall above the exhibits in the Yad Vashem Holocaust museum in Jerusalem.

11. A parallel process that occurred in the even more traumatic confrontation of German society to its racism following the collapse of the Third Reich. "[Gottfried] Appy describes the inability to mourn after the collapse of the Third Reich as one of the most frightening symptoms of German society. The horror over the inconceivable reality of the organized mass extermination of millions of people resulted in a complete repudiation of any kind of identification with Nazism. But splitting off Nazism and discarding it as belonging to a kind of psychopathological aberration and perversion of a criminal minority resulted in German society not acknowledging the minor or passive forms of identification with the Nazi ideology, which had been the case for the majority" (Granek, 1994, p. 635).

12. As Jeff Halper quipped talking to Jacqueline Rose, "Christians have to ask our permission before they can criticize Israel" (www.veoh.com/watch/v14134683E6HdGEz3?h1=In+conversation+Jeff+Halper+and+Jacqueline+Rose).

13. Yitzhak Laor (2009) has offered further reasons for European "semitophilia" and memorialization of the Holocaust: avoiding our guilt for slavery and the colonialism of the past, and serving as a cover for Islamophobia and the colonialism of the present.

14. See Israeli director Yoav Shamir's documentary on anti-Semitism, *Defamation*, for discussion of the socialization of Israeli youth in this regard.

15. "In the Israeli–Palestinian context, the delegitimization of the Palestinians did not begin with the occupation. The Arab residents of Palestine were labelled by Jewish newcomers . . . as primitive, uncivilized, savage and backward . . ." (Halperin et al., 2010).

16. Halperin et al. argue that the necessity to avoid guilt through the mechanisms of denial, repression, avoidance, and projection have driven Israeli attitudes towards the Palestinians such that: "as a result, [Israelis] remain unconscious of wrongdoings and offensive behaviour towards the occupied populations—all violations of accepted values—and therefore cannot experience guilt or pangs of conscience . . ." (Halperin et al., 2010). Furthermore, they argue that: "The attribution of hostility to the occupied group enables the perception of the ingroup's aggressive actions as self-defence. As a result, any guilt or distress that might have emerged had the opponent been perceived as more humane is reduced."

17. Gideon Levy, one of the only Israeli journalists to report from the West Bank and Gaza, has repeatedly stated that his work is intended to reveal the consequences of Israel's dehumanization of the Palestinians, which, he states, "has spread to every sector of Israeli society": see *Haaretz*, 29 May 2011 (www. haaretz.com/print-edition/opinion/daily-dehumanization-1.109322). See also Levy's interview with Johann Hari (www.huffingtonpost.com/johann-hari/ the-most-hated-man-in-isr_b_737411.html

18. The issue is not the unavailability of date concerning the conditions of life for Palestinians under Israeli control—international bodies, including the United Nations and Amnesty International, and both Palestinian and Israeli human rights organizations (e.g., Al Haq and B'Tselem), produce detailed reports that provide the relevant information. It is the apparent inconsequentiality of such reporting that presents us with a paradox.

19. A further indication of this might be seen in the way that discourse on anti-Semitism has often been over-determined by political agendas. Rather than imagining that anti-Semitism might be a factor in the whole range of attitudes towards Israel, it is asserted, even given quasi-official legitimization, that anti-Zionist opinions particularly are to be viewed as anti-Semitic or are particularly suspect in this regard (EUMC, 2005; Butler, 2003; Klug, 2004; Lerman, 2010).

20. General Director of Women against Violence and winner of the 2008 NIF Human Rights award for her work in combating racism.

21. See www.ofek-groups.org/en/index.php?option=com_content&task= view&id=43&Itemid=65

22. In 2002 Cherie Blair had to apologize for declaring that suicide bombers might be acting out of despair, and in 2004 Jenny Tonge lost her job on the Liberal Democrat front bench for expressing a similar view. In neither case was terrorism condoned or supported: the offence was to have humanized the person behind the outrage by implying that such behaviour could be seen to have meaning in context. This, one would think, would have to be the hallmark of any psychoanalytic contribution: their views are precisely those expressed by Ofer Grosbard (2003, pp. 96, 114). Consider also the stage play *Rachel*, based on the letters Rachel Corrie mailed to her family while undertaking solidarity work in Jenin, during which time she was killed by an Israeli bulldozer. Hostility in the United States resulted in the play's withdrawal, and its London production was the cause of highly emotive criticism. An attempt to represent the influence of history on Israeli attitudes towards the Palestinians, in *Seven Jewish Children: A Play for Gaza*, resulted in similar denunciations.

23. As an illustration, the predicament of Gilad Schalit, the Israeli soldier held by the Hamas government in Gaza, is given prominence in the media, while that of the many detainees in Israeli prisons likewise denied due legal process is not (see www.addameer.org/etemplate.php?id=342). Commentators explain Operation Cast Lead as a response to the rockets fired from Gaza that killed 28 people between 2001 and 2009. The many more Gazan civilians killed during that time appear to go unrecognized (see http://old.btselem.org/statistics/english/Casualties.asp). This footnote exemplifies a dilemma in writing about such a controversial subject. On the one hand, the need to include information to substantiate a point made in the text; on the other, the possibility that such statements might, by appearing crudely political, seem inconsistent with thinking psychoanalytically about a topic requiring sensitivity and tact. In a sense, the chapter offers a theorization of this dilemma.

24. In another, they have been compared with Gentiles who protected Jews during the Holocaust (Kane, 2005, p. 949).

25. "At the present time, an analyst who ventures beyond the confines of the armchair–couch relationship may well find himself confronted with 'the prohibition against thought issued by religion' of which Freud spoke, the first to level such reproaches being fellow psychoanalysts who have apparently forgotten that Freud's aim was not so much to care for the sick as to understand 'the riddles of the world'" (Chasseguet-Smirgel, 1990, p. 167).

26. There have been frequent references to the absence of a psychoanalytic response to the rise of fascism during the 1930s. More recently, using the search engine on the PEP Web archive, I found only one article published prior to 1994 that addressed the psychological consequences of Apartheid in South Africa for its victims (Straker, 1988). Of the 45 articles that mentioned "Vietnam" before the end of US military involvement there in 1973, none contributed to an understanding of the war or considered its humanitarian impact; those that offered a social analysis were concerned with understanding the dynamics of student rebellion, taking the position that the protest movement was the manifest expression of deeper, latent motivations. This has not meant refraining from an expression of political views that could be said to form a part of "received opinion", perhaps determined by what the liberal consensus endorses at any particular time: after the end of the Vietnam War and the overthrow of the system of Apartheid in South Africa, negative references to both became commonplace and did not need to be justified.

27. David Black cites an application of this principle in his exploration of values and moral judgements: "The psychoanalyst Erik Erikson spoke of Gandhi's struggle to attempt to overcome the tendency to create what Erikson called a pseudo-science, some group smaller than the human species as a whole, usually one to which we belong ourselves, that will have greater importance than all the rest" (Black, 2011, p. 168).

28. The conviction that "human rights are universal and indivisible" informs "A time to speak out", the declaration of the group Independent Jewish Voices (http://ijv.org.uk/declaration).

29. Landmarks include the United Nations Charter (1945), the Declaration of Human Rights (1948), and the Convention on the Prevention and Punishment of the Crime of Genocide (1948). A revised version of the Fourth

Geneva Convention (1949) has particular relevance, though Israel argues that its principles do not apply to Gaza and the West Bank as they deny these are under Occupation. Also of relevance to Israel/Palestine are Conventions on the Elimination of All Forms of Racial Discrimination (1966); the Suppression and Punishment of Apartheid (1973, which defined as a crime "inhuman acts committed for the purpose of establishing and maintaining domination by one racial group of persons over any other racial group of persons and systematically oppressing them"); against Torture (1983); and on the Rights of the Child (1989).

30. The philosophical doctrine that holds that ethical systems should be applied universally—that is, to everyone, regardless of culture, race, sex, religion, nationality, sexuality, or any other distinguishing feature.

31. Carlo Strenger (2011), an Israeli professor of clinical psychology, considers universalism to be a crucial factor in the alienation of many European and American Jews from Israel.

32. The full text of Freud's letter to H. Koffler declining to endorse Zionism is published in Bunzl and Beit-Hallahmi (2002, p. 159).

33. Over recent years the Oxford Research Group, with the participation of a number of psychotherapists, has continued work similar to that undertaken by Volkan with a focus on Israel/Palestine. Its papers provide an example of fresh thinking that has yet to permeate the wider society (see www.oxfordresearch-group.org.uk/projects/human_security_and_middle_east).

CHAPTER ELEVEN

The August 2011 Riots—them and us

Frank Lowe

"The condition of the individual-subject is paradoxical. The organizational qualities of the subject demand that we associate antagonistic concepts: exclusion and inclusion, the I, the they, and the it. This requires what I have called complex thinking, which is to say a thinking that is capable of unifying concepts which repel one another and are otherwise catalogued and isolated in separate compartments."

Morin (2008)

"Whilst we might thirst after the truth, 'to understand' is, more often than not to suffer. Thus whilst they might poison the mind, lies preserve us from conscious suffering."

Paul Hoggett (1992b, p. 61)

The August 2011 Riots started on 4 August in Tottenham, as a result of the suspicious shooting by the police of a young black man, Mark Duggan. The police's failure to engage with his family and supporters who went to the police station for answers became the trigger for the riot. From Tottenham, the rioting quickly spread over the next six days to 66 different areas across England and Wales. Five people died, at least 16 others were injured, and many lost their homes, businesses, and priceless possessions. It was estimated that 13,000–15,000 people took part in the riots and that overall the riots cost the country approximately half a billion pounds. Over 4,000 people were arrested, and about 1,483 were found guilty as charged (Riots, Communities and Victims Panel, 2012).

The causes of the August 2011 Riots were complex, and I think psychoanalysis can only help to contribute to our understanding of the riots rather than to provide an explanation. In this chapter, I aim to explore the idea put forward by Prime Minister David Cameron that the riots are the product of "pockets of our society that are not only broken, but frankly sick". But exactly what sickness is Cameron referring to—or what does he mean when he says the rioters are sick? I shall argue that to understand the "sickness" requires an examination not only of the rioters (them), but also of those who did not riot (us). I also put forward the idea that the riots were symptomatic of a malaise and, in addition, were an unconscious request for its recognition, understanding, and thoughtful containment.

Complexity theory is based on the view that all dimensions of existence are inseparable or interconnected (Morin, 2008). There is growing recognition of our tendency to avoid complexity in favour of simple or one-dimensional explanations for human behaviour. Morin argues that to take seriously the complexity of things will involve acknowledging that we can never be completely sure, and that we always need to work with varying degrees of uncertainty. The ideas put forward in this chapter are far from certain. I hope, however, that they engender a better appreciation of the complexity of the riots and, more importantly, stimulate more thinking and understanding about them and us.

I was in a holiday resort in Turkey, with mainly French and German tourists, when we heard a news report on the television about riots in London. The images on the screen of burning shops and looting were not those that my fellow tourists associated with England—the green and pleasant land of Queen Elizabeth, the Houses of Parliament, Wimbledon, Oxford and Cambridge, and so forth. The scenes of Tottenham and the rioters were disturbing, at many levels, not least because they jarred with the popular image of England and the English, but they were upsetting, embarrassing, even shameful to me, and they demanded an explanation.

The rioters—a sick pocket of society, a breed apart?

In the early days of the riots, there was an outpouring of contempt for the rioters. Government ministers, other public figures, and the media talked about the riots as a product of criminal gangs, feral children and teenagers, feckless and irresponsible parents, and young thugs who shared a culture of entitlement[1] and a disdain for responsibility and hard work. On 10 August 2011, David Cameron reassured the country that law and order will be restored on our streets. He said:

> It is all too clear that we have a big problem with gangs in our country. For too long there had been a lack of focus on the complete lack of respect shown by these groups of thugs. I'm clear that they are in no way representative of the vast majority of young people in our country who despise them, frankly, as much as the rest of us do. But there are pockets of our society that are not just broken, but frankly sick. When we see children as young as 12 and 13 looting and laughing, when we see the disgusting sight of an injured young man with people pretending to help him while they are robbing him, it is clear that there are things that are badly wrong with our society. For me, the root cause of this mindless selfishness is the same thing I have spoken about for years. It is a complete lack of responsibility in parts of our society, people allowed to feel the world owes them something, that their rights outweigh their responsibilities and their actions do not have consequences. [*Daily Telegraph*, 10 August][2]

Cameron seemed to be saying that the rioters are sick because they are mindless, selfish thugs who lack compassion, respect, and responsibility and feel the world owes them something.

Tony Blair, prime minister from 1997 to 2007, contends that neither social deprivation nor a lack of personal responsibility was the cause of the riots. In *The Observer* on 20 August 2011, he argued that Britain, like "virtually all" developed nations, needs to deal with a group of people who are "beyond the pale". In Blair's view, the rioters are alienated, disaffected youth who are outside the social mainstream and who live in a culture at odds with any canons of proper behaviour. They are not symptomatic of society at large, and Britain as a whole is not in the grip of "moral decline". "These young people are simply the product of families that are profoundly dysfunctional, operating on completely different terms from the rest of society, either middle class or poor."

Blair argues that what is needed is intervention family by family and a reform of criminal justice around antisocial behaviour, organized crime, persistent offenders, and gangs.

The Riots, Communities and Victims Panel set up by Prime Minister David Cameron reported in December 2012 that the riots were not carried out by children or teenagers or gang members, but by mostly young adults. "Our conclusion is that there was no single cause of the riots and no single group was responsible" (Riots, Communities and Victims Panel, 2012, p. 25). Tony Blair and David Cameron might also both note that the Panel's survey of local authorities found that only 5% thought there was an overlap between troubled families and riot families. I think the extreme demonization and pathologization of the rioters and their parents, which occurred during and shortly after the rioting, suggested the predominance of what Melanie Klein would describe as paranoid-schizoid thinking. The splitting of society into good and bad, responsible and irresponsible parents, law-abiding majority and criminal minority, involved the projection of all bad feelings into groups on one side of the split, and an idealization of the other groups as all good.

Paranoid-schizoid thinking: them and us

The rage of the rioters aroused anxiety about annihilation. According to Melanie Klein (1946), when under threat people are more prone to operate in the paranoid-schizoid position, where they project all their unbearable feelings onto the other and then can feel guilt-free, even self-righteous. During and shortly after the riots, a paranoid-schizoid state of mind seems to have predominated, and the society became one that was made up of the rioters and the non-rioters, them and us. They, the rioters, were seen as bad, immoral, irresponsible, criminals, or "frankly sick" in Cameron's words, and we, the non-rioters, were seen as different—that is, the normal, law-abiding, decent majority who aren't like them but who are in a position to judge and condemn. In this state of mind, the rioters were dehumanized and were seen in Tony Blair's words as "a breed apart". Although Cameron and Blair use different words, they both regard the rioters as different from the rest of us—a sick pocket of society. I would like to suggest that while those who rioted were not angels, they were through projection being asked to also carry for the dominant groups in society, and for society as a whole, unwanted feelings such as guilt and shame about their own lack of responsibility, compassion, and destructiveness.

The index patient: the dynamic context

Psychoanalysis is based on the idea that the individual's behaviour is affected by unconscious factors. An individual's personal unconscious, however, is influenced by his or her parents, family, and social environment. There is, though, a tendency within our society to ascribe a person's behaviour simply to personal factors (an approach that conveniently obscures or denies its roots in family, community, and society), and it is much more difficult to demonstrate how it may be linked to family, group, or wider societal dynamics. Central to psychoanalytic practice is the idea that one unconscious can communicate with the unconscious of another (Freud, 1912e), and there is increasing recognition that unconscious intersubjective processes affect the psyches of individuals much more than has been appreciated (Brown, 2011).

In my clinical experience, many young people who, for example, are referred to CAMHS struggle frequently not only with their individual problems, but also with their relationships with their families—primarily parents—and/or their social context. Often the young person is unconsciously bringing their parents, family, and sometimes school or society for treatment. From this perspective, the young person is accurately referred to as the index patient—that is, an indicator, sign, or emblem of a family or wider systemic problem.

Drawing on Winnicott's thinking, Teresa Bailey has written an interesting clinical paper in which she points out that there is no such thing as an adolescent, because their parents are always present in our work, even when we are working alone with a young person (Bailey, 2006, p. 180). Like the adolescent, parents and families are often unprepared for the loss of childhood, the pain of separation, and the aggression and emotional drama of the teenage years. Bailey points out that the intrapsychic and interpersonal dynamics of parents impact on the adolescent and their functioning in many different ways. There are a number of common risks that parents face, such as letting go too quickly (underestimating the need of the adolescent for supervision and guidance), as sometimes parents can feel resentful about still being needed. On the other hand, parents can hold on too long because of their own personal needs, such as for company or as a way of keeping the parental couple together. Some parents may not have worked through their own adolescent conflicts, and this can often unhelpfully dominate their approach to parenting their adolescent children, being unable to see their child's different needs and circumstances, and repeating mistakes made by their own parents.

The adolescent's growing independence and freedom to explore and experiment can also be envied by parents or be experienced as rejecting, and parents can become depressed or wish to hit back at them. Bailey stresses that whatever feelings the adolescents may stir up in their parents, they do need their parents to support their development, and sometimes parents need help to understand this vital role (Bailey, 2006). The difficult demands of adolescents are more likely to be met by parents who are able to find what Britton (1989) calls the "third" position internally or externally through links with others who can help them think about and adjust to the emotional needs and demands of their adolescents.

Vignette

A is a 15-year-old young man who lives with his 11-year-old sister and parents. He was referred to CAMHS because he was described as out of control and having a serious "anger management" problem. He had smashed up the living room in his house and had suffered serious cuts to his arms and hands in the process. His parents felt they could no longer cope with his behaviour, and they wanted him sorted out otherwise they might have to ask him to leave.

At the first appointment, I met with A individually, and a colleague met with his parents. A said he was "pissed off" with his parents and his little "goody two-shoes sister". His parents he described as over-controlling, because they objected to him smoking cannabis, which in his view was no worse than alcohol, and they would also prevent him from going to parties or, if they did allow him to go, wanted him to come home at ridiculously early times, like 11 or 12 o'clock. In subsequent appointments I learnt that at age 11, against his wishes, A was sent to a private school in another borough and, as a result, had lost contact with primary-school friends and had found it hard to settle at the private school. He couldn't relate to the children in the school because none came from his area, they were very middle class if not upper class, and most had been at the school since the age of 5. He felt an outsider at school and an outsider in his home area. By Year 9, age 13, unknown to his parents, he was depressed and was having suicidal thoughts. He began to smoke cannabis and became close to a few boys in the school who also smoked. He thought his parents were hopeless: they never really listened, and his father was never home because he worked all the time. Three years ago the family had moved into a bigger house, in a nicer part of their area, but he thought his mother was unhappy but always pretended otherwise. The whole thing is pointless, he would often say.

The parents presented as a united couple, confused about A's anger and increasingly unpleasant and irresponsible behaviour towards themselves and his sister. My colleague learnt that father was a successful plumber who had opened a plumbing shop but also continued to work as a plumber. Mother used to be bank clerk, and after A was born she began to work at home, managing her husband's business accounts and administration. Mr C was a charming and confident man who filled the room, and Mrs C was quiet and polite and tended to allow Mr C to speak for both of them. Mr C thought that in contrast to his own childhood, A had had it all and had probably been spoilt—had got things too easily and lacked discipline. However, their daughter was doing well. She had just started at the same school and seemed to be thriving. The two children, they said, were like chalk and cheese.

The work comprised individual psychotherapy appointments with A, parent appointments, and family appointments. However, as the work went on, Mr C often missed appointments or arrived extremely late. Mr C would be openly confronted by A in the family sessions, whose excuses and justifications became increasingly embarrassing. Mrs C, who had never challenged her husband, began to share her frustration and despair about him never giving the family priority. In a parents' appointment, while waiting for Mr C to arrive, she broke down and talked about her unhappiness, how she had a drink problem and had had an affair. The therapist felt compromised by having this secret information and, as Mrs C refused to share this information with her husband, encouraged her to seek individual help.

While on the surface appearing to be successful and thriving, this family was fundamentally unhappy and fragile. A's trashing of the family's expensive—but, we discovered, unused—living room was a symbolic communication about the lack of life, joy, and togetherness in the family. He had rung an alarm bell for himself and the family in his extreme destructive and self-destructive outburst. Consequently, the family were brought together to "sort out" A, but in effect he had arranged for the whole family to address its difficulties. In his individual therapy, A acknowledged how lost he was and how he felt locked on to a self-destructive trajectory. Cannabis, which had initially brought him some relief, had increasingly become a problem: he felt he had become highly dependent on the drug, it was adversely affecting his concentration, and he was putting himself at risk of being excluded from school or being arrested because of the activities of some of his associates. A was not conscious of his mother's depression and alcoholism, but I think he unconsciously knew that something vital had been lost in the family, that his mother was very unhappy, that his father needed to be around more, and that some urgent radical change in the family was needed.

I trust that this case has illustrated how an individual's behaviour can be a product of personal factors as well as of dynamic forces within the family and social context, and that much of this can be unconscious to those involved. We need to create a thinking space that enables thinking about the adolescent, the parental couple, the family and the social context, and their anxieties and defences. Such a space would ideally bring together all parties involved to consider their difficulties, with the support of a therapist who allied him/herself to seeking emotional truth and understanding and not allying too much with either the adolescent, the parent, or society, as this is likely to put the work and the possibility of change at risk.

I shall now try to show that the rioters of August 2011 can be thought about as index patients—an index of a deep malaise.

Riots as an index/symptom of malaise

Riots and revolt has been, for the past six centuries, a traditional
way of expressing and redressing the grievances of the poor and
powerless. [Webber, 1981, p. 245]

There have been riots by the poor and the powerless in Britain
for centuries as a way of expressing their pain and grievances.
Much has been written about the difference between the 2011 riots
and previous riots, leading many to regard the 2011 riots as not a
political riot or organized social protest, with a clear purpose or
message to deliver, but as simply mindless violence, criminality,
or "irrational outbursts of destructive if not self-destructive violence" (Žižek, 2011). However, in my view, the August 2011 Riots,
while unique in many ways, did also share elements in common
with previous riots—for example, the 1985 riots in Tottenham and
the 1981 and 2001 riots in Brixton, Toxteth, and Manchester. Many
reviews of riots (e.g., Bunyan, 1981) have shown that riots tend to
take place in deprived areas, are carried out predominantly by the
poor and powerless, and are triggered by a breakdown of communication between the police and local communities. These factors
also apply to the August 2011 Riots.

According to the *Guardian* and the London School of Economics
(*Guardian* & LSE, 2011) and the Riots, Communities and Victims
Panel (2012), the majority of the August 2011 rioters came from poor
neighbourhoods, with 41% of suspects living in one of the top 10%
of most-deprived places in the country. The data also show that
66% of neighbourhoods where the accused lived became poorer
between 2007 and 2010. Researchers found that in almost all of
the worst-affected areas, youth unemployment and child poverty
were significantly higher than the national average, while education attainment was significantly lower. The adverse impact of not
being at work on both physical and mental health has been grossly
underestimated (see Davies, 2011; Waddell, 1999).

People do not always know the full reasons for their behaviour,
or are not able to articulate what they are aware of. In fact, people
tend to communicate their most unmanageable/unbearable feelings
through projection into others, and it is only through the recipient
feeling these feelings—that is, if he or she can contain them—that
they can begin to make sense of the feelings communicated. As

Moylan (1994, p. 54) put it, we sometimes "communicate only with the primitive unconscious language of projective identification". Violence can be a way of the rioters evacuating into others their unbearable experiences—creating fear, vulnerability, and loss in the victim.

The case of A illustrated that there were conscious and unconscious reasons for his destructive and self-destructive behaviour. Understanding the reasons for this should include studying the dynamic context as well as listening carefully, not just to the content of what the rioters say, but also the way it is said and the atmosphere it creates—the feelings it produces in you, the listener. Noticing our experience and reflecting on it can help us gain some notion of what the rioters might have been communicating unconsciously. An examination of the context within which the riots occurred shows the following:

1. A financial crisis, starting in 2007–2008, led to a global economic recession, considered by many as one of the worst recessions since the 1930s. A major factor causing this recession was a credit bonanza driven by greed—in particular, by banks developing more and more high-risk credit and mortgage products, particularly in the United States, and lowering lending standards (otherwise known as the growth of sub-prime markets). When this market collapsed, it led to the collapse of Northern Rock, which had apparently made loans for more than four times what it had in its reserves. Northern Rock and other British banks were eventually rescued by the British taxpayer with loans of upwards of £850 billion.[3]

2. A government that had, in the face of the economic crisis, declared that "we are all in this together" instituted an austerity programme that placed the cost disproportionately on the poorer and weaker members of society (e.g., cutting public services, imposing a pay freeze on public sector workers, reducing tax credits, raising the age of retirement). This programme had been introduced in a country where income inequality had been rising faster than in any other Organisation for Economic Co-operation and Development (OECD) country since 1975. Their data show that the ratio of the average income of the richest 10% to that of the poorest 10% was nearly 12 to 1 (OECD, 2011).

3. A number of reports had noted that social mobility in the UK had stagnated, if not declined, and that people's occupational and economic destinations were increasingly dependent more on their social origins than on their personal ability. In other words, "equality of opportunity" in Britain has deteriorated in the past decade.

4. Youth (young people aged 16–24) unemployment in the UK was 1.04 million (22.5%) in December 2011, the highest it has been since 1986/87. According to the Centre for Social Justice (2011), the number of permanent school exclusions had almost doubled between 1997 and 2007. Klein (1999) argues that changes in the British educational system, such as an increasingly inflexible curriculum and emphasis on exam league tables, have contributed to the increase in school exclusions and disguised exclusions. The Social Exclusion Unit (2000) has pointed out that school exclusion is a risk factor for substance misuse, youth crime, mental health problems, and homelessness and in general is likely to increase a young person's disaffection.

5. Against this background of austerity, widening income inequality, and decreasing social mobility, a number of scandals were exposed that left the public outraged by the actions of those at the top of society who seemed to be self-serving, dishonest, and greedy. They include the parliamentary expenses scandal (June 2009), the Liberal Democrat Party breaking its election pledge to vote against any proposed increase in tuition fees, and the phone hacking of murdered schoolgirl Milly Dowler and victims of the 7/7 London bombings and many other people by Rupert Murdoch's News Corporation subsidiary, News International.

6. Finally, about two weeks before the riots, there were the resignations of two senior police officers, Sir Paul Stephenson, the Commissioner of London's Metropolitan Police Service, and Police Assistant Commissioner John Yates, due to concerns about their close links with News International.

A number of commentators saw the August 2011 Riots as a product of serious dysfunction in wider society. Slavoj Žižek (2011) regarded the manifesto of the Spanish Protest movement against austerity measures as expressing the attitude of many people not only in Spain but in other Western countries as well, including Britain. This manifesto, he reports, states that "Some of us have clearly defined ideologies, others are apolitical, but we are all concerned and angry about the political, economic and social outlook that we see around us: corruption among politicians, businessmen, bankers, leaving us helpless, without a voice" (Žižek, 2011). Claudia Webbe, a social worker who helped set up Operation Trident, a police unit aimed at combating drug-related gun crime, argued that there is no one single underlying cause of the riots, but believed that they were clearly linked to tensions that had arisen over issues ranging from the economy to social deprivation and policing. She saw the riots as a venting of anger about inequality, decades of generational unemployment, poverty, and police stop-and-search—in short, a wake-up call for society.

The role of the police is of particular importance, given their symbolic and actual relationship to the rioters. The police are supposed to be neutral, to enforce the law fairly, and to protect all citizens. But as a result of a number of reports (e.g., Hillsborough Independent Panel, 2012), police neutrality is seen not as an operational reality but more as a part of the legitimizing ideology of a class-dominated society. According to Kushnick (1981), there is a tendency for the police to see criminals as located within deprived poor areas, and consequently they are less concerned with and focused on "white-collar" crimes than with policing poor criminals. This approach tends to lead to the criminalization of the young and disadvantaged, through the stopping and searching of black youths and sections of white working-class youths. It is assumed that most criminality in Britain is a product of the unemployed, poor underclass in deprived areas. The reality is that there are discriminatory police practices that are reinforced by a discriminatory criminal justice system, through the "definition of crime itself, through selective, discretionary and discriminatory law enforcement, through differential access to bail and adequate legal representation, differential conviction and sentencing rates—all adding up to a disproportionate policing and criminalization and imprisonment of poorer members of society" (p. 191).

I think the August 2011 rioters, like Patient A above, can be thought of as index patients. Their behaviour is a symbol of a malaise not just in themselves, but in their families and communities and in society as a whole. In many ways, the rioters' behaviour mirrored the greed, lawlessness, and lack of compassion of bankers, politicians, and the police. Even the *Daily Mail*—not a left-wing paper by any measure—seems to share this view. Its Editorial on 14 October 2011 stated that "the bankers have the same contempt for the law abiding public as those looters and the same sense of entitlement to wealth as the teenagers who smash shop windows to steal flat-screen televisions". But the rioters are not simply an index of the greed, dishonesty, and lack of compassion of those at the top of society such as the bankers and MPs. They are an index of all of us. The financial crisis was also a product of oral greed: a widespread credit culture linked to an increasingly individualistic, narcissistic, and consumerist lifestyle across the whole of society. This is reflected in the decline of communal and mutual organizations (e.g., trade unions and building societies). Instead, there has been and there still is a common preoccupation in our society with individual status, fame, and the ability to participate in consumer markets (Morrow & Richards, 1996).[4] In short the rioters are also an index of our preoccupation with consumerism, with acquiring property, money, success, status, or fame at seemingly any cost. Davies (2011, p. 71) argues that "the culture of capitalism must keep individuals sufficiently dissatisfied that they continue to seek satisfaction from it, but not so dissatisfied that they reject or resist it outright". Advertising plays a key role in this process by subtly instrumentalizing dissatisfaction and unhappiness as a motivation for consumption and dissatisfaction (Davies, 2011). The August 2011 Riots I think say as much about "us", the non–rioters, as they do about "them". There is an old African saying that when one points a finger of blame at someone, there are three other fingers on the same hand that point back at you.

I believe the riots constituted at least in part an unconscious protest, on behalf of all of us, about the lies told by politicians and the media, widening social inequality, and a culture that seems to be driven by feathering one's own nest, consumerism, and the placing of money, power, and status above the welfare of human beings. I shall now go on to argue that the August 2011 Riots were largely adolescent in character and to draw on Donald Winnicott's ideas of "The Antisocial Tendency" (1956) and "Delinquency as a Sign of Hope" (1967) to further explore the meaning of the violence, stealing, and trashing of shops that characterized the riots.

The riots as a communication and a sign of hope

Although the rioters were made up of people of all ages, it was found that the majority of rioters (about 75%) were aged 24 or under. Of those brought before the courts, just under half were aged 18 to 24, with 26% aged between 10 and 17 years old, and only 5% over 40 (*Guardian* & LSE, 2011; Riots, Communities and Victims Panel, 2012). The riots had an adolescent character, not simply because most were under 25 years of age. But as Ward (2012) pointed out, the rioting also had an impulsive, risk-taking, and wild acting-out quality, with many of the rioters seemingly caught up in the delinquent excitement of the crowd, thinking that as everyone else was doing it, they would not be caught.

Winnicott argued in his classic paper "The Antisocial Tendency" (1956) that all children have an antisocial tendency, which is inherent in emotional development as no one's childhood is perfect and to a certain extent, frustration and a sense of deprivation are inevitable. Antisocial behaviour, according to Winnicott, is more likely to be a product of true deprivation—that is, when "there has been a loss of something good that has been positive in the child's experience up to a certain date, and that has been withdrawn; the withdrawal has extended over a period of time longer than that over which the child can keep the memory of the experience alive" (1956, p. 309). Such children, he argued, often unconsciously yearned for what they once had and had been deprived of. According to Ward (2012), the antisocial tendency is an expression that something is not right, and it could be better understood as an unconscious request to be held firmly but lovingly. The hope is that parents or family will hear the communication behind the antisocial act and respond appropriately. Otherwise, if not, the antisocial behaviour will spread to the school and then into society As Ward (2012) points out, the further it spreads beyond those who know and have any relationship with the young person, the less likely it is that the behaviour will be heard as a communication and the more likely it will receive a harsh, punitive response from society and its representatives. If the hoped-for response is not provided, the antisocial tendency begins to turn into delinquency.

Winnicott argues that because their request for help through antisocial behaviour is not understood, some young people become hardened and derive important secondary gains from their antisocial activity, which then makes it "much more difficult to see (what is still there, nevertheless) the SOS that is a signal of hope in the boy or girl who is antisocial" (Winnicott, 1967, p. 90). However, instead of a considered response to the antisocial behaviour of those who rioted, there was a severe retaliation against them. A petition signed by over 200,000 people was submitted to the government proposing that any convicted rioters have their benefit payments cut. On 10 August 2011, David Cameron reassured the country that law and order would be restored on our streets: "As I speak, sentences are also being passed; courts sat through the night last night and will do again tonight. It is for the courts to sentence but I would expect anyone convicted of violent disorder will be sent to prison. We needed a fight back and a fight back is under way" (*Daily Telegraph*, 10 August 2011). Some local councils stated that they intended to evict tenants who had rioted from their homes.[5] The Courts appeared to join the punitive frenzy, because defendants who would normally be released on bail were being routinely remanded in custody, and many of those found guilty seemed to be given disproportionately harsh sentences. Bawdon (2011) reported in the *Guardian* that Ken Macdonald QC described the courts as afflicted by a "collective loss of proportionality" after the riots. For example:

1. In London, Nicholas Robinson, 23, an electrical engineering student with no previous convictions, was jailed for the maximum permitted six months after pleading guilty to stealing bottles of water worth £3.50 from Lidl in Brixton. His lawyer stated that Nicholas had been walking back from his girlfriend's house in the early hours of the morning when he saw the store being looted, and had taken the opportunity to go in and help himself to a case of water. He explained that Nicholas was caught up in the moment and was ashamed of his actions. But the prosecution told Judge Alan Baldwin: "This defendant has contributed through his action to criminal activities to the atmosphere of chaos and sheer lawlessness" (*Guardian*, 12 August 2011).

2. Mother-of-two Ursula Nevin, from Manchester, was jailed for five months for receiving a pair of shorts given to her after they had been looted from a city-centre store.

3. A senior crown prosecutor, Ann Crighton (see the *Guardian*, 2 December 2011), with 18 years' experience with the Crown

Prosecution Service, said she has been reduced to tears by the severity of some sentences being handed out to teenage riot offenders by the youth court. She cited the case of a 17-year-old boy "from a very respectable family, who had never been anywhere near the police before", who was sentenced to 18 months' custody by West London youth court after handing himself in to police.

The former chairperson of the Criminal Bar Association, Paul Mendelle QC, said sentences were too long and harsh. He told BBC 5 Live: "When people get caught up and act out of character, in a similar way, there is a danger that the courts themselves may get caught up in a different kind of collective hysteria—I'm not suggesting violence or anything like that—but in purporting to reflect the public mood actually go over the top and hand out sentences which are too long and too harsh."

Eric Pickles (Secretary of State for Communities) told BBC Radio 4's *Today* programme: "We need to understand that people for a while thought that this was a crime without consequence— we cannot have people being frightened in their beds, frightened in their own homes for their public safety. That is why these kind of exemplary sentences are necessary. I think people would be rightly alarmed if that incitement to riot got off with just a slap on the wrist."

I am not saying that the rioters should not be punished but that our punishment should be considered and should assist with the development of the adolescent. The failure to understand or be interested in the meaning of the behaviour or the message behind the antisocial act can lead to more severe disaffection and more serious antisocial behaviour. I think the riots were also a manifestation of the antisocial tendency, an attempt to find the environmental care that has been lost, is needed, and which is arguably an entitlement. The riots could be thought of an expression of anger about the loss of and contact with good objects and a search for holding, containment, and environmental stability—a search for care so that development can occur. It implies hope and an attempt to not settle for deprivation and despair.

Since the riots, there has been further evidence that there is a deep societal malaise (banks found guilty of consciously mis-selling of Payment Protection Insurance, PPI; Barclays' illegal fixing of Libor rates; and the scandal of Hillsborough), which clearly demonstrates that those in authority can be unjust, inhumane, and corrupt. For 23 years, in the case of Hillsborough, the working-class victims were blamed by those in authority—the respectable classes who themselves had lied and fabricated evidence to avoid accountability and face justice.

Despite some recognition that these riots were "a wake-up call" to do something about gross hardship and despair at the bottom end of society, and that it mirrored our narcissistic, self-serving consumerist culture, there is as yet no evidence that the riots have led to the recognition that the national family is afflicted by a malaise and is in need of serious treatment.

Conclusion

The psychoanalyst Wilfred Bion (1992, p. 122) thought that there are two influential tendencies within the personality: one ego-centric (narcissism), the other socio-centric (socialism). We appear to be more dominated at the moment by the narcissistic tendency, in which notions of community and interdependence are dwarfed by the obsession with self. But although I think that psychoanalysis can make a useful contribution to thinking about unconscious dynamics in society, the contributions of other disciplines are also necessary to achieve a fuller understanding of societal functioning. In this chapter, I have drawn in particular on Klein's notion of the paranoid-schizoid position, where splitting, denial, projection, projective identification, and idealization are used to understand social anxieties about survival of the dominant or more powerful groups and the defences they use to ward them off and to protect themselves. But if we move beyond this defensive position or identification with the "haves", we will be more likely to be able understand and work with the emotional complexity of the riots. If we are in the depressive position, we will be less likely to split off unbearable feelings about the self and thus be more able to work holistically with all factors of internal and external reality for both them and us.

Threats to survival stir up primitive anxieties about annihilation. Very often, the response is to withdraw from reality in a way that seriously compromises the capacity for problem solving. Describing the riots as a medical or criminal condition reinforces notions of a pathological and deviant underclass and not only downplays that social and structural forces influence the development and course of disaffection but also conceals the deviance, criminality, and lack of compassion that is rife within our society. The riots are not just about "them", the rioters—they are also about "us", those who did not riot.

The roots of the riots lay in the individual developmental histories of each rioter, family dynamics, school milieu, and the social and economic context (see Kelloway & Harvey, 1999; Merton, 1997; Sanders & Hendry, 1997). There is an African saying that it takes a village to raise a child, a saying that seems increasingly to be quoted in Britain—I think for good reason, because the riots are not just about the people who took part in the riots, it is also says something about the village.

Notes

An earlier version of this chapter was published in *Psychodynamic Practice: Individuals, Groups and Organisations*, 2013, Vol. 19, No. 3, pp. 279–295 (www .tandfonline.com).

1. Theodore Dalrymple (real name Dr Anthony Daniels) has popularized the notion of "culture of entitlement", and he described British youth as barbarians and "the most unpleasant and violent in the world" (*Daily Mail*, 10 August 2011; *Wall Street Journal*, 15 August 2011).

2. The statement was published in full in the *Daily Telegraph* on 10 August 2011 and is available at: www.telegraph.co.uk/news/uknews/crime/8693134/UK-riots-David-Camerons-statement-in-full.html

3. Source: www.guardian.co.uk/politics/reality-check-with-polly-curtis/2011/sep/12/reality-check-banking-bailout

4. It is now a common ritual to get the latest version of a mobile phone, such as the iPhone, which is an example of the perpetual chase for "happiness" or "status" through the possession of consumer items. *The Independent* (19 September 2012) reported that there were more than 2 million pre-orders in just 24 hours of the launch of iPhone 5, more than double the number of the iPhone 4's pre-orders in the same time period previously, and that there were queues forming outside Apple's London Covent Garden store two days before the iPhone 5 launch on 14 October 2012.

5. On 13 August 2011, Wandsworth Council served the first such eviction notice, on the mother of an 18-year-old suspected of being a rioter.

Thinking Space events 2002–2013

2002

Apr. *The Emotional Roots of Anti-Racism: Some Personal and Institutional Reflections.* SPEAKER: Andrew Cooper, Adolescent Department, Tavistock Clinic

May *Whose Mind Is It On? Sameness and Difference in Work with an Adopted Mixed-Race Adolescent.* SPEAKER: Margaret Rustin, Child and Family Department, Tavistock Clinic

Jun. *The Psychic Geography of Racism.* SPEAKER: Julian Lousada, Adult Department, Tavistock Clinic

Oct. *Some Reflections on Work with Refugees.* SPEAKER: Maureen Fox, Child and Family Department, Tavistock Clinic

2003

Feb. *Exploring Racism. Between Fear and Blindness: An Exploration of the Relationship between a White Therapist and a Black Patient.* SPEAKER: Helen Morgan, BAP (Jungian Section)

Jun. *Some Problems with Psychoanalytic Engagement with Racism.* SPEAKER: Farhad Dalal, Psychotherapist, Training Group Analyst, and author of *Taking the Group Seriously* and *Race, Colour and the Process of Racialisation* (2002)

Nov. *Some Thoughts about Making Psychoanalytic Trainings in Work with Children More Accessible.* SPEAKER: Corrine Aves, Child Psychotherapist, Child and Family Department, Tavistock Clinic

2004

Jan.   *Some Reflections on Cross-Cultural Work with Adolescents.* SPEAKER: Stephen Briggs, Senior Clinical Lecturer in Social Work, Vice-Dean, Adolescent Department, Tavistock Clinic

Mar.   *Psychotherapy across Cultures: Challenging Assumptions.* SPEAKER: Kamaldeep Bhui, Psychotherapist and Professor of Cultural Psychiatry and Epidemiology, Queen Mary University, London

Apr.   *Black Caribbean Women and Mental Health.* SPEAKER: Elaine Arnold PhD, Visiting Fellow, University of Sussex, School of Social Work and Social Care

Oct.   *Working with Somali Fathers.* SPEAKER: Abdisamad Ghelle, Counsellor, Joint Camden/Tavistock Child and Family Department, Somali Children's Peace of Mind Project

Dec.   *Being Black in the Transference.* SPEAKER: Jonathan Bradley, Adolescent Department, Tavistock Clinic

2005

Jan.   *Reflection and Learning from Parent Work with a Black Couple.* SPEAKER: Trudy Klauber, Tavistock Clinic

May   *Minority Voices: Selected Research Findings and Thoughts on Good Practice in Providing Services for the Mental Health of Black and Minority Ethnic Young People.* SPEAKER: Cathy Street, Young Minds

Oct.   *The Experience of Unaccompanied Minors.* SPEAKER: Khurshid Meehan, Adolescent Department, Tavistock Clinic

Nov.   *Meeting of Cultures at the Boundaries: Implications for Institutions and BME Communities.* SPEAKERS: Agnes Bryan & Rameri Moukam

2006

Jan.   *Does Culture Matter in Psychotherapy?* SPEAKER: Britt Krause Consultant Systemic Psychotherapist, Child and Family Directorate, Training Development Consultant (Black and ethnic minority communities), Tavistock Clinic

Mar.   *Working with Black Children in Schools.* SPEAKERS: Frank Lowe & Onel Brooks, Adolescent Department, Tavistock Clinic

Apr.   *Learning from Supporting Excluded Black Children.* SPEAKER: Guy Command

May   *Working with Young Black Boys.* SPEAKER: Melvyn Davis, Coram Boys-2MEN Project

Nov.   *The Place of Muslim Spirituality in Therapy.* SPEAKER: Dr Eman Elizabeth Penny

2007

Jan.   *What Is Cultural Sensitivity?*   SPEAKER: Errol Francis, former Director of the Afro-Caribbean Mental Health Association and Project Leader at the Sainsbury Centre for Mental Health

Apr.   *The Interplay of Supervision in the Culturally Alert Organisation.*   SPEAKER: Ann Miller, Consultant Clinical Psychologist, Marlborough Family Services

May   *Containing Adolescents by Addressing Race and Culture.*   SPEAKER: Zack Eleftheriadou, Counselling Psychologist and Psychotherapist, Tavistock Clinic Visiting Lecturer, author of *Transcultural Counselling*

Jun.   *White Practitioners, Black Service Users: Working with African-Caribbean Pupils and Their Families.*   SPEAKER: Chris Glenn, Systemic Psychotherapist, Camden Secondary Education CAMHS Team, Tavistock and Portman NHS Trust

Oct.   *An Exploration of the Over-Representation of Young Black People in the Criminal Justice System.*   SPEAKER: Kjartan Sveinsson, Research and Policy Analyst, The Runnymede Trust

Nov.   *Providing Mental Health Services for Muslim Youth.*   SPEAKER: Aaliyah Shaikh, Chaplain, Winnicott Unit, St Mary's NHS Trust; Social Work Trainee and co-author of *The Muslim Youth Helpline Report*

2008

Jan.   *Help or Hindrance? Supremacy or Access? Therapy Across Race, Culture and Religion in an Unequal Society.*   SPEAKER: Yasmin Alibhai-Brown, Journalist

Feb.   *Eurocentric Thinking and the Treatment of Black Patients in the NHS.*   SPEAKER: Jules Pearson, Clinical Psychologist, North London Forensic Service, Chase Farm Hospital

Mar.   *Literality and Religion and Race in the Analytic Space.*   SPEAKER: David Morgan, Psychoanalyst and Consultant Adult Psychotherapist, Portman Clinic

Apr.   *The Experience of Delivering a Cross-Cultural Course in Social Care: What Can We Learn?*   SPEAKERS: Sonia Appleby, Adult Psychoanalytic Psychotherapist, Child and Family Directorate; Jina Barrett, Adult Psychotherapist, Adult Directorate; Maxine Dennis, Consultant Clinical Psychologist, Adult Psychotherapist, Adult Directorate, and South West London & St George's Mental Health NHS Trust; Rohina Ilyas, Organizational Consultant, Ilyas Jarrett & Co; Britt Krause, Consultant Systemic Psychotherapist, Child and Family Directorate, Training Development Consultant (Black and ethnic minority communities); Philip Stokoe, Psychoanalytic Psychotherapist, Clinical Director, Adult Directorate

May   *Inviting and Embedding Difference into the Organization: The Marlborough Cultural Therapy Centre.*   SPEAKER: Rabia Malik, Cross-Cultural Services Coordinator, Senior Family Therapist, Marlborough Family Service

Jun.   *Does an Employee's Colour Influence Their Experience with an Organization? Does Their Colour Affect the Way the Organization Responds to Them? Reflections Drawn from Consultancy Work in Local Government.* SPEAKER: Miranda Alcock, Analytical Psychologist, Individual, Group, and Organizational Consultant, the Bayswater Institute, and Founding Member of Training for Equality

Nov.   *Mixed-Race, Mixed-Heritage: Thinking About the Complexities.* SPEAKER: Yvonne Ayo, Systemic Therapist/Supervisor with research interest in children and families of mixed-race, mixed-heritages

2009

Jan.   *Issues of Identity and Belonging in a Psychotherapeutic Children's Group in an Inner-City Primary School.* SPEAKERS: Katie Argent, Child and Adolescent Psychotherapist, Tavistock Outreach in Primary Schools, & Fadumo Osman-Ahmed, Assistant Therapist, Tavistock Outreach in Primary Schools

Feb.   *Paradoxes and Blind Spots: Reflections on Being an Irish Woman Working in Mental Health and Organizational Consultancy in Britain.* SPEAKER: Aideen Lucey, Organizational Consultant

Mar.   *Mental Health in an Extraordinary Situation: Some Thoughts on Returning from a Tour of Palestine.* SPEAKER: Teresa Bailey, Child Psychotherapist, & Martin Kemp, Adult Psychotherapist

Oct.   *Issues Arising from Trying to Work with Cultural and Spiritual Diversity Sensitively.* SPEAKER: Rev. Cathy Wiles, Counsellor and Team Leader, Department of Spiritual and Pastoral Care, SW London and St George's Mental Health Services NHS

Nov.   *Intercultural Aspects of Working with Parents of Teenagers: The Open Door Approach.* SPEAKERS: Charlotte Jarvis, Consultant Child and Adolescent Psychotherapist, & David Trevatt, Open Door YPCS

Nov.   *On Being White in the Helping Professions.* SPEAKER: Judy Ryde, Co-Founder of the Bath Centre for Psychotherapy and Counselling and Past Chair of Psychotherapists and Counsellors for Social Responsibility

2010

Jan.   *Dark Side of the Soul: Some Thoughts on Racism and Psychoanalysis.* SPEAKER: Paul Gordon, Psychoanalytic Psychotherapist:

Feb.   *Institutional Racism: Can Psychotherapy Change?* GUEST SPEAKER: Professor Andrew Cooper; RESPONDENT: Dr Onel Brooks, Psychotherapist and Lecturer in Social Work, Tavistock Clinic

Feb.   *An Exploration of Some Social Class Issues in Psychotherapeutic Work.* SPEAKER: Joanna Ryan, UKCP Reg., Psychoanalytic Psychotherapist, Supervisor, and Researcher

Jun.   *Internal Racism: A Psychoanalytic Model.* SPEAKER: M. Fakhry Davids, Fellow of the Institute of Psychoanalysis, London, and a Member of the Tavistock Society of Psychotherapists

Nov.   *Black British Males in Search of a Place to Belong: A Psychological Under-standing of Joining and Leaving a Gang.* SPEAKER: Dr Kamisha Guthrie, Clinical Psychologist, Formerly Tavistock and Portman, NHS Trust

2011

Mar.   *Attachment as a Framework for Understanding Racism.* GUEST SPEAKER: M. J. Maher, Group Analyst, South London & Maudsley NHS Foundation Trust. CHAIR: Frank Lowe.

May   *Working with "Inter-racial" and "Intercultural" Couples.* GUEST SPEAKER: Reenee Singh, Consultant Systemic Psychotherapist/Research Specialist at the Tavistock and Portman NHS Foundation Trust, Founding Director of the Centre for Cross-Cultural Studies at the Institute of Family Therapy, Associate Editor for Qualitative Research for the Journal of Family Therapy. CHAIR: Yvonne Ayo, Systemic Family Therapist, Tavistock and Portman NHS Trust

Oct.   *Transcending the Legacies of Slavery.* GUEST SPEAKER: Barbara Fletchman Smith, Psychoanalytic Psychotherapist; CHAIR: Frank Lowe, Consultant Social Worker and Psychotherapist

Oct.   *A Deep Malaise: The August Riots.* SPEAKERS: Louise Lyon, Consultant Clinical Psychologist, Trust Director; Pauline Williams, Clinical Team Administrator, Child and Family Directorate; Julian Lousada, Consultant Social Worker, Head of Belsize Unit, Adult Directorate; CHAIR: Frank Lowe, Consultant Social Worker, Adolescent Directorate

Nov.   *Issues of "Race" in Supervision.* GUEST SPEAKER: Helen Morgan, Senior Member and Fellow of the British Association of Psychotherapists; CHAIR: Maxine Dennis, Consultant Clinical Psychologist and Psychotherapist

2012

Feb.   *Working with Lesbian, Gay, Bisexual or Transgender Young People Who Are Vulnerable.* GUEST SPEAKER: Debbie Killeen, formerly a Psychotherapist at the Albert Kennedy Trust

May   *Lesbian and Gay Couple Relationships: When Internalized Homophobia Gets in the Way of Couple Creativity.* GUEST SPEAKER: Leezah Hertzmann, Psychoanalytic Psychotherapist and Senior Psychoanalytic Couple Psychotherapist, Tavistock Centre for Couple Relationships; CHAIR: Elisa Reyes Simpson, Consultant Social Worker and Psychoanalytic Psychotherapist, Tavistock and Portman NHS Trust; RESPONDENT: Dr Onel Brooks

Jun.   *Khat: Culturally Appropriate or a Serious African Mental Health Issues in Britain?* SPEAKER: Abukar Awale, prominent Anti-Khat campaigner

Jun.   *Cultural Sensitivity and Forced Marriage: Exploring the Issues.* GUEST SPEAKER: Jasvinder Sanghera, Founder of the Karma Nirvana Project in 1993 to campaign against honour-based violence and forced marriage, and best-selling author of *Shame* and *Daughters of Shame*;

CHAIR: Dr Reenee Singh, Consultant Systemic Psychotherapist and Research Specialist at the Tavistock and Portman NHS Trust and Founding Director of the Centre for Cross-Cultural Studies at the Institute of Family Therapy

Sep.   *After the Riots and the Media Coverage Exploring the Psychological Impact of the Riots on the Tottenham Community.* VENUE: Tottenham Town Hall; SPEAKERS: Rt. Hon. David Lammy, Tottenham MP; *On "Mindless2 Violence*—Onel Brooks, Psychoanalytic Psychotherapist; *The Effects of Trauma*—Annette Wilson, Family Therapist, Haringey CAMHS; *On Community Therapy*—Victoria Lidchi, Psychologist, the Tavistock and Portman NHS Foundation Trust; *Moving Forward*—Shaun Collins, Assistant Director, Haringey Child and Adolescent Mental Health Service

Oct.   *Reflections on the Child Protection Issues Arising from Practices Linked to Beliefs in Witchcraft and Spirit Possession in London's African Communities.* SPEAKERS: Stephen Briggs, Centre for Social Work Research (UEL/Tavistock); Mor Dioum, Director, & Stephanie Yorath, Programme Director, Victoria Climbié Foundation

Mar.   *Who Do You Think You Are? Helping Young People from Marginalized Communities Liberate Themselves from Negative Identities.* SPEAKER: Gillian Hughes, Clinical Psychologist and Systemic Psychotherapist, Refugee Team, Tavistock and Portman NHS Foundation Trust; CHAIR: Lois Thomas, Clinical Psychologist, Tavistock and Portman NHS Foundation Trust

2013

Mar.   *Race and Gender Dynamics as a Defence against Anxiety in Organizations.* GUEST SPEAKER: Stuart Stevenson, Organizational Consultant and Psychoanalytic Psychotherapist in private practice. RESPONDENT: Agnes Bryan, Organizational Consultant, Psychotherapist and Associate Dean SAAMHS, Tavistock and Portman NHS Foundation Trust

May   *Seeing and Being Seen: A Psychoanalytic Exploration of the Impact and Risks of Internet Pornography.* SPEAKER: John Woods, Consultant Psychotherapist, Portman Clinic; CHAIR: Louise Lyon, Trust Director, Tavistock and Portman NHS Foundation Trust

Jun.   *Psychoanalysis and Homosexuality: Opening Up a Discussion.* GUEST SPEAKER: Juliet Newbigin, Psychoanalytic Psychotherapist, Senior Member of the British Psychoanalytic Foundation. CHAIR: Leezah Hertzmann, Psychoanalytic Psychotherapist and Senior Psychoanalytic Couple Psychotherapist, Tavistock Centre for Couple Relationships

Jul.   *"Adoption: All You Need Is Love?" What Happens to Identity in Transracial Adoption? A Personal Perspective from a Hong Kong–Chinese Adoptee Raised in a White British family.* GUEST SPEAKER: Lucy Sheen, actor, writer, filmmaker; CHAIR: Lois Thomas, Clinical Psychologist, Adolescent and Young Adult Service

REFERENCES

Allen, C. (1958). Homosexuality: Its nature, causation and treatment. In: C. Berg & C. Allen, *The Problem of Homosexuality*. New York: Citadel Press.

Alleyne, A. (2005). Invisible injuries and silent witnesses: The shadow of racial oppression in workplace contexts. *Psychodynamic Practice, 11* (3): 283–299.

Altman, N. (1995). *The Analyst in the Inner City*. Hillsdale, NJ: Analytic Press.

Altman, N. (2010). *The Analyst in the Inner City* (2nd edition). New York: Routledge.

Amin, A. (2010). The remainders of race. *Theory, Culture & Society, 27*: 1–23.

APA (1980). *Diagnostic and Statistical Manual of Mental Disorders*. Washington, DC: American Psychiatric Association.

Armitage, K. (2009). Young, lower middle class and black. *Sitegeist: A Journal of Psychoanalysis and Philosophy, 3*: 51–64.

Audit Commission (2004a). *The Journey to Race Equality: Delivering Improved Services to Local Communities*. London.

Audit Commission (2004b). *A Modern Approach to Inspecting Services*. London.

Awad, G. (2003). The minds and perceptions of "the others". In: S. Varvin & V. Volkan (Eds.), *Violence or Dialogue? Psychoanalytic Insights into Terror and Terrorism* (pp. 153–176). London: IPA.

Bailey, T. (2006). There is no such thing as an adolescent. In: M. Lanyado & A. Horne (Eds.), *A Question of Technique: Independent Psychoanalytic Approaches with Children and Adolescents*. London: Routledge.

Barden, N. (2011). Disrupting Oedipus: The legacy of the Sphinx. *Psychoanalytic Psychotherapy*, 25 (4): 324–345.

Barry, S. (2008). *The Secret Scripture*. London: Faber and Faber.

Barthes, R. (1957). *Mythologies*. London: Vintage, 1993.

Bawdon, F. (2011). Severe sentences for young offenders worries prosecutors. *Guardian*, 2 December.

Beck, J. (2002). Lost in thought: The receptive unconscious. In: J. Scalia (Ed.), *The Vitality of Objects: Exploring the Work of Christopher Bollas*. London: Continuum.

Beckett, J. C. (1981). *The Making of Modern Ireland 1603–1923*. London: Faber and Faber.

Benjamin, J. (1998). *Shadow of the Other: Intersubjectivity and Gender in Psychoanalysis*. London: Routledge.

Berger, J. (2008). *Hold Everything Dear: Dispatches on Survival and Resistance*. New York: Verso.

Bergler, E. (1956). *Homosexuality: Disease or Way of Life?* New York: Hill & Wang.

Berman, E. (2002). Beyond analytic anonymity: On the political involvement of psychoanalysts and psychotherapists in Israel. In: J. Bunzl & B. Beit-Hallahmi (Eds.), *Psychoanalysis, Identity and Ideology: Critical Essays on the Israel/Palestine Case* (pp. 177–200). Boston, MA: Kluwer.

Bhavnani, R. (2001). *Rethinking Interventions to Combat Racism*. Commission for Racial Equality. Stoke-on-Trent: Trentham.

Bhugra, D., & Bhui, K. (1998). Psychotherapy for ethnic minorities: Issues, context and practice. *British Journal of Psychotherapy*, 14 (3): 310–326.

Bhugra, D., & Bhui, K. (2006). Psychotherapy across the cultural divide. In: R. Moodley & S. Palmer (Eds.), *Race, Culture & Psychotherapy: Critical Perspectives in Multicultural Practice* (pp. 46–57). London: Routledge.

Bhui, K., Warfa, N., Edonya, P., McKenzie, K., & Bhugra, D. (2007). Cultural competence in mental health care: A review of models of evaluations. *BMC Health Services Research*, 7: 15.

Bieber, I., Dain, H., Dince, P., Drellich, M., Grand, H., Gundlach, R., et al. (1962). *Homosexuality: A Psychoanalytic Study of Male Homosexuals*. New York: Basic Books.

Bion, W. R. (1959). Attacks on linking. In: *Second Thoughts* (pp. 94–109). London: Karnac, 1993.

Bion, W. R. (1961). *Experiences in Groups and Other Papers*. London: Routledge.

Bion, W.R. (1962). *Learning from Experience*. London: Karnac.

Bion W. R. (1980). *Bion in New York and São Paulo*. Strathtay: Clunie Press.

Bion, W. R. (1992). *Cogitations*. London: Karnac.

Black, D. M. (2011). *Why Things Matter: The Place of Values in Science, Psychoanalysis and Religion*. London: Routledge.

Blackwell, D. (2002). Out of their class. *Group Analysis, 35*: 327–338.

Blackwell, D. (2005). *Counselling and Psychotherapy with Refugees*. London: Jessica Kingsley.

Bollas, C. (1992). *Being a Character: Psychoanalysis and Self Experience*. London: Routledge.

Botticelli, S. (2007). Return of the repressed: Class in psychoanalytic process. In: M. Suchet, A. Harris, & L. Aron (Eds.), *Relational Psychoanalysis, Vol. 3: New Voices*. Mahwah, NJ: Academic Press.

Bouquet, M. (1993). *Reclaiming English Kinship: Portuguese Refractions of British Kinship Theory*. Cambridge: Cambridge University Press.

Bourdieu, P. (1977). *Outline of a Theory of Practice*. Cambridge: Cambridge University Press.

Bourdieu, P. (1980). *Sociology in Question*, trans. R. Nice . London: Sage, 1993.

Bourdieu, P. (1986). *Distinction: A Social Critique of the Judgement of Taste*. London: Routledge.

Bracken, P. (1998). Mental health and ethnicity: An Irish dimension. *British Journal of Psychiatry, 172*: 103–105.

Breen, D. (1993.). Introduction. In: D. Breen (Ed.), *The Gender Conundrum: Contemporary Psychoanalytic Perspectives on Femininity and Masculinity*. The New Library of Psychoanalysis. London: Routledge.

Briggs, J. (1970). *Never in Anger: Portrait of an Eskimo Family*. Cambridge, MA: Harvard University Press.

Briggs, J. (1998). *Inuit Morality Play: The Emotional Education of a Three-Year-Old*. New Haven, CT: Yale University Press.

Britton, R. (1989). The missing link: Parental sexuality in the Oedipus complex. In: R. Britton, M. Feldman, & E. O'Shaughnessy (Eds.), *The Oedipus Complex Today: Clinical Implications* (pp. 83–101). London: Karnac.

Brown, L. J. (2011). *Intersubjective Processes and the Unconscious*. Hove: Routledge.

Brunner, J. (2002). Contentious origins: Psychoanalytic comments on the debate over Israel's creation. In: J. Bunzl & B. Beit-Hallahmi

(Eds.), *Psychoanalysis, Identity and Ideology: Critical Essays on the Israel/Palestine Case* (pp. 107–136). Boston, MA: Kluwer.

Bunyan, T. (1981). The police against the people. *Race & Class, 23* (2/3): 153–170.

Bunzl, J., & Beit-Hallahmi, B. (Eds.) (2002). *Psychoanalysis, Identity and Ideology: Critical Essays on the Israel/Palestine Case*. Boston, MA: Kluwer.

Butler, J. (1990). *Gender Trouble*. New York: Routledge.

Butler, J. (1995). Melancholy gender: Refused identification. *Psychoanalytic Dialogues, 5*: 165–180.

Butler, J. (2003). No, it's not anti-Semitic. *London Review of Books 25* (16), 21 August.

Butler, J. (2006). Israel/Palestine and the paradoxes of academic freedom. *Radical Philosophy, 135*: 8–17. Available at: www.ibrk.pwp. blueyonder.co.uk/foto_papers/butler_FOTO_revised.pdf

Calvo, L. (2008). Racial fantasies and the primal scene of miscegenation. *International Journal of Psychoanalysis, 89*: 55–70.

Canestri, J. (1999). Psychoanalytic heuristics. In: P. Fonagy, A. Cooper, & R. Wallerstein (Eds.), *Psychoanalysis on the Move*. London: Routledge.

Care Quality Commission (2011). *Count Me in 2010*. Newcastle upon Tyne: Care Quality Commission & National Mental Health Development Unit.

Centre for Social Justice (2011). *No Excuses: A Review of Educational Exclusion*. London.

Chakraborty, A., McManus, S., Brugha, T. S., Bebbington, P., & King, M. (2011). Mental health of the non-heterosexual population of England. *British Journal of Psychiatry, 198*: 143–148.

Chasseguet-Smirgel, J. (1990). Reflections of a psychoanalyst upon the Nazi biocracy and genocide. *International Review of Psychoanalysis, 17*: 167–176.

Chodorow, N. J. (1999). *The Power of Feelings*. New Haven, CT: Yale University Press.

Chomsky, N. (1999). *The Fateful Triangle: The United States, Israel and the Palestinians*. London: Pluto.

Churchill, W. S. (1957). *A History of the English Speaking Peoples: The Age of Revolution*. New York: Dodd, Mead.

Clarke, J., & Lemma, A. (2011). Editorial. *Psychoanalytic Psychotherapy, 25* (4): 303–307.

Cohen, S. (2001). *States of Denial: Knowing about Atrocities and Suffering*. Cambridge: Polity.

Cooper, A., & Lousada, J. (2005). *Borderline Welfare: Feeling and Fear of Feeling in Modern Welfare*. London: Karnac.

Covington, C., Williams, P., Arundale, J., & Knox, J. (2002). *Terrorism and War: Unconscious Dynamics of Political Violence*. London: Karnac.

Craib, I. (2002). What is social class? *Group Analysis, 35*: 342–350.

Curry, A. (1964). Myth, transference and the black psychotherapist. *International Review of Psychoanalysis, 45*.

Dalal, F. (1988). The racism of Jung. *Race and Class, 29* (3): 1–22.

Dalal, F. (1998). *Taking the Group Seriously*. London: Jessica Kingsley.

Dalal, F. (2002). *Race, Colour and the Processes of Racialization: New Perspectives from Group Analysis, Psychoanalysis and Sociology*. Hove: Brunner-Routledge.

Dalal, F. (2006). Racism: Processes of detachment, dehumanization and hatred. In: K. White (Ed.), *Unmasking Race, Culture and Attachment in the Psychoanalytic Space* (pp. 10–35). London: Karnac.

Dalal, F. (2012). *Thought Paralysis: The Virtues of Discrimination*. London: Karnac.

Das, V. (1995). *Critical Events: An Anthropological Perspective on Contemporary India*. Oxford: Oxford University Press.

Das, V. (2000). The act of witnessing: Violence, poisonous knowledge and subjectivity. In: V. Das, A. Kleinman, M. Lamphele, & P. Reynolds (Eds.), *Violence and Subjectivity* (pp. 205–225). Berkeley, CA: University of California Press.

Davids, M. F. (2010). *Thinking Space*. Lecture given at the Tavistock Clinic, London.

Davids, M. F. (2011). *Internal Racism: A Psychoanalytic Approach to Race and Difference*. London: Palgrave Macmillan.

Davies, W. (2011). The political economy of unhappiness, *New Left Review, 71* (September/October).

Dembo, T., Leviton, G. L., & Wright, B. A. (1975). Adjustment to misfortune: A problem of social–psychological rehabilitation. *Rehabilitation Psychology, 22*: 1–100.

Denman, C. (2004). *Sexuality: A Biopsychosocial Approach*. Basingstoke: Palgrave Macmillan.

Denman, F. (1993). Prejudice and homosexuality. *British Journal of Psychotherapy, 9* (3): 346–358.

De Zulueta, F. (1993). *From Pain to Destructiveness: The Traumatic Roots of Destructiveness*. London: Whurr.

Di Ceglie, R. G. (2013). Orientation, containment and the emergence of symbolic thinking. *International Journal of Psychoanalysis*. Online: Early View Website, 27 March 2013. doi:10.1111/1745-8315.12057

Dimen, M. (2006). Money, love and hate: Contradiction and paradox in psychoanalysis. In: L. Layton, N. C. Hollander, & S. Gutwill (Eds.), *Psychoanalysis, Class and Politics: Encounters in the Clinical Setting*. New York: Routledge.

DoH (2005). *Delivering Race Equality in Mental Health Care: An Action Plan for Reform Inside and Outside Services and the Government's Response to the Independent Inquiry into the Death of David Bennett*. London: Department of Health.

Domenici, T., & Lesser, R. C. (1995). *Disorienting Sexuality: Psychoanalytic Reappraisals of Sexual Identities*. New York: Routledge.

Donnelly, J. (2002). *The Great Irish Potato Famine*. Stroud: Sutton Publishing.

Drescher J. (1995). Anti-homosexual bias in training. In: T. Domenici & R. C. Lesser (Eds.), *Disorienting Sexuality: Psychoanalytic Reappraisals of Sexual Identities* (pp. 227–241). New York: Routledge.

Drescher, J. (1996). A discussion across sexual orientation and gender boundaries: Reflections of a gay male analyst to a heterosexual female analyst. *Gender and Psychoanalysis, 1*: 223–237.

Dyer, R. (1997). *White*. London: Routledge.

Eichenbaum, L., & Orbach, S. (1987). Separation and intimacy: Crucial practice issues in working with women in therapy. In S. Ernst & M. Maguire (Eds.), *Living with the Sphinx: Papers from the Women's Therapy Centre* (pp. 49–67). London: Women's Press.

Elias, N. (1994). *The Civilising Process*. Oxford: Blackwell.

Elmendorf, S., & Ruskin, R. (2004). Trauma, terrorism: Man's inhumanity to man. *International Journal of Psychoanalysis, 85*: 983–986.

Erlich, H., Erlich-Ginor, M., & Beland, H. (2009). *Fed with Tears—Poisoned with Milk*. Giessen: Psychosozial.

EUMC (2005). *Working Definition of Anti-Semitism*. Available at: www. european-forum-on-antisemitism.org/working-definition-of-anti-semitism

Fanon, F. (1967). *Black Skin, White Masks*. London: Pluto Press. 1986.

Feuerbach, L. (1841). *The Essence of Christianity*, trans. G. Eliot. First Neural Library Edition. Walnut, CA: MSAC Philosophy Group, Mt. San Antonio College, 2008.

Fitzgerald, B. (1999). Children of lesbian and gay parents: A review of the literature. *Marriage and Family Review, 29* (1): 57–75.

Fletcher, J. (1989). Freud and his uses: Psychoanalysis and gay theory. In: S. Shepherd & M. Wallis (Eds.), *Coming on Strong: Gay Politics and Culture*. London: Unwin Hymen.

Fletchman Smith, B. (2000). *Mental Slavery: Psychoanalytic Studies of Caribbean People*. London: Karnac.

Flower, S. (2007). On the slopes of Brokeback Mountain: Countertransference impediments to an analytic attitude in work with gay men. *British Journal of Psychotherapy, 23* (3): 431–443.

Fonagy, P. (2009). Introduction. In: B. Wilcox, R. C. Curtis, & L. C. Bohm (Eds.), *Taboo or Not Taboo: Forbidden Thoughts, Forbidden Acts in Psychoanalysis and Psychotherapy*. London: Karnac.

Fonagy, P., Steele, M., Steele, H., Moran, G. S., & Higgitt, A. C. (1991). The capacity for understanding mental states: The reflective self in parent and child and its significance for security of attachment. *Infant Mental Health Journal, 12* (3): 201–218.

Fonagy, P., & Taggart, M. (1966). Playing and reality I: Theory of mind and the normal development of psychic reality. *International Journal of Psychoanalysis, 77*: 217–233.

Fonagy, P., & Taggart, M. (1997). Attachment and reflective function: Their role in self-organization. *Development and Psychopathology, 9*: 679–700.

Forster, E. M. (1971). *Maurice*. Harmondsworth: Penguin Classics, 2005.

Foucault, M. (1976). *The History of Sexuality: An Introduction*. Harmondsworth: Penguin, 1978.

Frankenstein, E. (1943). *Justice for My People: The Jewish Case*. London: Nicholson & Watson.

Freud, S. (1905d). *Three Essays on the Theory of Sexuality. Standard Edition, 7.*

Freud, S. (1909d). Notes on a case of obsessional neurosis. *Standard Edition, 10*: 153–250.

Freud, S. (1910c). *Leonardo Da Vinci and a Memory of His Childhood. Standard Edition, 11*: 59–138.

Freud, S. (1912e). Recommendations to physicians practising psychoanalysis. *Standard Edition, 12*: 109–120.

Freud, S. (1912–13). *Totem and Taboo. Standard Edition, 13*: 1–161.

Freud, S. (1914g). Remembering, repeating and working-through (Further recommendations on the technique of psycho-analysis II). *Standard Edition, 12.*

Freud, S. (1917e). Mourning and melancholia. *Standard Edition, 14*: 243–58.

Freud, S. (1918b [1914]). From the history of an infantile neurosis. *Standard Edition, 17.*

Freud, S. (1920a). The psychogenesis of a case of homosexuality in a woman. *Standard Edition, 18*: 155–172.

Freud, S. (1922b). Some neurotic mechanisms in jealousy, paranoia and homosexuality. *Standard Edition, 18*: 221–234.

Freud, S. (1923b). *The Ego and the Id. Standard Edition, 19*: 3–66.

Freud, S. (1930a). *Civilization and Its Discontents. Standard Edition*, 21.

Freud, S. (1931b). Female sexuality. *Standard Edition*, 21: 221–243.

Freud, S. (1933a). *New Introductory Lectures on Psycho-Analysis. Standard Edition*, 22.

Freud, S. (1950 [1892–1899]). Extracts from the Fliess papers [Letter 71]. *Standard Edition*, 1.

Frommer, M. S. (1995). Countertransference obscurity in the psycho-analytic treatment of homosexual patients. In: T. Domenici & R. C. Lesser (Eds.), *Disorienting Sexuality: Psychoanalytic Reappraisals of Sexual Identities* (pp. 65–82). New York: Routledge.

Frosh, S. (1989). Psychoanalysis and racism. In: B. Richards (Ed.), *Crisis of the Self: Further Essays on Psychoanalysis and Politics*. London: Free Association Books.

Gabbard, G. O., & Williams, P. (2002). A boycott by passport [Editorial]. *International Journal of Psychoanalysis, 83*: 1001.

Gambini, R. (1997). The soul of underdevelopment: The case of Brazil. In: *Zurich '95, Proceedings of the Thirteenth International Congress for Analytical Psychology*. Einsiedeln, Germany: Daimon Verlag.

Garrett, P. (2002). No Irish need apply. *British Journal of Social Work, 32*: 477–494.

Gibbs, I. (2009). Race, culture and the therapeutic process. In: M. Lanyado & A. Horne (Eds.), *The Handbook of Child and Adolescent Psychotherapy: Psychoanalytic Approaches* (2nd edition, pp. 114–125). London: Routledge.

Gillespie, W. H. (1956). The general theory of sexual perversion. *International Journal of Psychoanalysis, 37*: 396–403.

Glass, C. (2004). It was necessary to uproot them. *London Review of Books, 26* (12): 21–23.

Goldberg, D. (1996). *To the Promised Land: A History of Zionist Thought*. London: Faber and Faber.

Goldberg, E., Myers, W., & Zeifman, I. (1974). Some observations on three interracial analyses. *International Journal of Psychoanalysis, 55*: 495–500.

Gordon, P. (1993a). Keeping therapy white? Psychotherapy trainings and equal opportunities. *British Journal of Psychotherapy, 10* (1): 44–49.

Gordon, P. (1993b). Souls in armour: Thoughts on psychoanalysis and racism. *British Journal of Psychotherapy, 10* (1): 62–76.

Gordon, P. (1996). A fear of difference? Some reservations about inter-cultural therapy and counselling. *Psychodynamic Counselling, 2*: 195–208.

Gordon, P. (2004). Souls in armour: Thoughts on psychoanalysis and racism. *British Journal of Psychotherapy, 21* (2): 277–294.

Granek, M. (1994). Review of *Persistent Shadows of the Holocaust: The Meaning to Those Not Directly Affected*, edited by R. Moses. *International Journal of Psychoanalysis, 75*: 635–639.

Greenslade, L. (1992). White skin, white masks: Psychological distress among the Irish in Britain. In P. O'Sullivan (Ed.), *The Irish in New Communities*. Leicester: Leicester University Press.

Grosbard, O. (2003). *Israel on the Couch: The Psychology of the Peace Process*. Albany, NY: State University of New York Press.

Guardian & LSE (2011). *Reading the Riots: Investigating England's Summer of Disorder*. Joint Report by the Guardian and the London School of Economics. Available at: www.guardian.co.uk/uk/interactive/2011/dec/14/reading-the-riots-investigating-england-s-summer-of-disorder-full-report

Habermas, J. (1972). *Knowledge and Human Interests*. trans. J. J. Shapiro. London: Heinemann.

Hacking, I. (1999). *The Social Construction of What?* Cambridge, MA: Harvard University Press.

Halperin, E., Bar-Tal, D., Sharvit, K., Rosler, N., & Raviv, A. (2010). Socio-psychological implications for an occupying society: The case of Israel. *Journal of Peace Research, 47* (1): 59–70.

Hartmann, S. (2005). Class unconscious: From dialectical materialism to relational material. *Psychoanalysis, Culture and Society, 10*: 121–137.

Hickman, M. J., & Walter, B. (1995). Deconstructing whiteness: Irish women in Britain. *Feminist Review, 50*: 5–19.

Hillman, J. (1986). Notes on white supremacy: Essaying an archetypal account of historical events. *Spring: A Journal of Archetype and Culture*: 29–58.

Hillsborough Independent Panel (2012). *Hillsborough: The Report of the Hillsborough Independent Panel*. House of Commons Papers, Volume 581 of C Series. London: Stationery Office.

Hoggett, P. (1992a). The art of the possible. In: *Partisans in an Uncertain World: The Psychoanalysis of Engagement*. London: Free Association Books.

Hoggett, P. (1992b). *Partisans in an Uncertain World: The Psychoanalysis of Engagement*. London: Free Association Books.

Holland, S. (1992). From social abuse to social action: A neighbourhood psychotherapy and social action project for women. In: J. M. Ussher & P. Nicolson (Eds.), *Gender Issues in Clinical Psychology* (pp. 68–77). London: Routledge.

Holmes, D. E. (1992). Race and transference in psychoanalysis and psychotherapy. *International Journal of Psychoanalysis, 73* (1): 1–11.

Holmes, D. E. (2006). Racial transference reactions in psychoanalytic treatment: an update. In: R. Moodley & S. Palmer (Eds.), *Race, Culture and Psychotherapy: Critical Perspectives in Multicultural Practice* (pp. 61–73). Hove: Routledge.

Horne, A. (2006). The Independent position in psychoanalytic psychotherapy with children and adolescents: Roots and implications. In: M. Lanyado & A. Horne (Eds.), *A Question of Technique: Independent Psychoanalytic Approaches with Children and Adolescents*. London: Routledge.

Isay, R. A. (1996). *Becoming Gay: The Journey towards Self-Acceptance*. New York: Henry Holt.

Joyce, J. (1916). *A Portrait of the Artist as a Young Man*. New York: Bantam, 1992.

Jung, C. G. (1990). *The Undiscovered Self*. London: Routledge.

Kane, B. S. (2005). Transforming trauma into tragedy: Oedipus/Israel and the psychoanalyst as messenger. *Psychoanalytic Review, 92*: 929–956.

Kareem, J. (2000). The Nafsiyat Intercultural Therapy Centre: Ideas and experience in intercultural therapy. In: J. Kareem & R. Littlewood (Eds.), *Intercultural Therapy*. London: Blackwell.

Kareem, J., & Littlewood, R. (Eds.) (2000). *Intercultural Therapy*. London: Blackwell.

Kelloway, E. K., & Harvey, S. (1999). Learning to work: The development of work beliefs. In: J. Barling & K. E. Kelloway (Eds.), *Young Workers: Varieties of Experience*. Washington, DC: American Psychological Society.

Kemp, M. (2005). On: A boycott by passport [Letter]. *International Journal of Psychoanalysis, 86*: 551–553.

Kemp, M., & Pinto, E. (2009). To resist is to exist: Notes on the psychological impact of military occupation in Palestine. *Therapy Today, 20* (2): 11–15. Available at: www.therapytoday.net/article/show/451

Khanna, R. (2003). *Dark Continents: Psychoanalysis and Colonialism*. Durham, NC: Duke University Press.

Kiberd, D. (1992). Introduction. In: J. Joyce, *Ulysses*. London: Penguin.

Kiberd, D. (1996). *Inventing Ireland*. London: Vintage.

Kinealy, C. (1995). *This Great Calamity: The Irish Famine 1845–52*. Dublin: Gill & Macmillan.

King, P. H. M., & Steiner, R. (1991). *The Freud–Klein Controversies, 1941–1945*. London: Tavistock Publications.

Klein, M. (1935). A contribution to the psychogenesis of manic-depressive states. In: *Love, Guilt and Reparation and Other Works 1921–1945*. London: Hogarth Press, 1975; London: Karnac, 1992.

Klein, M. (1946). Notes on some schizoid mechanisms. In: *Envy and Gratitude and Other Works 1946–1963*. London: Hogarth Press, 1975; reprinted London: Karnac, 1993.

Klein, R. (1999). *Defying Disaffection*. Stoke-on-Trent: Trentham.

Klug, B. (2004). The myth of the new anti-Semitism. *The Nation*, February. Available at: www.thenation.com/article/myth-new-anti-semitism

Kovel, J. (1988). *White Racism: A Psychohistory*. London: Free Association Books.

Krause, I.-B. (1998). *Therapy Across Culture*. London: Sage .

Krause, I.-B. (2002). *Culture and System in Family Therapy*. London: Karnac.

Krause, I.-B. (2010). "I feel therefore . . .": Being there in systemic psychotherapy practice. *Context, 107*: 4–7.

Krause, I.-B. (2011). *Reflexivity and Culture in Systemic Psychotherapy: Mutual Perspectives*. London: Karnac.

Krause, I.-B., & Miller, A. (1995). Culture and family therapy. In: S. Fernando (Ed.), *Mental Health in a Multi-Ethnic Society: A Multi-Disciplinary Handbook* (pp. 148–171). London: Routledge.

Kushnick, L. (1981). Parameters of British and North American racism. *Race and Class: A Journal of the Institute of Race Relations and the Transnational Institute, 23* (1): 187–206.

Lacan, J. (1973). *The Four Fundamental Concepts of Psycho-Analysis*, trans. A. Sheridan. London: Penguin, 1977.

Laor, Y. (2009). *The Myths of Liberal Zionism*. London: Verso.

Laplanche, J., & Pontalis, J.-B. (1973). *The Language of Psychoanalysis*. London: Karnac, 1988.

Lawrence, M. (2012). *Response to Paul Lynch*. Paper given at BPC Conference on Psychoanalysis and Homosexuality: Moving On (21 January).

Layton, L. (2004a). A fork in the royal road: Defining the "unconscious" and its stakes for social theory. *Psychoanalysis, Culture & Society, 9* (1): 33–51.

Layton, L. (2004b). This place gives me the heebie jeebies. *International Journal of Critical Psychology, 10*: 36–50.

Layton, L. (2006a). Attacks on linking: The unconscious pull to disassociate individuals from their social context. In: L. Layton, N. C. Hollander, & S. Guttwill (Eds.), *Psychoanalysis, Class and Politics: Encounters in the Clinical Setting* (pp. 107–117). London: Routledge.

Layton, L. (2006b). Racial identities, racial enactments, and normative unconscious processes, *Psychoanalytic Quarterly, 75*: 237–269.

Layton, L. (2006c). That place gives me the heebie jeebies. In L. Layton, N. C. Hollander, & S. Guttwill (Eds.), *Psychoanalysis, Class and Politics: Encounters in the Clinical Setting* (pp. 51–64). London: Routledge.

Leary, K. (2006). How race is lived in the consulting room. In: K. White (Ed.), *Unmasking Race, Culture and Attachment in the Psychoanalytic Space* (pp. 75–89). London: Karnac.

Lerman, A. (2010). *Trials of the Diaspora* by Anthony Julius [Review]. *Guardian,* 27 February. Available at: www.guardian.co.uk/books/2010/feb/27/trials-of-the-diaspora-julius

Lévi-Strauss, C. (1949). *Elementary Structures of Kinship.* Boston, MA: Beacon Press.

Levy, I. (2003). *Psychoanalysis, Identity and Ideology: Critical Essays on the Israel/Palestine Case* (2002), edited by John Bunzl & Benjamon Beit-Hallahmi [Review]. *International Journal of Psychoanalysis, 84*: 1642–1645.

Lewes, K. (1995). *Psycho-Analysis and Male Homosexuality.* Northvale, NJ: Aronson.

Limentani, A. (1977). Clinical types of homosexuality. In: I. Rosen (Ed.), *Sexual Deviation* (pp. 216–227). Oxford: Oxford University Press, 1979.

Lipsky, S. (1987). *Internalized Racism.* Seattle, WA: Rational Island.

Lousada, J. (1997). The hidden history of an idea: The difficulties of adopting anti-racism. In: E. Smith (Ed.), *Integrity and Change: Mental Health in the Market Place.* London: Routledge.

Lowe, F. (2006a). Containing persecutory anxiety: CAMHS and BME communities. *Journal of Social Work Practice, 20* (1): 5–25.

Lowe, F. (2006b). Racism as a borderline issue: The avoidance and marginalization of race in psychotherapy. In: A. Foster, A. Dickenson, B. Bishop, & J. Klein (Eds.), *Difference: An Avoided Topic in Practice.* London: Karnac.

Lowe, F. (2008). Colonial object relations: Going underground Black–White relationships. *British Journal of Psychotherapy, 24* (1): 20–33.

Macpherson Report (1999). *The Stephen Lawrence Inquiry: Report of an Inquiry by Sir William Macpherson of Cluny.* London: Stationery Office.

Maher, F. (1999). Coming out. In: C. Zmroczek & P. Mahoney (Eds.), *Women and Social Class.* London: Taylor & Francis.

Malcolm, N. (1980). *Ludwig Wittgenstein: A Memoir.* Oxford: Oxford University Press.

Mantel, H. (2009). Interview. *Guardian*, 12 September. Available at: www.guardian.co.uk/theguardian/2009/sep/12/hilary-mantel-booker-prize-interview

Marx, K. (1844). Economic and philosophical manuscripts. In: *Selected Writings in Sociology and Social Philosophy*, ed. T . Bottomore & M. Rubel. London: Watts, 1956.

Marx, K. (1973). Economic and philosophical manuscripts. In: *Early Writings*. London: Pelican & New Left Review.

Masson, J. M. (Ed.) (1985). *The Complete Letters of Sigmund Freud to Wilhelm Fliess, 1887–1904*. Cambridge, MA: Belknap Press.

McCann-Mortimer, P., Augoustinos, M., & LeCouteur, A. (2004). "Race" and the Human Genome Project: Construction of scientific legitimacy. *Discourse & Society, 15* (4): 409–432.

McDougall, J. (1990). *Plea for a Measure of Abnormality*. London: Free Association Books.

McNally, R. (2004). Conceptual problems with the DSM–IV criteria for posttraumatic stress disorder. In: G. M. Rosen (Ed.), *Posttraumatic Stress Disorder: Issues and Controversies* (pp. 1–14). Chichester: Wiley.

Mearsheimer, J., & Walt, S. (2006). The Israel lobby. *London Review of Books, 28* (6): 3–12.

Merton, B. (1998). *Defying Disaffection*. Stoke-on-Trent: Trentham.

Mitchell, J., & Rose, J. (Eds.). (1982). *Feminine Sexuality: Jacques Lacan and the Ecole Freudienne*. London: Macmillan.

Mitchell, S. A. (2002). Psychodynamics, homosexuality, and the question of pathology. *Studies in Gender and Sexuality, 3*: 3–21.

Mitchison, S. (2009). Class relations and individual consciousness: A neglected dynamic in analytic group therapy. *Psychotherapy and Politics International, 7* (1): 34–39.

Money-Kyrle, R. (1956). Normal counter-transference and some of its deviations. In: D. Meltzer & E. O'Shaughnessy (Eds.), *The Collected Papers of Roger Money-Kyrle* (pp. 330–342). Strathtay: Clunie Press, 1978.

Morgan, H. (1998). Between fear and blindness: The white therapist and the black patient. *Journal of the British Association of Psychotherapists, 3* (1): 48–61.

Morgan, H. (2002). Exploring racism. *Journal of Analytical Psychology, 47* (4): 567–588.

Morgan, M. (2001). First contacts: The therapist's "couple state of mind" as a factor in the containment of couples seen for consultation. In: F. Grier (Ed.), *Brief Encounters with Couples*. London: Karnac.

Morgan, M. (2005). On being able to be a couple: The importance of a "creative couple" in psychic life. In F. Grier (Ed.), *Oedipus and the Couple*. London: Karnac.

Morgan, M., & Ruszczynsky, S. (1998). *The Creative Couple*. Paper presented at the Tavistock Marital Studies Institute 50th Anniversary Conference, London.

Morin, E. (2008). *On Complexity: Advances in Systems Theory, Complexity, and the Human Sciences*. San Francisco, CA: Hampton Press.

Morrow, V., & Richards, M. (1996). *Transitions to Adulthood: A Family Matter?* York: Joseph Rowntree Foundation.

Moses, R. (2002). Unconscious defence mechanisms and social mechanisms used in national and political conflicts. In: J. Bunzl & B. Beit-Hallahmi (Eds.), *Psychoanalysis, Identity and Ideology: Critical Essays on the Israel/Palestine Case* (pp. 85–106). Boston, MA: Kluwer.

Moses-Hrushovski, R. (1996). Remaining in the bunker long after the war is over: Deployment in the individual, the group, and the nation. In: L. Rangell, & R. Moses-Hrushovski (Eds.), *Psychoanalysis at the Political Border: Essays in Honour of Rafael Moses* (pp. 165–188). Madison, CT: International Universities Press.

Moss, D. (2003). *Hating in the First Person Plural: Psychoanalytical Essay on Racism, Homophobia, Misogyny and Terror*. New York: Other Press.

Moylan, D. (1994). The danger of contagion: Protective identification processes in institutions. In: A. Obholzer & V. Zagier Roberts (Eds.), *The Unconscious at Work: Individual and Organization Stress in the Human Services*. London: Routledge.

Nietzsche, F. (1887). *The Gay Science*. New York: Vintage, 1974.

Nosek, L. (2003). Terror in everyday life: Revisiting Mr Kurtz. In: S. Varvin & V. Volkan (Eds.), *Violence or Dialogue? Psychoanalytic Insights into Terror and Terrorism* (pp. 31–52). London: IPA.

O'Connor, N., & Ryan, J. (2003). *Wild Desires and Mistaken Identities: Lesbianism and Psychoanalysis*. London: Karnac.

OECD (2011). *Divided We Stand: Why Inequality Keeps Rising*. Available at: www.oecd.org/unitedstates/49170253.pdf

Ogden, T. H. (1999). *Reverie and Interpretation: Sensing Something Human*. London: Karnac.

Olkin, R. (1995). *What Psychotherapists Should Know about Disability*. New York: Guilford Press.

Ó Siochrú, M. (2008). *God's Executioner*. London: Faber and Faber.

O'Toole, F. (2009). *Ship of Fools*. London: Faber and Faber.

Papadopoulos, I., Tilki, M., & Lees, S. (2004). Promoting cultural competence in healthcare through a research-based intervention in the UK. *Diversity in Health & Social Care, 1* (2): 107–116.

Papadopoulos, R. (2002). *Therapeutic Care for Refugees: No Place Like Home*. London: Karnac.

Pappe, I. (2006). *The Ethnic Cleansing of Palestine*. Oxford: Oneworld Publications.

Patterson, C. J. (1997). Children of gay and lesbian parents. In: T. Ollenick & R. Prinz (Eds.), *Advances in Clinical Child Psychology, Vol. 19* (pp. 235–282). New York: Plenum Press.

Philo, G., & Berry, M. (2011). *More Bad News from Israel*. London: Pluto.

Poland, W. (2005). On a boycott by passport [Letter]. *International Journal of Psychoanalysis*, 86: 902–903.

Rado, S. (1940). A critical examination of the concept of bisexuality. *Psychosomatic Medicine*, 2: 459–467.

Rattansi, A. (2007). *Racism: A Very Short Introduction*. Oxford: Oxford University Press.

Rattansi, A. (2011). Race's recurrence: Reflections on Amin's "The Remainders of Race". *Theory, Culture & Society*, 2: 112–128.

Reay, D. (2005). Beyond consciousness?: The psychic landscape of social class. *Sociology*, 39 (5): 911–928.

Reay, D. (2008). Reinvigorating democracy? White middle class identities and comprehensive schooling. *Sociological Review*, 56 (2): 238–256.

Riots, Communities and Victims Panel (2012). *After the Riots: The Final Report of the Riots, Communities and Victims Panel*. London.

Rivers, W. H. R. (1910). *Kinship and Social Organization: Together with The Genealogical Method of Anthropological Enquiry*. London: Athlone Press, 1968.

Rose, J. (1990). An interview with Hanna Segal. *Women: A Cultural Review*, 1 (2): 209.

Rose, J. (2005). *The Question of Zion*. Princeton, NJ: Princeton University Press.

Rosen, I. (Ed.) (1979). *Sexual Deviation*. Oxford: Oxford University Press.

Ross, W. D. (Trans.) (2005). *Aristotle: Nicomachean Ethics*. Available at: http://classics.mit.edu/Aristotle/nicomachaen.html

Rossiter, A. (1993). Bringing the margins into the centre: A review of aspects of Irish Women's Emigration. In: A. Smyth (Ed.), *Irish Women's Studies Reader*. Dublin: Attic Press.

Rustin, M. E. (1989). Encountering primitive anxieties. In: L. Miller, M. Rustin, J. Shuttleworth, & M. Rustin (Eds.), *Closely Observed Infants* (pp. 7–21). London: Duckworth.

Rustin, M. E. (2008). Work discussion: Some historical and theoretical observations. In: M. E. Rustin & J. Bradley (Eds.), *Work Discussion:*

Learning from Reflective Practice in Work with Children and Families.
Tavistock Clinic Series. London: Karnac.

Rustin, M. E. (2009). Work with parents. In: M. Lanyado & A. Horne
(Eds.), *The Handbook of Child and Adolescent Psychotherapy: Psychoanalytic Approaches* (2nd edition, pp. 206–219). London: Routledge.

Rustin, M. E, & Bradley, J. (2008). *Work Discussion: Learning from Reflective Practice in Work with Children and Families.* Tavistock Clinic
Series. London: Routledge.

Rustin, M. J. (1991). Psychoanalysis, racism and anti-racism. In: *The
Good Society and the Inner World.* London: Verso.

Ryan, J. (1998). Lesbianism and the therapist's subjectivity: A psychoanalytic view. In: C. Shelley (Ed.), *Contemporary Perspectives on Psychotherapy and Homosexualities* (pp. 44–57). London: Free Association
Books.

Ryan, J. (2004). *An Exploration of How Some Psychoanalytic Psychotherapists Conceptualise and Respond to Social Class Issues within
Psychotherapeutic Relationships* [Research report]. London: Tavistock
Institute of Medical Psychology.

Ryan, J. (2009). Elision and disavowal: The extrusion of class from
psychoanalytic discourse and practice. *Sitegeist: A Journal of Psychoanalysis and Philosophy, 3*: 27–39.

Rycroft, C. (1988). *A Critical Dictionary of Psychoanalysis.* London: Penguin.

Sabbagh, K. (2009). Perils of criticizing Israel. *British Medical Journal,
338*: a2066.

Said, E. (1984). Permission to narrate. In: M. Bayoumi & A. Rubin, *The
Edward Said Reader* (pp. 243–266). New York: Vantage, 2000.

Said, E. (1993). *Culture and Imperialism.* London: Vintage.

Said, E. (1997). *Covering Islam.* London: Vintage.

Samuels, A. (2006). Working directly with political, social and cultural
material in the therapy session. In: L. Layton, N. C. Hollander, &
S. Guttwill (Eds.), *Psychoanalysis, Class and Politics. Encounters in the
Clinical Setting* (pp. 11–28). London: Routledge.

Sand, S. (2009). *The Invention of the Jewish People.* London: Verso.

Sanders, D., & Hendry, L. B. (1997). *New Perspectives on Disaffection.*
London: Cassell.

Sandler, J. (1976). Counter-transference and role responsiveness. *International Review of Psychoanalysis, 3*: 43–47.

Sayer, A. (2005). *The Moral Significance of Class.* Cambridge: Cambridge
University Press.

Schacter, J., & Butts, H. (1971). Transference and countertransference in inter-racial analyses. *Journal of the American Psychoanalytic Association, 16*: 792–808.

Schafer, R. (1995). The evolution of my views on non-normative sexual practices. In: T. Domenici & R. C. Lesser (Eds.), *Disorienting Sexuality: Psychoanalytic Reappraisals of Sexual Identities* (pp. 187–202). New York: Routledge.

Schama, S. (2009). S. Sand, *The Invention of the Jewish People* [Review]. *Financial Times*, 13 November. Available at: www.ft.com/cms/s/2/b74fdfd2-cfe1-11de-a36d-00144feabdc0.html

Schwager, E. (2004). Transforming dualism and the metaphor of terror, Part II: From genocidal to dialogic mentality: An intergenerational struggle. *Psychoanalytic Review, 91*: 543–589.

SCIE (2006). *Are We There Yet? Identifying the Characteristics of Social Care Organisations That Successfully Promote Diversity*. Race Equality Discussion Paper 03. London: Social Care Institute for Excellence. Available at: www.scie.org.uk/publications/raceequalitydiscussionpapers

Segal, H. (1987). Silence is the real crime. *International Review of Psychoanalysis, 14*: 3–12.

Segev, T. (1991). *The Seventh Million: Israel and the Holocaust*. New York: Henry Holt.

Sennett, R. (2003). *Respect*. London: Penguin.

Sennett, R., & Cobb, J. (1972). *The Hidden Injuries of Class*. New York: W. W. Norton, 1993.

Shelley, C. (Ed.) (1998). *Contemporary Perspectives on Psychotherapy and Homosexualities*. London: Free Association Books.

Silver, C. B. (2008). Traumatic memories and the need to punish: The boycott of Israeli academics. *Psychoanalytic Review, 95*: 387–416.

Singer, T., & Kimbles, S. (2004). *The Cultural Complex: Contemporary Jungian Perspectives on Psyche and Society*. Hove: Brunner-Routledge.

Singh, R., & Dutta, S. (2010). *"Race" and Culture: Tools, Techniques and Trainings. A Manual for Professionals*. London: Karnac.

Skeggs, B. (1997). *Formations of Class and Gender: Becoming Respectable*. London: Sage.

Socarides, C. W. (1968). A provisional theory of aetiology in male homosexuality. *International Journal of Psychoanalysis, 49*: 27–37.

Social Exclusion Unit (2000). *National Strategy for Neighbourhood Renewal, Report of Policy Action Team 12: Young People*. Norwich: Stationery Office.

Steiner, H. J., & Alston, P. (2000). *International Human Rights in Context* (2nd edition). Oxford: Oxford University Press.

Steiner, J. (1985). Turning a blind eye: The cover up for Oedipus. *International Review of Psychoanalysis, 12*: 161–172.

Steiner, J. (1987). The interplay between pathological organisations and the paranoid-schizoid and depressive positions. *International Journal of Psychoanalysis, 68*: 69–80.

Stern, D. B. (2010). *Partners in Thought: Working with Unformulated Experience, Dissociation, and Enactment.* New York: Routledge.

Straker, G. (1988). Child abuse, counselling and apartheid: The work of the Sanctuary Counselling Team. *Free Associations, 10*: 7–38.

Strathern, M. (1992). *After Nature: English Kinship in the Late 20th Century.* Cambridge: Cambridge University Press.

Strenger, C. (2011). Israel is tearing apart the Jewish people. *Haaretz,* 24 June.

Suleiman, R. (2002). On marginal people: The case of the Palestinians in Israel. In: J. Bunzl & B. Beit-Hallahmi (Eds.), *Psychoanalysis, Identity and Ideology: Critical Essays on the Israel/Palestine Case* (pp. 71–84). Boston, MA: Kluwer.

Summerfield, D. (2004). Cross-cultural perspectives on the medicalization of human suffering. In: G. M. Rosen (Ed.), *Posttraumatic Stress Disorder: Issues and Controversies* (pp. 233–246). Chichester: Wiley.

Thomas, L. (1992). Racism and psychotherapy: Working with racism in the consulting room—an analytic view. In: J. Kareem & R. Littlewood (Eds.), *Intercultural Therapy.* Oxford: Blackwell.

Ullman, C. (2006). Bearing witness: Across the barriers in society and in the clinic. *Psychoanalytic Dialogues, 16*: 181–198.

Volkan, V. (1996). Intergenerational transmission and "chosen" traumas: A link between the psychology of the individual and that of the ethnic group. In: L. Rangell & R. Moses-Hrushovski (Eds.), *Psychoanalysis at the Political Border* (pp. 257–282). Madison, CT: International Universities Press.

Volkan, V. (2002). *Large-Group Identity: Border Psychology and Related Societal Processes.* Available at: http://vamikvolkan.com/Large-Group-Identity:-Border-Psychology-and-Related-Societal-Processes .php

Volkan, V. (2004). *Chosen Trauma: The Political Ideology of Entitlement and Violence.* Available at: http://www.vamikvolkan.com/Chosen-Trauma,-the-Political-Ideology-of-Entitlement-and-Violence.php

Volkan, V. (2007). Not letting go: From individual perennial mourners to societies with entitlement ideologies. In: F. Glocer Fiorini, S. Lewkowicz, & T. Bokanowski (Eds.), *On Freud's "Mourning and Melancholia"* (pp. 90–109). London: IPA.

Volkan, V. (2009). The next chapter: Consequences of societal trauma.

In: P. Gobodo-Madikizela & C. van der Merve (Eds.), *Memory, Narrative and Forgiveness: Perspectives of the Unfinished Journeys of the Past* (pp. 1–26). Cambridge: Cambridge Scholars.

Waddell, G. (1999). *The Back Pain Revolution*. New York: Churchill Livingstone.

Walkerdine, V., Lucey, H., & Melody, J. (2001). *Growing Up Girl: Psychosocial Explorations of Gender and Class*. London: Palgrave.

Ward, A. (2012). The "English Riots" as a communication: Winnicott, the antisocial tendency and public disorder. In: C. Reeves (Ed.), *Broken Bounds: Contemporary Reflections on the Antisocial Tendency*. London: Karnac.

Webber, F. (1981). Six centuries of revolt and repression. *Race & Class*, 23 (2/3): 245–250.

Wilson, M., & Francis, J. (1997). *Raised Voices: African Caribbean and African Users' Views and Experiences of Mental Health Services in England and Wales*. London: MIND.

Winnicott, D. W. (1956). The antisocial tendency. In: *Through Paediatrics to Psychoanalysis: Collected Papers* (pp. 306–315). London: Karnac, 1984.

Winnicott, D. W. (1967). Delinquency as a sign of hope. In: *Home Is Where We Start From: Essays by a Psychoanalyst*. London: Penguin, 1986.

Winnicott, D. W. (1971). *Playing and Reality*. London: Routledge, 2005.

Winnicott, D. W. (1986), Thinking and the unconscious. In: *Home Is Where We Start From: Essays by a Psychoanalyst*. London: Penguin

Witkon, E. J. (2008). *Freud in Zion: History of Psychoanalysis in Jewish Palestine/Israel 1918–1948* by Eran J. Rolnik [Review]. *International Journal of Psychoanalysis, 89*: 909–912.

Wollheim, R. (1987). Insults. *London Review of Books*, 9 June, pp. 12–13. Available at: www.lrb.co.uk/v09/n06/richard-wollheim/insults

Woodham-Smith, C. (1991). *The Great Hunger: Ireland 1945–1849*. London: Penguin.

Wright B. A. (1983). *Physical Disability: A Psychosocial Approach* (2nd edition). New York: Harper & Row.

Yeats, W. B. (1933). *Remorse for Intemperate Speech*. In: *Collected Poems of W. B. Yeats*. London: Macmillan.

Yi, K. (1998). Transference and race: An intersubjective conceptualization. In: R. Moodley & S. Palmer (Eds.), *Race, Culture and Psychotherapy*. London: Routledge.

Young, A. (1995). *The Harmony of Illusions: Inventing Post-Traumatic Stress Disorder*. Princeton, NJ: Princeton University Press.

Young, R. (1994a). *Mental Space*. London: Process Press.

Young, R. (1994b). Psychoanalysis and racism: A loud silence. In: *Mental Space*. London: Process Press.

Zarkowski, C. (2000). Trauma stories: Violence, emotion and politics in Somali Ethiopia. *Transcultural Psychiatry, 37*: 383–402.

Zarkowski, C. (2004). Writing trauma: Emotion, ethnography and the politics of suffering among Somali returnees in Ethiopia. *Culture, Medicine and Psychiatry, 28*: 189–209.

Zeldin, T. (1995). *An Intimate History of Humanity*. New York: Harper-Collins.

Žižek, S. (2011). Shoplifters of the World Unite: The meaning of the riots. *London Review of Books Online*, 19 August.

Zmroczek, C., & Mahoney, P. (Eds.) (1999). *Women and Social Class*. London: Taylor & Francis.

Zuckerman, M. (2002). Towards a critical analysis of Israeli political culture. In: J. Bunzl & B. Beit-Hallahmi (Eds.), *Psychoanalysis, Identity and Ideology: Critical Essays on the Israel/Palestine Case* (pp. 59–70). Boston, MA: Kluwer.

Zureik, E. (2011). Colonialism, surveillance, and population control: Israel/Palestine. In: E. Zureik, D. Lyon, & Y. Abu-Laban (Eds.), *Surveillance and Control in Israel/Palestine: Population, Territory and Power* (pp. 3–46). London: Routledge.

adolescent(s), ix, 40, 215, 216, 218, 226
adolescent omnipotence, 47
African slaves, 20
age, as protected characteristic, 147
ageism, 1
Alderdice, J., 204
Al Haq, 208
Allen, C., 156
Alleyne, A., 17
Altman, N., 13, 17, 127
American Psychiatric Association
    (APA), 149
American Psychoanalytic
    Association, 147, 149
    1991 Position Statement on
    Homosexuality, 149
Amin, A., 112, 114, 126
Amnesty International, 208
"Analytic Third", 161
annihilation anxiety(ies), 214
    primitive, 227
anti-racist initiatives, 3
anti-Semitism, 8, 190, 191, 192, 197
antisocial behaviour, 214, 224–226
antisocial tendency, 223, 224, 226
apartheid, 62, 168
appearances, assumptions on basis
    of, 114
Appy, G., 207
Aristotle, 9
Armitage, K., 144
Arundale, J., 204
Association for Psychoanalytic
    Psychotherapy, 148
attachment(s):
    homosexual, 154
    secure, 23
    sexual, 154
attachment relationship, reflexivity
    of, 118

Audit Commission, 2, 9, 14
Augoustinos, M., 114
August 2011 Riots, UK, 211–228
    causes of, 212
    austerity programme, 220
Awad, G., 199, 200, 204, 205

Bailey, T., 215, 216
Baldwin, A., 225
Barden, N., 148
Barry, S., 174
Bar-Tal, D., 205
Barthes, R., 126
basic-assumption functioning, 29
Bawdon, F., 225
Bebbington, P., 158
Beck, J., 26
Beckett, J. C., 168
behaviour, antisocial, 214, 224–226
Beit-Hallahmi, B., 190, 192, 197, 210
Beland, H., 197
benevolent neutrality, as therapist's
    correct/normal attitude to
    patient, 86, 88, 108
Benjamin, J., 111, 112
Bereaved Families Forum, 206
bereavement, 92
Berger, J., 75
Bergler, E., 156
Berman, E., 199, 202
Berry, M., 185
Bhavnani, R., 15
Bhugra, D., 12, 13, 109, 110
Bhui, K., 12, 13, 109, 110
Bieber, I., 149, 156
Bion, W. R., 5, 21, 29, 33, 89, 91, 111
    capacity to think (K), 9, 23, 24, 86
    containment, 159
    curiosity, disturbance of impulse
        of , 11

Bion, W. R. (*continued*):
"knowing" and "knowing about",
distinction between, 11
minus K (−K), 25
narcissistic tendency, 227
PS–D (paranoid-schizoid–
depressive) balance, 34
reflecting and thinking, 115
"restraint" in interpretive work,
102
reverie, 24
bisexuality, 150, 155
black, negative connotation of, 112
Black, D. M., 186, 202, 204, 209
Black and White Minstrel Show, 75
"blackness", images of in patient's
dreams (case study), 102–107
black patient and white therapist
(case study), 68–73
Blackwell, D., 122, 123, 129, 141, 144
Blair, A., 213, 214
Blair, C., 208
blank screen therapist, 87
blind eye, turning a, and Irish identity
in Britain, 170
blind spots regarding Irish identity
in British organizations and
society, 166–183
BNP: *see* British National Party
Bollas, C., 5, 21, 34
genera, 25–27
borderline condition, homosexuality
as, 155
borderline phenomenon, white
racism as, 59
Botticelli, S., 144
Bouquet, M., 113
Bourdieu, P., 115, 126, 162
BPC: *see* British Psychoanalytic
Council
Bracken, P., 172
Bradley, J., xiii, 6, 19, 85–108
Breen, D., 152, 153
Briggs, J., 111, 116–119
British Council for Psychotherapy
and Counselling, 158
British Nationality Act, 1948, 171
British National Party (BNP), 62
British Psychoanalytic Council (BPC),
7, 147–149, 157, 164
Britton, R., 111, 216
Brooks, O., xiii, 5, 35–55
Brown, L. J, 215
Brugha, T. S., 158
Brunner, J., 194
B'Tselem, 208

bulimia, 120, 121
Bunyan, T., 219
Bunzl, J., 190, 192, 197, 210
Butler, J., 154, 155, 162, 199, 208
Butts, H., 88

Calvo, L., 145
Cameron, D., 8, 212–214, 225
CAMHS: *see* Child and Adolescent
Mental Health Service
Canestri, J., 128
cannabis, 216–218
capitalism:
culture of, 223
global, 176
capital punishment, 186
Care Quality Commission, 172
categorization, 70, 111, 112, 125
gender, 161
Catholic Church, in Ireland, 32, 174,
175
Centre for Social Justice, 221
Chakraborty, A., 158
Chasseguet-Smirgel, J., 189, 209
Child and Adolescent Mental Health
Service (CAMHS), 91, 92, 107,
215, 216
child poverty, 219
Chodorow, N. J., 158
Chomsky, N., 200
"chosen traumas", of social group,
188
CHRE: *see* Council for Healthcare
Regulatory Excellence
Churchill, W. S., 168
circumcision, 78–80
Clarke, J., 148
class: *see* social class
class difference, 127–131, 133, 135, 137
experiences of, 128
classification, 112, 122
Linnaean, 113
class relations, internalization of, 129,
144
class unconscious, 144
power of, 143
Clay, C. (Muhammad Ali), 75
clinical relationship, changing views
of, 158–165
Cobb, J., 128, 133, 144
Cohen, S., 205
collective hysteria, 226
collective memory, 123
collective psychic structures, 189
colonialism, 7, 81, 112, 167–170, 174,
177–179

British, in Ireland, 168–183
  psychic legacy of, 167, 177
  colonial object relations, and psychic
    relationship between black
    and white people in Britain,
    167
Combatants for Peace, 206
competence, cultural, 109–126
complexity theory, 212
conscience, ego-function of, 186
consumerism, 223
containment, 9, 159, 212, 226
  importance of, 23–24
Controversial Discussions, 157
Cooper, A., 112
Corrie, R., 208
Council for Healthcare Regulatory
    Excellence (CHRE), 147
countertransference, 39, 68, 78, 80, 82,
  class-related, 131, 134–143
  confused, 81
  and homosexuality, 159, 160, 162
  in infant observation, 90
  and negative thoughts about
    patient, 69
  transference and, 127, 130, 137
Covington, C., 204
Craib, I., 129, 141
creative thinking, 25
Crighton, A., 225
Criminal Bar Association, 226
critical theory, 18, 33
Cromwell, O., 168
cross-cultural psychotherapeutic
    practice, 111
Crown Prosecution Service, 225
cultural competence, 6
  complexity of, 109–126
  training of, 110
cultural complex, concept of, 187
cultural diversity, 1, 12, 15
culture:
  boundaries of, xviii
  contested, particularized,
    fragmented, 119
  of entitlement, 213, 228
  issues, 2, 13
  lack of thinking about in
    psychotherapy, 12–14
  as shared patterns, 119
curiosity, 11
  lack of, 18–19
Curry, A., 71

Dalal, F., 19, 60, 85, 86, 88, 90, 112, 113,
  159, 187, 201, 203, 206

Dalrymple, T. [A. Daniels], 228
Daniels, A. [T. Dalrymple], 228
Das, V., 124
Davids, M. F., iii, xvii–xx, 17, 60, 89,
  90, 108, 112, 159
Davies, W., 219, 223
Davis, M., 75
Declaration of Human Rights, 204,
  209
decontextualization, 114
defence mechanisms, 205
DeGruy Leary, J., 20
dehistoricization, 114
dehumanization, 62, 205
  of Jews, 189–191
  of Palestinians, 8, 189, 192–197
delinquency, 224
  as sign of hope, 223
Dembo, T., 159
denial, 16, 52, 57, 63, 65, 67, 73, 192,
  227
denigration, 59, 70, 137, 195
Denman, C., 148
Denman, F., 148
Department of Health (DoH), 109
depersonalization, 62
depressive position, 21–23, 44, 61, 227
deprivation, early, 102, 103
depth psychology, xviii
De Zulueta, F., 189
Di Ceglie, R. G., 165
difference, stigmatization of, 159
Dimen, M., 143
disability, as protected characteristic,
  147
discrimination, 30, 32, 110, 171, 172
  Equality Act of 2010, 147–148
  racial, 86
  and training of psychotherapists:
    issue of, 1–2
  lack of thinking about, 12–15
displacement, 44, 123, 141, 193, 195
diversity, 1–6, 11, 15, 18, 24, 76
  in clinical setting, 75
  issues, in psychotherapy, 2, 19
  lack of meaningful discussion
    about, 3
  lack of thinking about in
    psychotherapy, 12–14
  racial, 75
  thinking about, 4, 33
  understanding of, 6
  working with, 3, 14
diversity learning events, 11
diversity legislation, 3
diversity training, 3

divorce, 92
Domenici, T., 158
Donnelly, J., 169
Dowler, M., 221
doxa, 119
    as normative unconscious, 115
Drescher, J., 151, 163, 164
Duggan, M., 211
Dutta, S., 109
dyadic therapeutic relationship, 161
Dyer, R., 172

early deprivation, 102, 103
economic inequality, 12
economic recession, global, 220
Edonya, P., 109
education attainment, 219
ego-function of conscience, 186
ego psychology, 42
Eichenbaum, L., 13
Elias, N., 60, 128
Elmendorf, S., 199
empathy, importance of, in
        therapeutic stance, 91
enactment, 19, 20, 69
    as therapeutic tool, 159
Enlightenment, 110, 112
entitlement, culture of, 213, 228
Equality Act of 2010, 147
equal opportunity policies, 14, 57
Erikson, E., 209
Erlich, H., 197
Erlich-Ginor, M., 197
erotic transference, 160
essentialism, 203
Ethiopian Community Association,
        121
Ethiopian–Ogaden war, 123
ethnicity, 33, 35, 37, 75, 78, 79, 85–88,
        107, 187
examination league tables, 221
exhibitionism, 150

families, dysfunctional, 213
Fanon, F., 17, 114, 167, 170
fascism, 205, 209
father, phallic role of, denial of, 157
Ferenczi, S., 54
fetishism, 150
Feuerbach, L., 16
financial/economic crisis, 172, 176,
        177, 220, 223
Fitzgerald, B., 165
Fletcher, J., 154
Fletchman Smith, B., 206
Flower, S., 160

Fonagy, P., 14, 23, 200
Forster, E. M., 163
Foucault, M., 114
Foulkes, S. H., 60
fragile narcissism, 194
Francis, J., 17
Frankenstein, E., 193
free association, xviii, 25, 28, 29
Freud, A., 33
    Controversial Discussions, 157
Freud, S., 33, 44, 54, 55, 149, 158, 202,
        205, 209, 210
    benevolent neutrality, as therapist's
        correct/normal attitude to
        patient, 86, 88, 108
    Civilization and Its Discontents, 42,
        45
    The Ego and the Id, 152, 154
    "Female sexuality", 152
    "From the history of an infantile
        neurosis", 145
    homosexuality, 151
    Leonardo Da Vinci and a Memory of
        His Childhood, 151
    "Mourning and melancholia", 154
    narcissism of minor differences, 42
    New Introductory Lectures on Psycho-
        Analysis, 18, 152
    "Notes on a case of obsessional
        neurosis", 151
    phallic monism, 152
    "The psychogenesis of a case of
        homosexuality in a woman",
        151, 152
    "Recommendations to physicians
        practising psycho-analysis",
        215
    "Remembering, repeating and
        working-through", 21, 177
    resistance to becoming conscious of
        unconscious, 16
    "Some neurotic mechanisms
        in jealousy, paranoia and
        homosexuality", 151
    Three Essays on the Theory of
        Sexuality, 150, 151, 153, 154
    Totem and Taboo, 203
    Wolf Man, 145, 151
Frommer, M. S., 160, 161
Frosh, S., 61
fundamentalism, 61, 63

Gabbard, G. O., 198, 199
Gambini, R., 61
Gandhi, M., 209
Garrett, P., 171, 172

gender:
    as habitus, 162
    issues of, xviii
gender categorization, 161
gender identification, 154
gender identity, 152, 161, 162
gender reassignment, 161
    as protected characteristic, 147
genera, 25–27
generation difference, issues of, xviii
Geneva Convention, Fourth (1949),
    209–210
genocide, 63, 190–192
genotype, vs. phenotype, 113
Gibbs, I., 88
Gillespie, W. H., 149
Glass, C., 194
global capitalism, 176
global economic recession, 220
globalization, 59, 176
    social dislocation attendant on,
        199
Glover, E., 149
Goldberg, D., 193
Goldberg, E., 88
good breast, idealization of, 41
Gordon, P., 2, 12, 57, 59
Granek, M., 207
Greenslade, L., 172
Grosbard, O., 194, 195, 208
group identification, 206
group identity, and inter-ethnic
    conflict, 187

Habermas, J., 18
habitus, 120, 124–126
    concept of, 115
    gender as, 162
    Inuit, 119
Hacking, I., 122
Halper, J., 207
Halperin, E., 205, 207, 208
Hartmann, S., 143, 144
Harvey, S., 228
Hendry, L. B., 228
here-and-now transference, 159
Herzl, T., 192, 193
heterosexuality, 7, 151, 153, 154, 158
Hickman, M. J., 172
Higgitt, A. C., 23
Hillman, J., 61, 62
Hillsborough Independent Panel, 222
Hippocratic Oath, 202
Hirschfeld, M., 150
Hitler, A., 37
Hoggett, P., 64, 65, 211

Holland, S., 13
Holmes, D. E., 71, 88, 107
Holocaust, 76, 188–192
    survivors of, 192
homelessness, 221
homophobia:
    and diversity, 3
    internalized, 158, 160, 163
    as psychic retreat, 155
homosexual attachments, 154
homosexuality, 3, 7, 19, 147–165
    attitude of the psychoanalytic
        profession in Britain to, 148
    as borderline condition, 155
    as perversion, 157
    psychoanalytic thinking about, 160
    psychoanalytic view of, as
        pathology, 156
homosexual orientation, 7, 147, 151
homosexual patients, 149, 151, 155,
    156, 158, 160
Horne, A., 40, 42–44
Horney, K., 152
Human Genome Project, 113
hysteria, collective, 226

ideal internal objects, 40
idealization(s), 5, 59, 214, 227
    pathological, 40
    preventing thinking, 35–55
    psychoanalytic definition of, 41
idealized object, flight to, 41
identification(s):
    group, 206
    with oppressor, 188
    preventing thinking, 35–55
    psychoanalytic definition of, 40
IJPA: see International Journal of
    Psychoanalysis
Inclusion Strategies, 14
income inequality, 220, 221
Independent Jewish Voices, 209
Independent school of
    psychoanalysis, 44
index patient, 215–218, 222
inequality, perverse seductive power
    of, 140
infantile structure of the individual,
    problem with working with,
    100
infant observation, 90
infertility, 125
insight, flight from, effect of, 100
institutional racism, 36
institutions, established, superego
    control by, 61

inter-communal conflicts,
    psychoanalytic study of,
    187–189
intercultural therapy, 2, 13
inter-ethnic conflict, and group
    identity, 187
internalized projection, 175
internal objects, ideal, 40
internal racist, 36, 73, 90
international behaviour, standards
    of, 204
International Journal of Psychoanalysis
    (*IJPA*), 198, 199, 202
interpretive work, "restraint" in, 102
intersubjective processes,
    unconscious, 215
intrapsychic processes, 145
introjection, 24, 70
Inuit habitus, 119
Inuit morality, 119
Inuit toddler, ethnography of
    (case study), 116–119
Inuktitut, 118
inverted snobbery, 140
IRA bombings in Britain, 171
Ireland:
    British colonialism in, 168–183
    Catholic Church in, 32, 174, 175
    creativity and rich literary/cultural
        tradition of, 178
    potato blight, effects of, 169
Irish identity, 7
    blind spots regarding, in British
        organizations and society,
        166–183
Irish people in Britain, as at receiving
    end of negative projections
    (case study), 179–183
irredentist ideologies, 188
Isay, R. A., 158, 164
Israel, 8
    boycott of, 198, 206
    and Palestinians, 184–210
    and the West, emotional linkages in
        the relationship between, 186
Israeli Committee Against House
    Demolitions, 206
Israel–Palestine situation, 8
Israelis, 185, 192–208

Jews, dehumanization of, 189–192
Jones, E., 151, 152
Joyce, J., 169, 178
Jung, C. G., 17

Kane, B. S., 192, 193, 196, 209

Kareem, J., xvii, 2, 12, 13
Kelloway, E. K., 228
Kemp, M., xiii, 8, 184–210
Khan, M., 33, 76
Khanna, R., 112
Kiberd, D., 166, 169, 178
Kimbles, S., 187
Kinealy, C., 169
King, B. B., 75
King, M., 158
King, P. H. M., 157
kinship, patrilineal principles of, 124
Klein, M., 5, 33, 41, 42, 111, 152
    Controversial Discussions, 157
    depressive position, 21–44, 61, 227
    idealization of good breast, 41
    paranoid-schizoid position, 21–23,
        214, 227
    paranoid-schizoid thinking, 22,
        214–215
    projective identification, 227
Klein, R., 221
Klug, B., 208
"knowing" and "knowing about",
    distinction between, 11
Knox, J., 204
Koffler, H., 210
Kohon, G., 42
Kohut, H., 194
Kosminsky, P., 185
Kovel, J., 17
Krause, I.-B., xiv, 6, 109–126
Ku Klux Klan, 62
Kushnick, L., 222

Lacan, J., 41, 152, 153
Laor, Y., 207
Laplanche, J., 40, 41, 202
large-group dynamics, 184–210
large-group identity, 187, 190
large-group psychology, 187
"large-group tent", 187, 189, 195, 205
Lawrence, M., 157
Lawrence, S., xix, 15, 157
Layton, L., 19, 112, 115, 119, 126, 129
league tables, of examinations, 221
Leary, K., 112
LeCouteur, A., 114
Lees, S., 109
Lemkin, R., 190
Lemma, A., 148
Lerman, A., 208
Lesser, R. C., 158
Lévi-Strauss, C., 124
Leviton, G. L., 159
Levy, I., 202, 208

Lewes, K., 150, 151, 156
Limentani, A., 157
Linnaean classification, 113
Lipsky, S., 17
Littlewood, R., 12
London bombings (7/7), 221
loss of functioning, catastrophic,
    defence against, 89
Lousada, J., 63, 112
Lowe, F., xiv, xvii, xix, 1–9, 11–34, 59,
    159, 167, 211–228
Lucey, A., 7, 30–32, 166–183
Lucey, H., xiv, 7, 30, 141, 166

Macdonald, K., 225
Machsom Watch, 196
Macpherson Report (Stephen
    Lawrence Inquiry), 15
Maher, F., 137
Mahoney, P., 128
Malcolm, N., 37–39, 44
manic defence, 83, 176
Mantel, H., 175
marginalization, 85, 201
marriage and civil partnership, as
    protected characteristic, 147
Marx, K., 16, 18
maternity, as protected characteristic,
    147
Matte-Blanco, I., 60
McCann-Mortimer, P., 114
McDougall, J., 157
McKenzie, K., 109
McManus, S., 158
McNally, R., 122
Mearsheimer, J., 200
Melody, J., 141
Mendelle, P., 226
mentalization, 23, 143
Merton, B., 228
middle-class patients, with working-
    class and lower-middle-class
    therapists, 131–136
Middle East, problems in, and
    psychoanalysis, 197–201
Miller, A., 110
minus K (–K), 23, 25
Mitchell, J., 153
Mitchell, S. A., 149, 161
Mitchison, S., 144
Mograbi, A., 207
Money-Kyrle, R., 86, 87, 91, 108
moral relativism, 204
Moran, G. S., 23
Morgan, D., xv, 5, 75–84
Morgan, H., xv, 5, 12, 56–74, 159

Morin, E., 211, 212
Morrow, V., 223
Moses, R., 194, 195, 197
Moses-Hrushovski, R., 188, 195
Moss, D., 19*
Moylan, D., 220
Murdoch, R., 221

Nafsiyat Intercultural Therapy
    Centre, London, xvii, 13
narcissism, 44, 194, 227
    fragile, 194
    of minor differences, 42
    as obstacle to thinking, 40–42
    psychoanalytic definition of, 41
narcissistic attachments, 55
narcissistic object relations, 189
narcissistic tendency, 227
national character, 37, 38
National Socialism, 189
Nazareth Conferences, 197
Nazi genocide, 190, 191
Nazism, 58, 189–193, 202
negative transference, 88, 131
neutrality, therapist's, 8, 202, 203, 205,
    222
    benevolent, as correct/normal
        attitude to patient, 86, 88, 108
Nevin, U., 225
Newbigin, J., xv, 7, 147–165
New Israel Fund, 185
New Savoy Partnership, 148
Nietzsche, F., 38, 39, 43, 44, 54
normative unconscious, doxa as, 115
Northern Ireland, The Troubles in, 171
Nosek, L., 199

objects:
    paranoid splitting of, 59
    transitional, 111, 119
O'Connor, N., 148, 151, 154, 158
OECD: see Organisation for
    Economic Co-operation and
    Development
oedipal dynamics, xix
Oedipus complex, 39, 49, 152, 157
    positive and negative, 153
OFEK, and Tavistock Institute of
    Human Relations, 197
Ogden, T. H., 161
Olkin, R., 159
omnipotence, adolescent, 47
Operation Cast Lead, 209
Operation Trident, 222
oppressor, identification with, 188
Orbach, S., 13

Organisation for Economic
    Co-operation and
    Development (OECD), 220
organizing internal template, 60
Ó Siochrú, M., 168
O'Toole, F., 172, 176
Ovesey, L., 149
Oxford Research Group, 210

Palestine, 8, 184, 186, 188, 190, 193,
    199, 200–202, 204
Palestine–Israel situation, 8
Palestinian resistance movement, 199
Palestinians:
    dehumanization of, 8, 189, 192–197
    and Israel, 184–210
Papadopoulos, I., 109
Papadopoulos, R., 123
Pappe, I., 194
paranoid-schizoid–depressive
    balance (PS–D), 34
paranoid-schizoid position, 21–214,
    227
paranoid-schizoid thinking, 214–215
    racism as example of, 22
paranoid splitting, 59, 90
paranoid transference, 89
parents, intrapsychic and
    interpersonal dynamics of,
    impact of, 215
parliamentary expenses scandal, 221
particularism, 203, 204
pathological idealization, 40
pathological organization, 60
patient, black, and white therapist,
    56–74
patrilineal ideology, 125
patrilineal principles of kinship, 124
Patterson, C. J., 165
Penal Laws, Ireland, 168, 182
persecutory anxiety, 41
personal transference, 71
phallic monism, 152
phenotype, vs. genotype, 113
Philo, G., 185
Physicians for Human Rights-Israel,
    206
Pickles, E., 226
Pinto, E., 185
Poitier, S., 75
Poland, W., 31, 33, 198
police:
    neutrality, 222
    and racism, xix, 15
    role of in riots, 211, 222
political correctness, 54, 57

culture of, 14
polymorphous perversity, 151, 153
Pontalis, J.-B., 40, 41, 202
post-traumatic stress disorder
    (PTSD), 121, 122
pregnancy, as protected characteristic,
    147
prejudice, 9, 12, 13, 15, 22, 76, 77, 83,
    159, 172, 191
pre-transference, 71–73
primitive anxieties, 5, 9, 227
primitive experiences, patient's
    communication of, 91
primitive splitting, 191
projection(s), 6–8, 26, 29, 31, 32, 44, 67,
    70, 106, 191, 208
    baby's, containment of, 23
    and class, 142, 145
    and colonizer/colonized, 170–172,
        175, 177, 179, 182
    container for, 62
    criticism of reliance on, 89
    defensive, 88
    denigrating, 142
    of failure and rejection, 83
    of feeling of guilt, 89, 194, 195
    in groups, 187
    of hated feelings, 61
    and homophobia, 155, 160
    hostile, 18
    internalized, 175
    of masculine/feminine qualities,
        66–67, 137
    mutual, 3
    negative, 167, 177, 179
    object as transient container for, 26
    and racism, 17, 22, 63, 90, 166, 167
    and rioting, 214, 215, 220, 227
    and role of chairperson in Thinking
        Space, 29
    shadow, 61–62, 70
    and splitting, 22
    of stupidity, 182
    of unwanted feelings and
        characteristics, 16, 22, 60, 219
    use of, to feel better about
        ourselves, 8
projective identification, 6, 39, 44,
    88–91, 107, 227
    communication via primitive
        unconscious language of, 220
    patient's use of, 159
psychic determinism, 87
psychic retreat, 82, 155
PS–D (paranoid-schizoid–depressive)
    balance, 34

psychoanalysis, narcissistic
    attachment to, 43
psychoanalytic work, issues of racism
    in, 85–105
psychotherapy:
    ethics of, 201–204
    and social sciences, tension
        between, 109
PTSD: *see* post-traumatic stress
    disorder

Qipisa Inuit, Baffin Island, Eastern
    Canada, 116, 118

race (*passim*):
    biological, 58
    boundaries of, xviii
    concept/idea of, 89, 113, 126
        as empty category, 58, 89
    issues, xviii, 2, 13
    naturalization and internalization
        of, 114
    not a natural category, 112
    as protected characteristic, 147
    thinking about:
        difficulties of, 54
        and lack of thinking, 35–55
        in practice in institutions, 45–50
    see also racism
race equality, 1, 18
Race Equality Plans, 14
race equality training, poor reputation
    of, 14–15
racial difference, xix, 88, 107
    between analyst and patient, 56–74,
        75–84, 107
    conceptualizations of, xviii
racial discrimination, 86
racial diversity, 12, 75
racialization, of unconscious, 201
racism (*passim*):
    denial of, 172
    early, basis of, 113, 114
    as example of paranoid-schizoid
        thinking, 22
    experience of being subjected to,
        140
    as form of pathology, 58
    impact of on work in the consulting
        room, 56–74
    inner, template of, 60
    institutional, 36
    internal, 17, 89
    issues of, in psychoanalytic work,
        85–105
    likened to parasites, 85, 90

murderous potential of, 190, 191
    in police, xix, 15
    psychoanalytic perspective, 59
    as psychotic state of mind, 59
    in self, resistance to thinking about,
        16–18
    as splitting or projective
        mechanism, 63
    theory of, 8, 59
    thinking about, 2, 4, 14, 16–18
    and transference, 50
    traumatic aspects of, 63
    white, 62
        as borderline phenomenon, 59
racist, internal, 36, 73, 90
racist states of mind, 36
Rado, S., 155
Rank, O., 151
Rattansi, A., 110, 112, 113, 126
Raviv, A., 205
Rayner, E., 42
Reay, D., 145
re-enactment, 19
    risk of, 20–21
    trans-generational, 193
relational self, 119
relativism, 109, 114, 203
    moral, 204
religion or belief, as protected
        characteristic, 147
reparative drive, 87
repressed, return of, 177, 196
reverie:
    capacity for, 43
    importance of, 23–24
Richards, M., 223
riot(s):
    Brixton, 1981, 219
    as communication and sign of
        hope, 224–227
    as index/symptom of malaise,
        219–223
    Manchester, 1981, 219
    role of police, 222
    Tottenham, 1985, 219
    Toxteth, 1981, 219
    UK, August 2011, 4, 8, 211–228
Riots, Communities and Victims
        Panel, 212, 214, 219, 224
Rivers, W. H. R., 113
Robinson, N., 225
Roman Catholicism, Irish, 168
Rose, J., 153, 165, 193, 207
Rosen, I., 157
Rosler, N., 205
Ross, W. D., 9

Rossiter, A., 172
Ruskin, R., 199
Rustin, M. E., 19, 90, 92, 108
Rustin, M. J., 58–59, 89–90
Ryan, J., xv, 6, 127–146, 148, 151, 154, 158, 160
Rycroft, C., 40, 41

Sabbagh, K., 187
Said, E., 170, 199, 200
Samuels, A., 112
Sand, S., 207
Sanders, D., 228
Sandler, A.-M., 159
Sayer, A., 144
Schacter, 88
Schafer, R., 151, 161, 165
Schalit, G., 208
Schama, S., 190, 207
schizophrenia, 156
school exclusion, 221
Schwager, E., 193
Segal, H., 33, 202
Segev, T., 190
self-idealization, 23
self-love, 54, 55
    as obstacle to thinking, 40–42
semitophilia, 207
Sennett, R., 128, 133, 135, 139, 140, 144
sex as protected characteristic, 147
sexism, 1
sexual abuse, 120
sexual attachments, 154
sexuality, issues of, 13
sexual orientation, 75, 148, 149, 151, 156, 160, 161, 164
    as protected characteristic, 147
    and social stigmatization, 158
Shamir, Y., 207
Sharvit, K., 205
Shaw, G. B., 178
Shelley, C., 148, 158
sibling rivalry, 117
Silver, C. B., 198
Singer, T., 187
Singh, R., 109
Skeggs, B., 145
slavery, 20, 21, 63, 167, 186
Socarides, C. W., 148, 149, 156
Social Care Institute for Excellence (SCIE), 2
social class, 6, 7, 127–130
    boundaries of, xviii
    definitions, criteria for, 128
    dynamics, 127

issues of, 7, 13, 127, 129–131, 137
    in psychotherapeutic work, 127–146 [middle-class therapists with working-class patients, 136–140; working-class and lower-middle-class therapists with middle-class patients, 131–136]
    research, 129–130
    self-definition of, 128
Social Darwinism, 110
social and economic inequality, 12, 223
Social Exclusion Unit, 221
social group, "chosen traumas" of, 188
social mobility, 128, 141, 221
    upward, 144
social sciences, and psychotherapy, tension between, 109
social unconscious, concept of, 60, 187
Socrates, 1
Spanish Protest movement, 221
Spencer, H., 110
split-off parts of self, 31
splitting, 3, 8, 16, 22, 62, 168, 171, 178, 199, 214, 227
    paranoid, 59, 90
    primitive, 191
splitting mechanism, racism as, 63
Steele, H., 23
Steele, M., 23
Steiner, H. J., 204
Steiner, J., 13, 60, 170
Steiner, R., 157
Stephen Lawrence Inquiry (Macpherson Report), 15
Stephenson, P., 221
stereotyping, 3, 30, 32, 159, 192
Stern, D. B., 161
stigmatization, 158, 201
    of difference, 159
Straker, G., 209
Strathern, M., 113, 126
Strenger, C., 210
substance misuse, 221
Suleiman, R., 194
Summerfield, D., 122
superego, 61
    moralizing, 186
superego control, by established institutions, 61
suspicion, atmosphere of (case study), 92–102
symbolization, 111

taboos in psychotherapy, 14
Target, M., 23
Tavistock Clinic, xvii, 2, 11, 19
    Adolescent Department, 104
Tavistock Institute of Human
        Relations, and OFEK, 197
terrorism, psychoanalytic
        commentaries on, 199
therapeutic frame, 159
therapeutic relationship, dyadic, 161
therapist:
    blank screen, 87
    neutrality of, 8, 86, 88, 108, 202, 203,
        205, 222
    and patient, difference between:
        racial, 56–74, 75–84, 92–102, 107
        racial, cultural, gender (case
            study), 80–82
        religious and cultural (case
            study), 77–80
therapy, relational model of, 161
thinking:
    creative, 25
    definition of, 21–23
    development of, 25–27
    self-love or narcissism as obstacle
        to, 40–42
Thinking Space:
    aim of, 19
    forum, xvii, 4, 12, 24
    key values and methods, 27–28
    model, 11–34
    project, xvii
    role of the chairperson, 29
third position, 111–112, 114, 126, 216
    reflective, 128
Thomas, L., 12, 71
Tigrayan People's Liberation Front,
    120
Tigrayan woman, psychotherapy
        with (case study), 120–125
Tilki, M., 109
"time collapse", 188
tokenism, 2, 14, 76
Tonge, J., 208
Touma-Sliman, A., 197, 200
transference:
    attacking, 135
    being "black" in, 85–108
    and class, 127, 130, 135–139, 142
    in consultancy work, 167, 168
    and countertransference, 127, 130,
        137
    erotic, 160
    here-and-now, 159

negative, 88, 131
paranoid, 89
personal, 71
and power differential in
        therapeutic relationship, 74
and racism, 5, 6, 50, 66, 69, 71, 72
in supervision, 79
true, 88
transference resistances, 58
trans-generational re-enactment, 193
trans-ideological acknowledgement,
    42–45
transitional objects, 111, 119
transitional phenomena, 115, 119,
    126
traumatic experiences, 8, 122
turning a blind eye, and Irish identity
        in Britain, 170

Ullman, C., 196
unconscious:
    racialization of, 201
    resistance to becoming conscious
        of, 16
unconscious intersubjective
        processes, 215
unemployment, youth, 221
United Kingdom Council for
        Psychotherapy, 158
United Nations:
    Charter, 209
    Convention on the Elimination
        of All Forms of Racial
        Discrimination, 210
    Convention on the Prevention and
        Punishment of the Crime of
        Genocide, 209
    Convention on the Rights of the
        Child, 210
    Convention on the Suppression
        and Punishment of Apartheid,
        210
    Convention against Torture, 210
universalism, 8, 109, 114, 203, 205
universalist ethic, 202, 205

value system, 80, 135
Volkan, V., 187–190, 195, 201, 205, 206,
    210

Waddell, G., 219
Waddell, M., ix–x
Walkerdine, V., 141
Walt, S., 200
Walter, B., 172

Ward, A., 224
Warfa, N., 109
Webbe, C., 222
Webber, F., 219
West, the, 8
    bystander position of, 205
    ethnocentric approaches of, 205
    and Israel:
        emotional linkages in
            relationship between, 186
        and Palestinians, 184–210
white supremacist culture, 61
white therapist:
    and black patient (case study),
        68–73
    and white patient (case study),
        65–68
Wilde, O., 178
Williams, P., 198, 199, 204
Wilson, M., 17
Winnicott, D. W., xxii, 25, 47, 215
    antisocial behaviour, 224
    antisocial tendency, 223–225
    delinquency as sign of hope, 223
    external reality, 64
    holding, 159
    transitional objects, 111–112, 119
    transitional phenomena, 115, 119,
        126
Witkon, E. J., 192

Wittgenstein, L., 5, 37–39, 43, 44, 51, 54
Wolfenden Committee, 149
Wolf Man, 145, 151
Wollheim, R., 198
Women against Violence, 208
Women's Therapy Centre, 13
Woodham-Smith, C., 169
Work Discussion Group, Tavistock
    Clinic, 19
Wright, B. A., 159

Yad Vashem Holocaust museum,
    Jerusalem, 207
Yates, J., 221
Yeats, W. B., 173, 174
Yi, K., 87, 88, 107, 108
Young, A., 122
Young, R., 4, 9, 12, 57
youth crime, 221
youth unemployment, 219, 221

Zarkowski, C., 122–124
Zeifman, I., 88
Zeldin, T., 1
Zionism, 185, 188, 190, 192–195, 210
    political, 193, 195
Žižek, S., 219, 221, 222
Zmroczek, C., 128
Zuckerman, M., 192, 194
Zureik, E., 192